Wally Went to Ouagadougou

G000127887

Previous books by the same author

Wally by Name:
A Monkey's Tale (Volume One)
iUniverse 2005
ISBN: 0-595-34650-2

A Minority of One:
A Monkey's Tale Continued (Volume Two)
iUniverse 2005
ISBN: 0-595-35110-7

For further information on Volume One, see
www.diadembooks.com/payne.htm
For further information on Volume Two, see
www.diadembooks.com/wally.htm

Wally Went to Ouagadougou:
A Monkey's Tale Continued (Volume Three)
All Rights Reserved. Copyright © 2014 Wally Payne

No part of this book may be reproduced or transmitted in any form or by any means, graphic, electronic, or mechanical, including photocopying, recording, taping or by any information storage or retrieval system, without the permission in writing from the copyright holder.

The right of Wally Payne to be identified as the author of this work has been asserted in accordance with the Copyright, Designs and Patents Act 1988 sections 77 and 78.

Published by Diadem Books

For information, please contact:

Diadem Books
16 Lethen View
Tullibody
ALLOA
FK10 2GE
Scotland UK

www.diadembooks.com

The views expressed in this work are solely those of the author and do not necessarily reflect the views of the publisher, and the publisher hereby disclaims any responsibility for them.

ISBN: 978-1-291-98836-9

Wally Went to Ouagadougou

A *Monkey's Tale* Continued
(Volume Three)

by

Wally Payne

DIADEM BOOKS

About the Author:

A defrocked police constable, Wally Payne joined the Royal Military Police in 1964 and, following an often bumpy ride on the promotion roller coaster, rose to the dizzy heights of captain before retiring from the service in 1991.

Good fortune aplenty, the odd dash of nepotism and some old fashioned bluff saw him secure employment, oft times a little too 'exciting' for comfort, in various far flung outposts. Visas and work permit stamps of Algeria, China, Hong Kong, Mali, Mozambique, the Philippines, South Africa and Thailand all grace his passport.

Now domiciled in his native north-east of England, his feet continue to itch unmercifully as he ponders what may lie on the other side of the hill.

Erratum

On page 316 of my second volume *A Minority of One*, I erroneously commented that the officer who replaced me in Detmold had been sent back by the Canadian Armed Forces before the completion of his tour of duty. I now understand this to be untrue and wish to apologise to the officer concerned.

To NGBC - World renowned vampire
and anecdotal assassin.

Table of Contents

Chapter 1

Thailand

FOLLOWING more than twenty-seven years of 'meritorious and distinguished' service, I left the Army on 5th August in the year of our Lord one thousand, nine hundred and ninety-one. There are people who served with me who might take exception to such a lofty description of my time in the Royal Military Police, but that's what my discharge papers say! The array of medals awarded during my service were testimony to exactly what the Army was going to miss: after all, they don't just give the General Service Medal with Northern Ireland clasp and the Long Service and Good Conduct Medal to any old Tom, Dick or Harry you know? Despite having landed a plum posting in Hong Kong, I'd simply grown tired of wearing a uniform and, despite a plethora of happy memories, it was high time for me to try something new. Like every long-serving soldier finally hanging up his boots, however, I was about to be afflicted by the malaise of being unable to settle back into civilian life. In my case, a short fuse and inability to stick at a job for longer than five minutes were to be cruelly exposed.

No matter how cheesed off you get in the Army, there's no running home to mummy. One has pledged one's troth to Her Majesty and, even in adversity, there's nothing for it but to soldier on. I'd battled on for longer than most, although there had been plenty of times when I'd come precariously close to packing my kit bag, giving my superiors the soldiers' farewell and heading for the hills. Now though, finally freed from the strictures of military discipline, there were no longer any compulsion to grin and bear it when faced with arrogance and stupidity. If inclined, I could now tell my boss he was a buffoon and that he could stick his job up his backside, with no fear of ramifications more serious than having my P45 prepared by the secretary.

Whilst still enjoying my discharge leave and even before I'd drawn my last month's salary from the Crown, I was gainfully employed by a company in Hong Kong. Securing a civilian job before leaving Her Majesty's employ had afforded me the opportunity of bucking the military system one last time, by failing to attend my pre-release interviews and by refusing absolutely to accept the offer of a pre-release course. The Army offers an astonishing array of courses, designed to prepare soldiers for the difficult transition to civilian life. Just the same, they ran neither 'Beekeeping for Beginners' nor 'Practical Ark Building' classes and nothing else really took my fancy.

My first employers were a company rejoicing under the name of Infoprobe, one of the two founder members being an old military friend. They were a gang of private detectives and made money by investigating intellectual property rights— trademark violations to the layman. From day one, I knew this wasn't the job for me. Walking into business premises with a hidden camera or microphone and trying to get incriminating evidence was just too devious for my style. Apart from reading a few files and roaming the streets with an experienced 'Infoprober', my input to the company's war effort was minimal. To compound my new boy's insecurity, the company's Chinese partner clearly resented my presence. He was a man who recognised nepotism at work, although his opinion counted for little. His fellow director was my chum Adam Kenworthy and it was Kenworthy, a former Royal Military Police comrade, who had engaged me.

As well as making money out of international companies trading in Hong Kong, Infoprobe had a branch down in

Thailand. It did precious little by way of business, although its continued existence gave the two directors a bona fide excuse to visit Bangkok every couple of months at the company's expense. Their visits had little to do with drumming up trade, needless to say. The incumbent of the manager's chair in Thailand was a bloke with an honour's degree in alcoholism and it was Kenworthy's intention to replace him with me, a man of altogether more sober habits. So, after a mere fortnight of learning the basics as an investigator in the complicated trademark violations business in Hong Kong, I sallied forth for Bangkok.

Kenworthy elected to accompany me over to Thailand, on the pretext of showing me the ropes. In reality, he wanted to give me a guided tour of the best bars, clubs, massage parlours and assorted dens of iniquity. Nothing wrong with that of course! We had first class tickets on Thai International and were the last to board the plane at Kai Tak airport. Befitting passengers of our importance, they closed the doors the moment we turned left towards the posh seats. When faced with unlimited supplies of free drink, Royal Military Police tradition demands a doughty performance and we dutifully dispatched considerable quantities of champagne, wine and brandy. We were both pretty mellow by the time we alighted in the Kingdom of Thailand.

Following a bawdy weekend, a fair proportion of which was spent in the splendid Wheatlander Massage Parlour, Kenworthy boarded an airport bound taxi early on Monday morning. He hadn't considered a visit to the company offices necessary, nor did he deem to give me a briefing on exactly what was expected of me. With trade mark violations on every street corner in Bangkok, the company's bread and butter, some advice on company policy and tactics would have been appreciated. As it was, I really didn't have a clue how to set about things. More convinced than ever I wasn't embarking on a long-term career, I made my way from my weekend hotel to the company's office, located in the Bangkapi area of the city.

Alighting from a taxi and making my way towards the Infoprobe office, I felt distinctly apprehensive. There was, though, an even bigger fish out of water wandering abroad in Bangkapi that morning. An itinerant palm reader approached and, for a modest number of baht, he undertook to tell my fortune. Having perused my palm for a period, he embarked upon the worst soothsaying performance of all time:

"You are happily married with three children," he declared.

"No, I'm not."

"You are happily married with two children," he suggested.

"No, I'm not."

"You are married though?" he asked with an air of desperation.

"No, I'm not."

"You are divorced."

"No, I'm separated," I said, putting him out of his misery.

"You are very happy in your job."

"Most definitely not!"

"You are on holiday in Thailand."

"No."

"You are going on a long journey."

"Only as far as the offices over there. How far is that?"

"Where do you stay in Bangkok?"

"At the Rex Hotel on Sukhumvit Road."

"Tonight you will meet an attractive young lady and have a good time," he suggested, grasping at straws.

"You're probably right on that one," I said and gave him his money.

The reason for Kenworthy's reluctance to accompany me to the company's modest piece of real estate became apparent the moment I arrived. The company secretary, who also happened to be the landlady of the building, met me and directed me towards the small flat abutting the office to deposit my belongings. The living room and bedroom were in an appalling condition, but were eclipsed by the squalid state of the bathroom. The bath had more rings than the Olympic banner and, what I found most repellent, a light switch covered with dirt, grease and goodness knows what other germ-laden organisms. The place clearly hadn't seen a squirt of Flash or a yellow duster since time immemorial. Moving on to the office complex, I discovered a disorganised array of papers, files and samples of counterfeit products. Following some preliminary niceties, the secretary hit me with a real low ball. In her view, things weren't going at all well at Infoprobe. In recent times there had been just too many managers for her liking and, furthermore, she confessed to having had her fill of the whole organisation. She tendered a week's notice as secretary and then, in her capacity as landlady, gave me a week's notice to vacate the premises!

Next morning I called Kenworthy and asked for some much needed advice. He instructed me, rather too curtly for my liking, to find alternative office space and somewhere else to live. That wasn't particularly helpful counsel, given I possessed neither the wherewithal to pay rent, nor any local knowledge of the area. Hell, I hadn't even found the nearest noodle shop yet!

Fatigued following a futile Tuesday afternoon's office hunting, I ventured down to Soi Cowboy, an area renown for all the wrong reasons. Sitting outside a bar in this boisterous street of adult entertainment, I happened upon an old Army acquaintance. He was a former SAS man, who wouldn't tell me what he was doing in Bangkok, but who quickly had me sussed.

"Don't tell me you're working for Infoprobe?"

"Yes, I am."

"You've not replaced that drunken idiot of a manager have you?"

"Yes, I have."

"How old are you, Wally?"

"Forty something."

"Do you want to be forty something plus one?"

"Yes, of course."

"Then get your arse out of that company," he advised.

It was serious food for thought.

My dipsomaniac predecessor had made some investigations over in Vietnam and Laos, into the manufacture of 'look-alike' sound systems of a famous brand name. A shady entrepreneur was importing these items into Thailand and distributing them through his factory outlet in Bangkok. I had been left instructions to visit this factory; to confirm whether or not they had the items in stock and, if so, to establish both cost and delivery times for orders. Taking over someone else's incomplete investigation has never appealed to me and as I climbed the stairs to the dodgy sound system repository, it was without great enthusiasm. Very conveniently, there were actually some samples of the suspect products in the importer's office foyer and, given they were only orange boxes covered with veneer; they looked and sounded very reasonable to me. Once I'd gathered any evidence, Infoprobe would pass the information onto the genuine manufacturer's solicitors, who would then take up the legal battle. The fee for this kind of work was considerable and was, quite frankly, money for old rope.

My conversation with the managing director of the dodgy company appeared to be proceeding in the right direction and I was in the process of arranging to buy some of his counterfeit gear, when he opened his desk drawer. I imagined he was about to present me with a leather-bound diary, or perchance an expensive pen sporting his company's logo. How wrong can you be? From the drawer he pulled a Smith & Wesson 9mm pistol and put it onto his desk, with the business end pointing in my direction.

"Mr. Payne, I think it is time for you to leave my country," he said slowly.

His supposition was spot on; but what, or who, had given me away? This wasn't a good time to ask probing questions though and so I never did find out.

"Mr. Chatratpatdipong, you are absolutely right. With your kind permission, I shall take my leave of you forthwith and catch the very next flight out of your magnificent country."

It wasn't a classic speech, but brief and to the point. It probably saved me from getting a beating from a few of Chatratpatdipong's henchmen, or an even worse fate! Without standing on ceremony, I sped down the stairs, took a taxi to the Infoprobe office, packed my gear, took another taxi to the airport and put my first class Thai International ticket to good use. I didn't need any convincing to bin Infoprobe and get out of Thailand before any real mischief befell me. I tarried at Hong Kong airport just long enough to visit the Cathay Pacific office and splash out on a business class ticket back to the UK. My first, puny attempt at earning a living in Civvy Street hadn't lasted a month.

My Uncle Mark died as my Heathrow-bound flight was winging its way westwards; I knew there had to be some reason why fate had decreed my return to Blighty.

Chapter 2

Hong Kong

WHILST ATTENDING FUNERALS and contemplating my navel in the UK, I wrote to Adam Kenworthy at Infoprobe to explain the rationale behind my swift departure from Thailand. The letter was penned in what, for me, passes as a conciliatory style. It was made clear that I'd taken their job on the understanding it would be interesting, there would be scope to develop things as I saw fit and that my living conditions would be reasonable, at the very least. As I've already explained, the office and flat were in a perfectly disgraceful condition; Kenworthy gave me no advice or instructions whatsoever and even refused to talk about business during our weekend together in Bangkok. To make matters worse, Infoprobe had been exceedingly sparing with the information they were willing to divulge about the running of this operation. The truth is, the Thailand office existed for two simple reasons: firstly, to add the name of another major city to their company letterhead and, secondly, to give the directors a reason to visit Thailand regularly for a spot of sexual gratification at the company's expense. No flies on that pair!

Kenworthy's response to my missive was to lambaste me in no uncertain terms and demand reimbursement for the cost of my airfare from Bangkok to Hong Kong. Since I'd never received a penny piece from them by way of remuneration, I suggested they take the cost of the fare from my wages and give the residue to a charity of their choice. There was no further correspondence on the topic.

By the time I returned to Hong Kong some six weeks later, everyone had cooled down and the matter had been brushed under the carpet—part of the way. Just the same, there had been some strange goings on and Kenworthy had clearly made an effort to extract his pound of flesh. Several important pieces of mail addressed to me at the Bangkok office, including letters regarding my military pension rights and reserve commitment, along with letters from a lady friend in Hong Kong, had mysteriously disappeared. My lady friend began receiving correspondence from a person claiming to be Robert Robertson, an Englishman living in the Mei Foo Sun Chuen area which, coincidentally, was Kenworthy's place of abode. In his subsequent letters to her, he was brazen enough to mention her allegedly insatiable sexual appetite and asked if he might be of service. What a bounder! Despite her status as something of a lush, this upset the lady somewhat; enough for her to withdraw my common law conjugal rights. It cost me a considerable sum in gifts to regain her confidence, which was hard to bear since I was totally innocent for once. I know full well who penned those letters and it smelt very nasty, but since my hasty departure from Bangkok hadn't exactly covered me in glory, I let the matter go. Nevertheless, I would neither forget, nor forgive this unethical performance.

I had first met the aforementioned Filipina lady at one of my pal Lin Hung Yee's parties. She was quite presentable and fate dictated our paths should cross again. She would, I decided, do admirably as 'my bit on the side', someone to use for lewd purposes whenever the mood took me. For no other reason than to see how she would react to being propositioned thus, I invited her for supper in a posh restaurant. The meal and small talk safely negotiated, I wasted no time in putting my impure suggestions to her. She was somewhat taken aback, but mellowed considerably when the subject of a retainer was mentioned and promised to think about the proposal. By the time I returned from a routine visit to the lavatory, she had thought about it and accepted my roguish scheme. What this lady did to make ends meet I'm not sure, but if the size and location of her living quarters were anything to go by, it didn't pay very well. It was in this modest abode that I did my bit for the Philippines' balance of payments deficit. In fact, one of the most interesting sexual encounters of my life took place there, when my concubine's niece dropped in for a bite to eat as I was paying a flirtatious visit. Quite unperturbed by my disgraceful behaviour with her aunt, she demolished her Garoupa and Seaweed flavoured noodles, before washing her hands and joining in the fray.

Some time later, I uncovered Kenworthy's compulsion for making a play for the lady friends of his acquaintances. The salacious bugger was often guilty of sailing pretty close to the wind; far too close on the occasion he surreptitiously opened the address list on my mobile phone, noted the number of my current Filipina favourite and later called her to arrange a dinner date. My fury was considerable, especially when I discovered that the wanton hussy had actually accepted his invitation. My retaliation was both swift and savage; she was struck off my Christmas card list with no further ado! He was a deviate, albeit inventive man when it came to obtaining sexual gratification. One of his favourite ploys was to visit a massage parlour during the afternoon and allow the duty harlot to pleasure him until, when nearing the point of no return, he would telephone his secretary and chat to her about work related subjects. Each to their own I suppose.

Whether feeling guilty for his misdeeds, or simply for the joy of my sparkling company, Kenworthy continued to invite me out socially. We took lunch in the finest restaurants a couple of times a week, with the substantial bills invariably finding their way to his expense account. His reputation as a generous tipper ensured exemplary service and resulted in

10

some thoroughly pleasant nosebags in restaurants I certainly couldn't have afforded to patronize.

Other highlights of my week were our visits to the race tracks at Sha Tin and Happy Valley where, as part owner of a horse called Royal Blue, Kenworthy was always able to book tables in the superior owners' restaurants. Furthermore, his insider knowledge and personal form analysis system ensured a fair proportion of winning bets. His intimate knowledge of what was going on in Hong Kong, his pre-eminence as a whoremonger of the first polish and undoubted generosity ensured some truly enjoyable times for me. If only he would have stopped trying to steal my latest flame!

One evening's entertainment with the rogue will always stick out in my mind. It was the time he coerced me into accompanying him to the Annual General Meeting of the Hong Kong MENSA Society, held at the Royal Hong Kong Police Officers' Club in Causeway Bay. Kenworthy boasted of an IQ only a point or two short of him being declared a genius, although I believe he may have obtained his high standing and probably even his membership via the back door. My presence at the meeting was in the capacity of 'member's mate', as I had never considered applying to join what I have always perceived to be something of a screwball organisation. Before official business got underway, the president of the society rose to give his opening address and to bid a hearty welcome to any newcomers.

"I see there are several new faces at the meeting this evening. You sir, would you care to rise and introduce yourself?" he said to a man dressed in a shirt almost loud enough to hear.

"Evenin' y'all," drawled a southern state American, "I'm Leroy Goldblatt the Third and I'm a member of Mensa in Tuscaloosa, Alabama," he declared with pride.

"Welcome to Hong Kong, Leroy," replied the president, "I trust you'll enjoy your time with your brothers here in the Far East."

"And you sir?" he said, addressing a man sporting a natty line in Lederhosen.

"Schön guten Abend zusammen. My name Fritz von Menninghausen ist and my Mensa club locates from Augsburg in Germany."

There was applause, albeit somewhat muted, for the man from the Fatherland.

I was the third visage unknown to the president.

"And you sir, would you care to tell us who you are?"

I rose slowly to my feet.

"My name is Wally Payne and I am an alcoholic," I falsely confessed.

"Don't be a prat! Our AA meetings are on Tuesdays, today's Friday," said Kenworthy, the straight man in our well-rehearsed routine.

There was a stunned silence. Perhaps our little joke wasn't deserving of a belly laugh, but surely it merited a titter or two. They may all have been brighter than me academically, but at the cost of a sense of humour apparently.

I can always rely on my mate Lin Hung Yee to fix things when I'm in Hong Kong and he responded to my plea for some reasonably cheap, long-term accommodation by booking me into the Bonham Hotel, in the Bonham Strand area of Western district. The Bonham was probably one of the tallest, surely the thinnest and definitely the shortest-lived hostelry in the history of Hong Kong. It was built, performed its task as a hotel and was converted into an office complex, all within eighteen months.

It was in my postage stamp sized room on the thirteenth floor of this billet that it finally dawned on me. The prospects of a person of my vintage landing gainful employment in the colony weren't altogether rosy. Being a freemason would have enhanced my prospects considerably I learnt retrospectively, but I wasn't, am still not and don't ever aspire to being 'on the square'. I read every job ad appearing in the *South China Morning Post* and the *Hong Kong Standard* for two months, replied to anything even vaguely in my line and waited in vain for replies.

My solitary job interview was for a position as the controller of a Vietnamese Boat People Camp, located on a forlorn island somewhere in the South China Sea. Having been an Army administration officer, it was a position for which I considered myself ably qualified. Alas, the longhaired, bearded, Liverpudlian UNHCR scruff who interviewed me didn't share my view. This archetypal member of the 'do-gooder' brigade, a man possessed of a particularly irritating guttural accent, couldn't get it through his thick, socialist skull that soldiers actually left barracks from time to time. I'm certain he considered us self-sufficient creatures who remained battened down in our little cantonments until we were ready to fade away. The bearded buffoon! Have you ever noticed how everyone associated with supposedly benevolent organizations: like Greenpeace, Amnesty International, Oxfam, Shelter, Médecins sans Frontiers, Save the Children and the likes, sports a beard? I don't like people with beards and, on women; I consider them particularly unbecoming.

Fortunately, being the inmate of lodgings as humble as the Bonham didn't prevent me from inviting the odd female member of the species back to take a look at my etchings. Standing in the 'Wanch Bar' one evening, I found myself sharing a packed corner with a couple who had been playing badminton. He was a boring fart, although his buxom partner was rather easy on the eye and, unless I was sadly mistaken, ripe for the plucking. Having just downed my fifth pint of the amber nectar, something rather unusual occurred. Exiting the latrines following a routine discharge, I discovered the short-skirted badminton player waiting for me.

"Are you staying in a hotel?" she enquired.

That wasn't an easy question to answer. The Bonham hardly merited such a lofty description, but I nodded to indicate the affirmative just the same.

"Would you care to take me back to your room and fuck me?" asked the brazen temptress.

Now this question wasn't nearly as difficult to answer and so I took her by the hand, initially. Her badminton partner wasn't best pleased to see his red-hot promise going off with a substitute, but he didn't offer any stern resistance. I can report my subsequent behaviour with this lewd lady to have been of a purely functional nature. This brief tryst, though, actually cost me money. Part of my post coital patter with a female I have not the slightest interest in seeing again, is to take her address and telephone number. This prevents them from getting maudlin and they leave the field of combat with hope in their hearts. This lady contrived to leave her badminton gear behind in my room and, rather than consign it to the bin, I posted it onto her. Almost HK$10 down the drain!

Her Majesty had been gracious enough to deposit a sizeable sum of money into my bank account when I finished working for the crown. I elected to take the maximum amount of gratuity and smaller monthly pension; this way, more of my filthy lucre was available in a lump sum and could be disposed of as I saw fit. And there's no easier place to be parted from your money than in Hong Kong, ask anyone who lives there. Nevertheless, nowhere on earth suits me better than Honkers does and I was perfectly happy to take a year or so off, to do whatsoever took my fancy.

There lurks within me a trace of talent as a storyteller, or so I'd been told. It occurred to me; therefore, that since I had nothing better to do, perhaps committing my numerous tales to paper might be a worthwhile undertaking. So, whilst indulging in my passion for walking the hills, I carried with me a notebook into which the briefest details of any memories I could dredge from the darkest recesses of my memory could be recorded. Hundreds of stories came to mind in this fashion and many of them found their way, firstly into my notebook, and then into my autobiographical volumes.

Only a fool would walk the hills of Hong Kong in the dark and so, whilst honing my mind and body to perfection during the day, there remained ample time to socialize in the evenings. The naughty Wanchai area was only three stops away from my hotel on the MTR underground system and, since I had the requirement to replace the bodily fluids expended during my often strenuous walks, several of the bars in the area benefited from my patronage. The company of a lady was easy enough to come by whenever a gentleman had the urge; the Hong Kong Cultural Centre always had something on to stimulate my highbrow musical tastes; one could gamble for twenty-four hours a day in nearby Macau, as well as throw one's money away at the Sha Tin and Happy Valley racetracks; my chum Lin was forever organising Chinese dinners and, when I tired of the flesh pots, the Methodist Church was always there as my spiritual home. I was a contented retired soldier.

One Saturday morning, I arranged to go hiking on Lantau Island with County Tyrone's very own Jackie Currie. Having waited in vain as three ferries deposited their passengers at Mui Wo, I reluctantly accepted that the unreliable Ulsterman wasn't going to show. Meanwhile, I'd noticed a chap dressed in walking gear doing exactly the same thing as me; waiting patiently. He turned out to be an American who, thinking he was in Discovery Bay, was waiting for his walking partner to arrive. Discovery Bay was several miles away; his map-reading skills had failed him at the first hurdle. Rather than forego a day's exercise however, we agreed to walk together. As a stranger to the area, he was glad to accept my plan for a trek of perhaps a dozen miles, but he wasn't aware my proposed route would take us over some exceedingly severe terrain. Hong Kong is awash with splendid hiking routes; the pity is that the ambient temperature and humidity can make the going very tough indeed for the better part of the year.

My newly found victim and I took the Inter-island ferry as far as Chi Ma Wan, walked around the Vietnamese Boat People's prison camp and headed up towards the hills. This was an area I knew intimately and which, at this hot and humid time of the year, was a very testing place to hike. Being well used to trekking around the Lantau hills, even in high summer, my planned walk would be well within my capabilities. Whether this soft Yank would last the distance was debatable. Having set a hot pace up and down the slopes, I expected to see the American dropping behind, but he remained right behind me. The final ascent before getting back to our starting point at Mui Wo was very hard going indeed, but my transatlantic cousin stuck like glue, right up to the time we turned into Papa Doc's hostelry for some well-deserved liquid refreshment.

For a chap who had only been in the humid summer climate of South East Asia for a couple days, especially someone who had been in temperate Scandinavia for the previous eight weeks, his fitness was remarkable.

"By the way Tyler, exactly what were you doing in Norway?" I enquired over an ice-cold pint of San Miguel.

"Oh, I was part of the USA national team taking part in the World Orienteering Championships," he said modestly.

And I'd tried to test him for stamina!

The Hong Kong Football Club soccer team was in the First Division at this time and my chum Gordon Ross was their physiotherapist. Bumping into him one afternoon, he enquired whether I fancied watching the Club's match against Eastern at the Government Stadium that evening. Nothing appeals to me more than watching a match, so along I went. My seat was directly behind the team benches and, when Gordon spotted me, he promptly invited me down to join the Club's hierarchy on the touchline. Thus, the bench was graced by the presence of the manager and his number two, Gordon and the club trainer, a brace of substitutes and me.

Halfway through the first-half, there was a mighty coming together of players and a member of the Eastern team was left pole-axed on the ground. The frantic waving of arms by players of both teams indicated something seriously amiss with the fallen hero. In Hong Kong, it takes the combined efforts of the managers, coaches, trainers, ambulance men and substitutes to sort out a serious injury and the wounded man left the field of combat on a stretcher, surrounded by a phalanx of helpers, well-wishers and those who just fancied getting their pictures in the paper next morning. The mass evacuation left a total of two lonely souls to man the Club team's dugout—one of the substitutes and me. Sod's Law dictated there would be trouble before the rest of the management crew returned and, sure enough, one of the Club players went down. The substitute ran on to attend him, but before he could walk him back to the bench, another player bedecked in the Club's royal blue hit the dirt. He required medical assistance too and, as I was the only person left in the dugout, the referee called me on. Attired in a bespoke suit, silk tie and hand-made shoes, I must have cut a dapper figure as I sped, gazelle-like, onto the pitch. My St. John's Ambulance Brigade first-aid certificate had expired decades previously and it came as a blessed relief to discover that my patient was suffering from nothing more serious than a kick in the nether regions. Following a few 'knees bend' and a splash of water, he was soon ready to resume the battle. I defy this player, or any other player for that matter, to say he was ever sluiced down by a more sartorially elegant magic 'sponge man' than me.

Lin Hung Yee, one of my oldest and best friends, was the leader of the gang of Chinese with whom I socialized on a regular basis. Our twice-weekly social evenings were held at whatever restaurant was giving the best deal on the night; the only constant being that the restaurant would most certainly never previously have celebrated the presence of a *gwai-lo* customer. Our parties were often rowdy affairs.

One of our regular watering holes was the Pigeon Restaurant in Chai Wan, an establishment boasting a capacity for some four-hundred patrons. The restaurant's special attraction one November evening, in addition to the usual invitation to 'eat and drink all you can', was the appearance of Taiwan's chanteuse of high repute—Felicity Wong, the Taipei Nightingale. This was an offer too good to miss and our gang trooped along en masse to make an attempt on the Chai Wan all-comers' brandy drinking record. Both Felicity Wong and the chefs were in top form and, by half-time in the proceedings, life had taken on a rosy glow. The *maître d'* suddenly appeared at our table and began to chat to my pal Cecil Chan. I heard my name mentioned and noticed the *maître* taking notes.

"W-A-L-L-Y. Warry," Cecil replied to a question posed in Cantonese and therefore unintelligible to me.

"P-A-Y-N-E. Paynee," he replied to the second question.

"What's going on Cecil?" I asked.

"You only 'gwai-lo' in restaurant; he want know what is your name."

By this time I'd consumed sufficient brandy and beer to accept his implausible response without delving deeper. After the half-time break, it was time for Felicity to start her second set of songs. The lights all went out; there was a roll of drums; an announcement in Cantonese and a bright spotlight picked out the scantily clad Taipei Nightingale. A second roll of drums was followed by another announcement in Cantonese, which included the words, 'Mister Warry Paynee'. The blinding, million candle power spotlight then picked me out and a dozen of my pals pushed me forward towards the stage. Felicity, I discovered as we stood together on the boards, was both a charming lady and fluent in English. My sudden appearance was clearly as big a surprise to her, as it was to me

"You can't sing anything in Mandarin I suppose?" she enquired, with more than a hint of desperation.

"Strangely enough, I can," I answered to her obvious relief, "I know Rose, Rose, I love you."

The band, having been thus informed, burst into tune and Felicity and I gave it our best effort. When we finished, the audience erupted into ecstatic applause and I ran off stage with the words 'encore, encore' ringing in my ears. Strange the Cantonese should use the French expression of appreciation, but they do. There was no chance of an encore from me however, I'd already returned to our table to berate my inscrutable friends; the bastards! On subsequent visits to this restaurant, my first priority was to establish a quick escape route, just in case.

On Armistice Day 1991, I took my daily dose of caffeine in the Delifrance coffee shop at World Wide Plaza in Central. Having drained a second cup, I vacated my seat with the intention of heading towards the GPO, to post some letters. At precisely the same moment, whether by accident or design, an attractive Filipina also happened to be leaving the cafe. We nodded. Crossing the pedestrian overpass leading towards to post office, I noticed the lady again. She turned around, saw me trudging along behind her and then carried on. To my dismay, she turned around several more times and despite the serpentine route, on each occasion, there I was still marching along behind her. Finally, I felt obliged to speak, just in case she imagined a stalker was at his work.

"I'm not following you miss; simply heading for the post office," I explained. "Me too," she replied.

We went to the Post Office together and then for another cup of coffee. I used to drink far too much coffee in those days! This lady was subsequently to play an important part in my life.

My pleasing lifestyle continued through to Christmas and now there was the added enjoyment of seeing my latest lady friend at weekends, on weekdays too if she could escape the gaze of her tyrannical Chinese employers. The New Year saw me accommodated in the altogether plusher Wesley Hotel in Wanchai, where I stayed for a couple of months before making yet another trip to the UK on the scent of a job. My search for gainful employment in Leicester having fallen on stony ground, I soon returned to Hong Kong. Then, before you could say 'Confucius', summer was upon us and, with it, the realisation I'd been living the Life of Riley for a very long time and getting nowhere quick. To make matters worse, I was living the good life in one of the most expensive cities in the world. My Filipina and I were getting pretty close and, as she was mightily cheesed off with her employers, I suggested we move to the Philippines for a while and test the water over there. There were no arguments from the blue corner and, once she'd settled things with the Chinese family for whom she worked, we booked our tickets to Manila. With two days remaining in Hong Kong before our flight, Nelia undertook the task of finding us a transit hotel. In all innocence, she chose a place that looked good and was reasonably priced. The Beverley Hotel in Lockhart Road however, was a hotel not best known for its long term guests and a two-night sojourn qualified us as exceedingly long-stay visitors indeed. I took the precaution of removing the contraceptives placed in the bathroom for the use of the short timers before she had a chance to see them. None too soon, the pair of us were aboard an eastbound Philippine Airlines 747, sitting in Mabuhay Class of course.

Chapter 3

Philippines

IN MANILA, Nelia booked us into a rather shabby looking hostelry called 'Robelle House'. From the ring of its name, one would be forgiven for imagining the establishment to be an Anglican Retreat House, although judging from the cut of our fellow residents, the place clearly did business along the same lines as the Beverley Hotel in Hong Kong. The lady will confess to having a poor track record when it comes to selecting hotels of an acceptable standard.

After a couple of days doing the tourist rounds of Manila, we set off in an overcrowded and under-maintained bus to do some house hunting. Exactly why we headed south and alighted at a place called Pacita Complex has never been satisfactorily established, but this sprawling residential mess in Laguna Province was to become *chez-nous* for the next few years. We rented a place in Antique Street, (named after an area in the Philippines incidentally and in no way indicative of the ages of the residents), which had remained unoccupied since it was built some years previously. Although a most acceptable residence by Filipino standards, it seemed terribly compact to me. Now, I'm no civil engineer, but there were things about the way Number 24 had been cobbled together that worried me considerably and probably explained why the house had never attracted any previous tenants. Not the least of my concerns was a double-socket electrical plug fitted inside the shower cubicle! Health and Safety considerations assume an exceedingly low profile in the Philippine Islands.

Little did I know when signing the lease, but hidden under a few inches of poor topsoil in the garden lay not only a builder's spoil tip, but also the Regimental Headquarters and three battalions of the San Pedro Armoured Cockroach. These facts only became apparent after I'd acquired the necessary tools and made my first foray into the garden. Once disturbed by my horticultural endeavours, the insects crashed out from their peacetime location and took up defensive positions in the area I'd designated for my herbaceous border. A battle plan needed to be formulated to stop these loathsome creatures from infesting the house and so I made a rapid military appreciation of the situation. Cockroaches don't like water you know, so, by giving their nest a good sluicing to bring all the buggers to the surface, I set about them with a flat piece of wood. The battle swung to and fro, the outcome remaining in the balance; until chemical warfare, in the shape of a tetramethin and propoxus combination contained in a can of insect repellent finally won the day.

I planted the whole area with quick growing 'kamote' plants; sweet potatoes to us. They were coming along splendidly and I was looking forward to a bumper harvest, when the Barangay captain and a delegation from the street committee descended upon me. The shade created by komote leaves, I was reliably informed, is the favourite habitat of snakes and the plants were not welcome in urban gardens. They were promptly dug up and, as a reward for my compliance, an invitation to the next men's street party was delivered. At this gathering, the topic of handguns was uppermost in the conversation and the Barangay captain, a sort of a local sheriff, was aghast to discover that the Payne household didn't possess a firearm. He called at our house the very next evening and presented me with his spare pistol; a weapon which stayed with me for a couple of years without ever being used in anger. The captain also gave me an assurance: in the event of me needing to shoot any burglars, then a phone call to him would suffice to have the problem resolved without any questions being asked. In the Philippines, the attitude towards burglars and intruders is to shoot them first and sort the paperwork out with the police afterwards; although a small financial consideration would probably be expected to smooth the matter away. What's wrong with such a sensible approach most rational people might ask?

My military acquaintances would have been amazed to see how well the man who couldn't screw in a light bulb, or perform the simplest of practical chores, set about gardening and painting. Perhaps I'd inherited some of my Dad's practical skills after all. Meanwhile, Her Ladyship set about planning exactly where best to site our new household appliances, to ensure the neighbours could see them to full advantage. Whether equipment actually functions is secondary to showing it off in Filipino eyes.

My aversion to dogs dictated that we would be the only family in the whole of Pacita Complex without a canine companion. "No bloody mongrel will ever see the inside of my place of abode," I'd vehemently declared. So, just where did Bingo come from and why the hell did I allow him to stay? The fact is, the little fellow melted even my hard heart. Alas, he was a sickly chap from the outset and died whilst still in his infancy. He was interred in secret, to prevent any passing Roman Catholic priests praying over the grave and demanding a fee for performing the obsequies. When we had our deep-water well sunk a week later, the drilling team, by my reckoning, went straight through the mortal remains of our Bingo. Consequently, I was never too keen on the water drawn from our private artesian source thereafter.

To my considerable surprise, there were two other white inhabitants living within a stone's throw of our abode in Antique Street. Alec Lanchester was a Brummie and, as if such an accident of birth wasn't tragic enough, he was an Aston Villa supporter to boot. He claimed to be a descendent of the Lanchester car family, but didn't appear to have two centavos to rub together. All his waking hours were dedicated to planting and tending vegetables on a piece of waste ground near his home and he was inordinately proud of his efforts; until he arrived to water them one morning and discovered that some rotten swine had stolen the lot. He never continued with his agricultural endeavours thereafter. Gardening is simple and, from my point of view, if you can't grow things in the hot and humid conditions prevailing in the Philippines, then you haven't much chance of lifting a prize at the Chelsea Flower Show. There's many a time I've left a stick in the garden overnight, only to discover it bearing fruit next morning.

The other lost soul, who lived at the corner house in Antique Street, was an East German. Judging from his standoffishness and the number of defensive installations that sprang up around his house, he was expecting a visit from the Stasi at any moment. Try as I might, this guy was determined not to reveal his antecedents and he took to slipping back indoors the moment he espied me approaching his fortified ramparts. On reflection though, confessing my erstwhile service as a British Military Policeman perhaps wasn't the best way of gaining his trust. It was his young son who finally spilt the beans, by telling me his father was an ex-policeman from East Berlin and that 'Onkel Hermann' had paid for them to resettle in the Far East. Some months later they all disappeared, without a word, never to be seen again.

If you are a tall, well-built, football-loving gentleman who has lived an orderly life in the military and has an aversion to dogs, with the possible exception of winning greyhounds, then let me tell you something: Pacita Complex isn't for you! For a start, it isn't known as the 'dog shit capital' of South East Asia for nothing. Dogs with a loud bark are particularly cherished, for their ability to scare away potential burglars and Jehovah's Witnesses. Another prime annoyance is the constant sound of a large ball being bounced, rather than kicked, by playing children. It can be very wearing, especially since absolutely everyone plays basketball and every other house has a hoop erected in the garden. Why didn't they kick the ball? Then I might have gone and played with them and passed on a few of my silky skills! It has often occurred to me that, since the average height of a Filipino is around 5 feet 3, surely basketball is a bird-brained game to select as a national sport?

No right-minded European would ever contemplate a visit to Pacita Complex but, should you ever be smitten with an overwhelming urge, then make it brief. In no particular order, here is a list of things that will drive you progressively insane:

Power Brown Outs – Black outs to us British, but in a country so heavily influenced by the USA, they call them brown outs to be more politically correct. They invariably occur during the exciting part of a film; when you haven't 'saved' on the computer, or whenever Leicester City are on Match of the Day and one of our players is bearing down on goal.

Dog shit – Almost every house in Pacita Complex has at least one dog, specifically trained to bark whenever a burglar approaches within fifty yards. As dogs can't tell the difference between a burglar, the postman and any law-abiding citizen, they bark constantly. They also shit constantly, making torches a prerequisite whenever strolling at night, especially during a brown out.

Burning Rubbish – For reasons that have baffled sociologists for centuries, Filipinos feel compelled to carry a box of matches with them at all times. Thus, they are perfectly 'tooled-up' for setting fire to anything combustible and, should the resulting smoke be offensive or, better still, toxic; they feel fulfilled. Like the Olympic Flame, the rubbish tip at the San Pedro Cockfighting Arena is permanently alight; thereby rendering this den of iniquity a place to be given a wide berth by asthmatics and bronchitis sufferers.

Balut – A balut is a duck egg with an embryonic duckling inside. It is boiled and eaten, with salt, whilst still warm. It looks disgusting and, to the British palate, tastes disgusting too. Vendors toting trays of the offending objects patrol the street in the evenings booming, "Baluuuuuuuuuuut!" This not only alerts balut devotees of their presence, but also has the effect of waking all the babies and dogs in the neighbourhood.

Mosquitoes – The hybrid strain of mosquito prevalent in Antique Street is a cross between the Hungarian Horned Horsefly and a Griffon Vulture. They are most certainly not creatures to be trifled with.

Buses – The average Filipino is rarely much more than five feet tall and has a proportionately minute bottom. Consequently, three adults can fit into the bench seats of buses imported from Japan with consummate ease. Conversely, the standard, cuddly, British bum cannot and, thus, travel by bus becomes an ordeal. The answer is to buy all three seats, goodness knows they are cheap enough, but that gives the green light to every sad-looking old lady in town to come and join you for a free ride. Filipinos are mentally incapable of settling into the first seat they occupy and, upon boarding the vehicle, a mass outbreak of 'musical bus seats' ensues. Once seated, passengers are next overtaken by a 'lemming style' compulsion to twiddle with the cold-air adjusters. Unless his vehicle is full to capacity, no bus driver would dream of departing from the terminus. This can prove a time consuming business should there be a European aboard, since no Filipino will sit next to a white man, unless forcibly required to do so.

Motor Tricycles – These are also made for a nation of midgets and, unless you are willing to risk life and limb by sitting on the pillion, it is necessary to cock your head to one side when wedged into the sidecar. Despite this enforced contortion, you are still guaranteed to hit your head on the roof each time the driver negotiates a bump in the road. I'm convinced my spondylosis came about as a direct result of travelling in tricycles.

The Jeepney – This vehicle is peculiar to the Philippine Islands, something for which the rest of the world should be truly grateful and being a passenger in such a conveyance should to be avoided at all costs. A 14-seater will contain a minimum of 16 passengers, all of whom will be crammed in like sardines. An added annoyance for anyone of average European height is the roof, which is constructed to suit only the perpendicularly challenged. Drivers are manic and the vehicles never roadworthy. Tyres seldom sport any tread and spares aren't considered worthy of attaching to the vehicle unless they have material showing through the rubber. Indicators are not normally fitted and, if they are, then they are most certainly never used. The vehicle will swerve regularly from lane to lane and will stop anywhere to pick up or disgorge passengers, invariably in a spot that causes maximum inconvenience to other road users. Jeepney drivers are often drunk, drugged or both and will seldom be in possession of insurance, or a driver's licence.

An unwritten code of honour exists amongst Filipino public service transport drivers: their vehicles must remain under maintained and in contravention of as many construction and use regulations as possible. Clouds of burning oil emanating from the exhaust pipe, a condition known locally as 'smoke belching', is particularly encouraged. With roads invariably narrow, it follows that the speed of the slowest jeepney dictates the pace attainable by all other means of transportation.

Driving – Journeys in the Philippines are measured in one of two Ministry of Transport officially sanctioned methods: the kilometre (km) and the Near Death Incident (NDI). The distance from home to my daughter's school was 5 x NDI and was a journey I undertook four times a day. My Valium dependency cannot be disassociated from this ordeal. A fundamental tenet of all Filipino drivers is to remain blithely unaware of whatever is going on around you. Take my advice and hire a driver.

Mail – The Philippines Postal Service must surely be the most inept postal organization in the world. If the post office should perchance have any stamps in stock, letters to Europe will gather dust before being considered worthy of onward transmission. Arriving mail will be stamped with the date it's received at the post office, although this date in no way indicates the letter will be delivered any time soon. If the postman designated to an area should be sick or on leave, then his mail will remain undelivered until he returns, bronzed, from his fortnight on Boracay Island. There are no post boxes in the Philippines; the letters therein wouldn't last five minutes before being stolen, or set alight.

Wet Toilet Seats – Filipinos consider anal and rectal cleanliness to be next to godliness. They also consider toilet paper unhygienic and so, in the absence of a bidet, they wash their nether regions with water, usually contained in a plastic bucket lodged adjacent to the WC. The result is a shit and water mixture, which is retained on the lavvy seat for the next visitor to sit on. Should you be foolhardy enough to take up residence in this blighted land, then do what I did and have a second lavatory installed and marked, "For European Use Only!" Slightly racist I'll grant you, but well worth the risk of prosecution.

Water Bucket – Despite the fact the Philippines is awash with water for the majority of the year, perceived water shortages are never far from the mind of the inhabitants. Consequently, all Filipino lavatories and showers contain at least one large plastic pail full of water, just in case there should ever be a drought. It serves no discernable purpose, other than to cause maximum annoyance and prove an ideal object for stubbing one's toe upon.

Noise – The pandemonium prevalent in any residential area, especially during the hours when normal human beings are intent on sleeping, tests the limits of tolerance. Imagine if you can, a fusion of noise incorporating Battersea Dogs' Home, a maternity ward, a lunatic asylum and the second Battle of the Somme and you're getting somewhere near. Music is invariably played at maximum volume, with the bass turned up full to produce sound waves strong enough to resonate throughout the neighbourhood.

Compulsion to Urinate – Filipinos, both male and female, find it physically impossible to pass a public convenience without taking advantage of the facilities. Moreover, males of the species feel biologically compelled to urinate in public, oblivious of passing girls' school buses or flocks of nuns.

Police – A pre-requisite for entry into the ranks of the Philippine Police Department is to be grossly overweight, to have as little knowledge of English (the language in which they operate) as possible and possess the sleight of hand to move a bribe from hand to pocket at a velocity greater than that of a speeding bullet. The ability to detect a foreigner at the wheel of an approaching vehicle still several hundreds of yards distant, and then stop him to extort money for some spurious moving traffic offence, is considered a promotion enhancing quality.

Death Wishes – I've weighed more than 200 lbs for a long time but, if a 400 lb man was bearing down on me in a shopping mall, then, as sure as God didn't make little green apples and it don't rain in Indianapolis in the summer time, I'd get out of his way. Why then, do 100 lb Filipinos insist on flirting with disaster by running across my path at every opportunity? Similarly, what drives Filipinos to gather in large numbers to engage in conversation at the top and bottom of escalators, oblivious of those stepping on or alighting?

During the days of my incarceration in Antique Street, my Friday evenings were occasionally illuminated by a visit to Makati City's 'P Burgos' bar area, along with a crowd of expatriate senior citizens. In deference to the age of our group, our evenings rarely extended beyond 2200 hrs, although we enjoyed some jolly times nevertheless. In truth, by this time I was ready for a rest anyway. In such antiquated company you see, my comparative youth made me the primary target for swooping colonies of bar girls. Naturally, I strove to uphold the standards expected of a military policeman, but there are limits to a chap's stamina.

The senior member of the 'jolly boys' was John Kent, a fellow Englishman and all-round good guy. John decided to eschew the hustle and bustle of the big city, by moving down to the south of Luzon, to enjoy the hustle and bustle of Legaspi City. A couple of years later he died and Alex McNee, the

Aussie representative of our little band, went down south to pay his final respects to our old drinking companion. Upon his return, Alex arranged to meet me at the Prince of Wales pub in Makati City, to tell me all about his pilgrimage to Lagaspi. I arrived rather earlier than scheduled, intent on drinking a couple of beers before steeling myself for the unenviable task of looking at funeral photographs. At the bar I fell into conversation with an amiable Norwegian and, when Alex arrived, we invited Lars to join us for lunch. As I'd feared, Alex produced the mandatory Filipino funeral photos, which I waded through with scant interest before passing them onto Lars. He gave the photos a cursory glance too and handed them back to Alex. It was when Alex produced his *pièce de résistance*, a photo of John lying in his coffin, that Lars sat bolt upright.

"Oh my God, it's John Kent!" he said.

"You know him?"

"Very well indeed! We drank together for many years at the Scandinavian Seamen's Club!"

When I first arrived in the Philippines, it simply wasn't possible to buy British foodstuffs. True, on the odd occasion, the Makati Supermarket saw fit to stock the kind of treats that had kept the British Army on the move throughout the centuries. The most sought after commodity was HP Sauce and, whenever news of the delivery of a consignment became common knowledge, then the rush of expatriates towards the store was, to say the least, undisciplined. On the day of the 'Great HP Sauce Riots', they had all but sold out by the time I arrived from Laguna Province. My swift reconnaissance of the store revealed, standing in supreme isolation on the top shelf of the condiments section, a solitary, orphaned bottle of the splendid preparation. I wasn't alone in having spotted the prize and it was a three-way race for this last bottle; between me, an attractive, big-breasted beauty in high-heels and an old biddy sporting a tweed suit and sensible shoes. It was a 'no contest' really, although the old lady showed commendable speed out of the blocks and had actually made a grab for the bottle, before I felled her with a sharp elbow to the ribs. The resultant fracas showed the British in the worst possible light, as various factions took the side of the old lady, or me. Both material and physical damage was done and, to be frank, my performance would have won me no awards for sportsmanship. Just the same, I hung on pugnaciously to my bottle and the sauce tasted 'gradely' on my chip sandwiches. How tragic that Heinz now makes the stuff in the Netherlands.

The shore of Laguna de Bay, the second biggest freshwater lake in South East Asia, lay not a mile from our abode. Not that you could get remotely close to the shoreline, since all the land surrounding the lake appeared to be in private hands. After yet another failed attempt to be the first Briton to roll up his trouser legs and paddle in the lake, I was returning home defeated when I happened upon a small, ramshackle house. In the garden were a battalion's worth of fighting cocks, all tethered to stakes knocked into the ground and strategically placed to keep them from attacking each other. Whilst taking a few pictures, the owner emerged from his hovel to pass the time of day. Not unnaturally, the conversation turned to his fighting cocks; the finest in the whole of San Pedro by all accounts. It had been his intention to enter his supreme pair in the forthcoming San Pedro Cockfighting Derby he confided, but financial difficulties meant he couldn't raise the required entry fee. For the peso equivalent of a fiver, my fiver, Carlos and I entered the two cocks for the Derby taking place on Saturday evening. Despite Carlos' optimism, both of his birds were killed in their first fight! The owners of the triumphant roosters even exercised their winners' prerogative, by taking our poultry home for Sunday lunch. How terribly unsporting! I promptly announced my retirement from the cock-fighting game.

Nelia had been much taken by the pronounced Leicester accent of my cousin Jim, whom she'd met when he paid a visit to Hong Kong. Along with dropped aitches, the Leicester vernacular requires words containing the letter 'i' to be articulated as if they were spelt 'oi'. Consequently:

> bike = boike
> like = loike
> nice = noice.

You can clearly pick out this idiosyncrasy in almost every overheard conversation in the fair city. Thus, a 'question and answer' session with Jim might have gone thus:

"Did you like the fried rice Jim?"

"Yes, it were noice, very noice."

"How's that for a view Jim?"

"It's noice. Very noice."

"How was your leg-over last night?"

"Noice. Very, very noice."

We attended the Union Church in Lagaspi Village in those days, a church run along Methodist and Baptist lines. Eucharist was only taken on a monthly basis and, because of the immense size of the congregation, communicants were served in the pews by a bevy of acolytes. The bread could be dispatched at one's leisure, but it was traditional to save the glass of wine, or fruit juice, in a rack set into the pew in front and drink it once everyone had been served. Nelia always took fruit juice but, one day, in a moment of reckless abandon, she selected the wine. The minister administered a prayer; everyone drank and then settled back for a few moments of pious contemplation. There wasn't a sound to be heard, not until a solitary voice was heard to whisper, "Noice, very noice." Thereafter, the word 'noice' became *de rigueur* in our family conversations.

My journey home from church on Sundays took me along one of the world's widest racetracks; Epifanio de los Santos Avenue, mercifully known as EDSA for short. Despite multiple lanes in each direction, traffic along this highway is manic and impossibly heavy at all times. At one point, my route home made it necessary to swerve from the inside lane to the extreme outside lane in order to make the flyover heading to Alabang and the south. This is a manoeuvre best undertaken at top speed, with a prayer on your lips and most definitely with the eyes closed. One particular Sunday however, the enormous overhead sign for 'Alabang' had been relocated from the outside, to a middle lane. In the erroneous assumption they had made some road changes, I drove in the lane indicated, before needing to swerve violently at the last moment as the 'Alabang' sign re-appeared, three lanes to my right. A lurking policeman, sensing the possibility of a bribe, signalled for me to halt. As he fumbled for his pencil and notebook, I watched two-dozen other vehicles, all driven by Filipinos, perform exactly the same last-gasp manoeuvre I'd just needed to make. The corpulent policeman didn't raise an eyebrow when I pointed out this mass motoring infraction, although he did make a half-hearted, but ultimately futile attempt to stop a couple of cars, before returning to the more pressing business of extorting coin of the realm from an 'Americano'. My flat refusal to pay a bribe forced him to issue me with a fixed-penalty ticket. Miffed at his failure to get a bung, he threw the book at me and I was cited not only for the bizarre sounding offence of 'dangerous swerving', but also for 'reckless driving'. He incurred my considerable wrath, by attempting to use my car boot as a convenient place on which to lean his book of tickets. Once he had desisted and used his thigh as a substitute, I also took him to task about the accusation of reckless driving and asked him if he could define 'reckless'. He couldn't. I considered fighting the case, but the combined fine for both offences amounted to the peso equivalent of a mere £7. Considering this to be cheap at twice the price and simply for the experience, I paid the fine at the Coconut Planters' Bank as required.

We were invited to our neighbours' church wedding, which was being held some fifteen years after their registry office ceremony. Actually, it's quite a common occurrence for Filipinos to forgo the non-mandatory church wedding altogether, on the grounds of expense. The neighbours belonged to a group called 'Couples for Christ' however and, along with another dozen pairs from the organisation, they had agreed on a mammoth-sized church wedding, with the costs shared thirteen ways, at the suggestion of their local priest. The groom asked me to be his sponsor and, as this involved only standing next to him at the altar and, more importantly, minimal financial outlay, I accepted the undertaking. I arrived at the church at the prescribed hour, resplendent in a suit constructed of material altogether too heavy for the prevailing weather conditions, only to discover that, apart from the priest, no one else was present. Nothing happens on time in the Philippines it seems, not even a wedding. A couple of hours later, once everyone had located San Lorenzo Church in Biñan, Laguna, the priest got the show on the road. The poor chap was suffering from malaria and wasn't in the best of form, but he succeeded in marrying the whole crowd in record time just the same.

From the church, it was on to the reception held in a large garden somewhere nearby. A lawn sloped upwards from the entrance to a concreted plinth, on which stood an enormous oaken table simply groaning with food. Places for the happy couples were set around this structure, with hangers-on like us seated willy-nilly on the grassed area. Drink was taken and a few happy-clappy types sang 'Kumbaya' to the accompaniment of a group of particularly proficient guitarists. Finally, it was time to get down to the eating and one of the organizers called for quiet. To my considerable surprise, he signalled for me to approach the top table.

"Sir, I wonder if you'd be gracious enough to read the Gospel Reading of the Day?" he enquired.

"It would be my pleasure," I replied and read from the sheet of paper he produced.

With this task accomplished, he had another question for me.

"Sir, I wonder if you would now read the Prayer for the Day?"

"Most certainly," I replied and read a prayer to a hundred or more bowed heads.

He wasn't done with me yet, though.

"Sir, before we start eating, would you be good enough to bless the food?"

"I fear I'm not qualified for such an undertaking," I avowed.

"But surely Father," he said, before I interrupted him.

"You didn't think I was a priest, did you? I was sitting holding hands with my lady when you asked me to come forward for goodness sake," I pleaded.

"But you are wearing a suit," he said, "and only priests wear suits."

The food went unblessed.

As well as my criminal record for alleged reckless driving in the Philippines, I'm not unknown to the South Yorkshire Police either. Once a criminal, always a criminal you see! During a short trip back to the UK, I was to fall seriously foul of the law as it pertains to the Rotherham area! It shames me to admit the fact, but Wally Payne is a *bona fide* malefactor. My case even has an official Criminal Records Office number and, what's more, I've had my fingerprints taken! It all happened in the early hours of a Monday morning, as I was driving down the M1 with my mother following a visit to see relatives in Sunderland. The southbound motorway was chock-a-block with traffic, as drivers waited with commendable patience for their turn to squeeze around two transporters, each carrying an enormous turbine. These giant beasts took up two and a half lanes and moved at a pedestrian five mph. We were somewhere near Rotherham before we managed to clear the obstruction and continue our journey towards Leicester. Remarkably, within a minute of overtaking the transporters, I found myself driving along at 70mph with no sign of another vehicle, either in front or behind. I decided to afford myself the luxury of driving in the middle lane, especially since, in the far distance, I could now make out the tail lights of a lorry in the inside lane.

A precautionary glance in my rear view mirror revealed a car speeding up behind me. As he neared us, the driver flashed his lights several times before driving into the outside lane until he was level with me. Following an unmistakable gesture, one much beloved of the Longbowmen of Agincourt back in days of yore, he made it clear he considered my rightful place to be in the inside lane. I ignored him. He dropped back and drove up the inside lane until he was level with me once again and made a similar longbowman's gesticulation. I ignored him again so, in a fit of road rage, he dropped back and sped up the middle lane to ram me from behind. Apparently fulfilled, he drove off at high speed.

The episode had an unnerving effect on my mother, so a tea-break at the next service area was the order of the day. As I indicated to turn off the motorway however, there was my new-found chum, waiting at the side of the road with his four-way indicators flashing. I drove on and found a slot on the car park but, before I could alight, he had raced into a nearby parking slot and was advancing on foot towards my vehicle. He came up to my driver's side window and began to scream abuse. He ranted, raved and blasphemed, suggesting that foreigners of my ilk ought not to be driving on British roads. Now I may have been a touch browner than the average Anglo-Saxon at the time, but after years in the Orient one does tend to sport something of a tan. It was the sleight on my lineage that made this former British soldier see red and, despite my reluctance to display the violent side of my nature in front of my Mam, I suggested he stay put. I stepped out of my car, resigned to settling this matter in the time-honoured military fashion.

In front of me stood an exceedingly slight opponent, standing barely 5 feet tall in his built-up shoes. This fellow would comfortably have made the flyweight limit. Towering over him by almost a foot and outweighing him by at least six stones, I sensed a definite mismatch and felt obliged to comment in a somewhat threatening fashion in the hope he would simply disappear:

"I bet you feel a real twat now, don't you short-arse? Do you realise you're offering to take on someone twice your size? Now, my diminutive friend, before I eat you for breakfast, get back into your car and piss off," I suggested uncharitably.

"Are you going to make me?" he enquired.

"I'll be happy to oblige," I volunteered.

"Oh yes. You and who's Army?" he was foolish enough to ask.

I don't suppose my left hook travelled more than a foot. He, though, went back considerably further and landed on his backside. Arising somewhat groggily, with his right eyebrow streaming blood, he staggered off in the direction of his car. Rather than beating a retreat however, he went directly to the boot, opened it and started to rummage inside. Having just been subjected to road rage bordering on the manic, only to have the perpetrator follow me to my place of refuge and verbally abuse me, I assumed my opponent was looking for a weapon of some kind with which to continue the contest. I tapped him on the shoulder. As he turned around, he was treated to another rather fine left hook, this time to the right side of his bearded jaw. This man clearly wasn't built for bare-fist combat, because he split open along his jaw line and looked a rather sorry sight when he finally heeded my advice and drove away. As he departed, I noticed a young lad sitting, weeping, in the front seat of his car. Would you believe it, this jackass had his eight-year old son with him!

The phone was ringing as I made a dawn entry into my house in Leicester. At the other end of the line was a policeman from Rotherham.

"Mr Payne?" enquired a Yorkshire accent.

"It is," I replied, "With whom do I have the pleasure of conversing?"

"PC Jobowski of the Rotherham Police. Mr Payne, you were involved in an incident earlier this morning at the Howell Service Station."

"Yes, I was."

"There has been a complaint against you Mr Payne and I require you to be at Rotherham Police station at 1100 hrs this morning."

"And if I were to decline your kind invitation?"

"Then we'll come and fetch you. The offence you've committed carries the power of arrest."

"So PC Jabowski, without witnessing the occurrence and without questioning me, you have already established my guilt, have you? Do you perhaps mean you wish to interview me with regard to an offence I'm alleged to have committed?" I suggested.

"Yes, my mistake! I wish to make enquiries into an incident that occurred earlier this morning."

"In which case, I'll be delighted to meet you at the prescribed hour."

I took the train up to Rotherham and had enough time to have breakfast at Subway, before walking along the main street to the Police Station.

There must have been a lot of crime in the Rotherham area the previous night, because the waiting room was awash with unsavoury sorts awaiting their turn to face the music. I was the oldest person present by at least twenty years. The congregation in the waiting room were a sartorially inelegant bunch for sure and I was the only person dressed in a suit and tie. A Dunn's overcoat, Cheney shoes and a furled copy of *The Times* completed the upper class image I was trying to present. A policeman came into the room at precisely 1100hrs, took a look around and walked out again. Five minutes later he reappeared, a puzzled look on his face and called out, "Is there a Mr Payne here?" He seemed genuinely surprised to discover that the previous evening's alleged assailant wasn't a young lout, but an elegantly dressed, middle-aged lout. PC Jabowski invited me to accompany him to the interview room.

With almost thirty years of police experience under my belt, failure to present a plausible defence to the allegations would have been unforgivable on my part. After giving me the caution and turning on his tape recorder, PC Jabowski was subjected to a high-quality, bull-shitter's performance. It clearly impressed him. He switched his tape recorder off and confessed, "If I'd been in your shoes Walter, I'd have decked the bastard before you did." I suggested he switch his machine back on and record his comments for posterity, but he declined. Thereafter, we had a pleasant conversation, during which time I discovered he was a former Military Police NCO; a brother-in-arms no less.

There was no denying I'd cracked my opponent with a couple of decent left-hooks and done him considerable damage, but my assertion was that he'd asked for it. PC Jabowski agreed whole-heartedly and decided to cut me a deal: sign a formal caution in front of the Duty Inspector and I was a free man. It was a fair enough offer, but it meant accepting I was the guilty party. It was my belief the charge wouldn't have had a chance in court, so I declined. The officer's next offer wasn't so hot. Since my return to the Philippines was imminent, he would need to lock me up until I could be brought before the magistrates. Spending some time as a guest of the Rotherham Police wouldn't have bothered me in the least; it would have been an experience in fact, but my Mam would have had the vapours. As the option of signing a formal caution remained extant, I signed on the dotted line after all. Then, just as everything appeared tickerty-boo, they took me down the stairs to be photographed and have my fingerprints taken. So there you have it, I'm a fully qualified criminal.

Before making my first trip to the Philippines, I'd once taken an old American chap to task in a branch of McDonald's on Nathan Road in Hong Kong. He'd been berating a throng of Filipinas gathered for their Sunday lunch in such a vitriolic fashion that several of them were crying. I required him to leave the premises and apologised to the Filipinas for his insulting behaviour. Much later, it occurred to me that there was a lot of truth in what the old Yankee had had to say!

Visiting the Union Church in Lagaspi Village on my first Sunday in Manila, an amiable American and long-time resident of the Philippines introduced himself. Being the new boy in town, Tom kindly took me for lunch after the service and proceeded to impart words of wisdom. He summarised his warnings about survival in the Philippine Islands, gleaned over decades living in this part of the world, with the acronym –

GLINT. This acronym, he maintained, summed up the average Filipino. It stood for:

G - Greedy
L – Lying
I – Insecure
N – Nationalistic
T – Thieves

That seemed frightfully harsh to me at the time. Now, many years later, I could add several other letters to form an altogether longer mnemonic. In fact, I'm still to find a single redeeming feature about the Philippines and three months is the absolute maximum length of time I can stick the place before taking a break. The term, 'Couldn't organise a booze-up in a brewery' could have been coined specifically for Filipinos and, were I the President of the blighted land, my plans to bring the country screaming into the 21st century would include replacing all public service vehicle drivers with chimpanzees and sending the entire population back into the jungle for a million years, to evolve into Homo Sapiens. As far as I'm concerned, the Philippines can sink back into the ocean.

Chapter 4

Maximum Security Asia

ON A TRIP from Manila to Hong Kong, undertaken in the sure and certain belief there must be a job for me somewhere up in the Old Colony, I bumped into my old Army chum Colin Dodge. Now working for a local security company, he was on his way to meet his bosses for a couple of sundowners and invited me to accompany him. At the watering hole in Admiralty, I met Chris Harding, another old face from my military past and Joe Champagne, his American partner. They were Colin's bosses and ran the very first security company in the Colony to use former British Army Gurkha soldiers as guards; many other organisations were to follow suit. Harding had come up with the idea of employing Gurkhas during a walking holiday in Nepal, where he'd encountered hundreds of unemployed former soldiers, all still in fine shape and all desperate to find employment. Since jobs were all but impossible to find in Nepal, why not employ these men as high-end security guards in Hong Kong was the conception that came to him. He formulated a business plan to establish a security company and presented it to the like-minded Champagne, the man with the money. Harding resigned from the Army and set about fulfilling his dream in the colony. What an inspired, money-making enterprise it turned out to be. By all accounts, he and Champagne were making considerable amounts of filthy lucre.

    Their first contract had been to provide guards to secure a large construction site up in the New Territories; a location where the theft of materiel was running into millions of Hong Kong dollars each month. During the first month with Gurkhas manning the ramparts, losses dropped to precisely zero. A passing Chinese did steal a solitary brick one evening, but he was chased for a couple of miles until he ran out of steam and meekly handed the swag back to the pursuing Nepalese. Newspaper reports of this incident did the company's name no harm at all. Neither did the reports of another incident that served to illustrate to potential customers just how tenacious the men from Nepal really were.

Enjoying a rare day off up in the New Territories, Officer Gurung had fancied a beer and so wandered down to a bar in the town of Fanling, where he ordered a pint of the amber nectar and sat down to enjoy it. Inadvertently, he had made a serious error of judgement, by selecting a watering-hole known to be the haunt of a local triad gang. The leader of the gang wasted no time in approaching the interloper, rolled up his sleeve and displayed his triad membership tattoo. Instead of quaking with fear, the amiable Gurkha complimented him on such fine needlework and rolled up his own sleeve, revealing his regimental tattoo. Gurung never got to the bottom of his pint; the gang set about him, gave him a sound beating and, to the ring of mocking laughter, threw him bodily out of the premises.

Now, the triad leader may have been well-versed in the art of running a gang of bullying thugs, but he clearly hadn't been briefed on the subject of the fighting men from the foothills of the Himalayas. He severely underestimated the courage of Johnny Gurkha and especially his capacity for revenge. Officer Gurung returned to his accommodation, tidied himself up, strapped on his kukri and went back into the bar. He headed straight up to the triad leader and, without a word, sliced off his ear. He immediately gave himself up to the police, entered a guilty plea in court and went to jail for eighteen months. His honour, though, had been satisfied and he did the time standing on his head; especially since he was secure in the knowledge the company had retained his services, on full pay, until his sentence was served.

I appear to have created the right kind of impression over cocktails that evening because, shortly afterwards, Joe Champagne invited me to attend an interview. His proposal was, once the necessary permission had been obtained, would I be interested in running the Vietnamese arm of their operation? Indeed I would! Getting permission to open an office in Saigon turned out to be a convoluted business and, in fact, the call forward to start work in Vietnam never did come. Instead, tired of me pestering them for updates every couple of days, Chris and Joe took me onto their payroll in an alternative capacity. The Vietnam option was finally abandoned and instead, I became the sole employee of an offshoot company called Maximum Security Asia.

Since Hong Kong companies had proved their willingness to pay well over the odds for top quality security guards, might there be a market for high quality security equipment too? This was the rationale behind them giving me a job. I was given an office the size of a broom cupboard inside the premises of another of Joe's companies; someone threw the catalogue of an organisation called Police Product Stores of Oakland, California at me and I became Maximum Security Asia. My task was to establish a joint venture company with PPS and conduct a feasibility study, to see if there was a market for top quality security gear in South-East Asia.

The only thing my bosses did during those first three months was to pay me and phone once a week, just to confirm I hadn't passed away prematurely. Actually, I was content to be left alone, although a little more hands-on commitment from them wouldn't have gone badly amiss. Once permits of various sizes and hues had been obtained, licences for this and that secured and stationery printed, it was time for me to let the joint venture company in Oakland know we were open for business. I penned them a letter, electing to open my missive with a snippet of old English: Yanks like that kind of thing. I scribbled out my draft and handed it to the Chinese girl who, despite all her kicking and screaming, had been nominated as my part-time secretary. A premonition that our relationship was going to be fraught with difficulties was confirmed the moment she presented the typed draft of her first effort on my behalf. My opening gambit had been, "Greetings from Far Cathay!" Clarissa Chang, like a host of secretaries before her, had found my handwriting all but impossible to decipher. Misreading my scribble, she had typed, "Greetings from Fat Cathy!" I fell to the ground and kicked my legs in the air in a bout of uncontrollable mirth. Being Chinese, Clarissa was smitten with an immediate and massive loss of face. It took much fawning, many sweet words, copious quantities of green tea and two shrimp and seaweed flavoured Pot Noodles to win her round.

I actually put a lot of effort into those early months and did everything necessary to get the company up and running. Then, a couple of things happened to knock me back. Firstly, the joint venture partners in the USA decided upon a subtle change of policy. With a view to penny pinching, they decided to dispense with the feasibility study, declaring that the volume of goods sold would be used to gauge business potential. In my view, these tactics changed me from being a manager and administrator, into a salesman. I wasn't interested in being a salesman and had no intention of becoming one. Then, on one of my rare forays into the world of commerce, the boss of a security company to whom I was trying to sell some of our wares confirmed my worst fears. After listening to my humble line of patter, this plain speaking Chinaman declared, "You no fucking good salesman!" I could offer no defence to this harsh, albeit astute observation.

I promptly sought out an old chum of many years standing, a man who had been in the security business in Hong Kong for twenty-five years and made his pile. With no axe to grind whatsoever, he assured me there was no market in Hong Kong for our range of products. The Chinese, he convinced me, invariably went for the cheap and cheerful option when it came to equipping their men. Security guards in Hong Kong, he maintained, stood barely above toilet cleaners on the social ladder and good quality equipment, especially pricy American wares, would be wasted on them.

Within a couple of days of sending out copies of the PPS catalogue to every company in Hong Kong with even a tenuous connection to the security business, there was a call from a guarding company based in Wanchai. Without even trying, I sold this company's CEO several pieces of body armour at well over the going rate; perhaps I wasn't such a lousy salesman after all? It's a fair bet the stuff went straight up to China, to be torn apart, copied and appear back in Hong Kong—on sale for a quarter of the price. Despite a trifling success, Mr. Chan made me feel a complete novice at the game, by asking some perfectly reasonable questions about the capability of 'Second Chance' body armour for which I had no answer. Sure, I was able to spout a load of bullshit, but my knowledge was inadequate and my performance wouldn't stand up to a serious inquisition. A fact-finding visit to our American supplier would be essential if I was ever to really know the ropes about body armour. Joe Champagne agreed unequivocally and, within a week, I was aboard a Singapore Airways flight bound for San Francisco.

Jim Cunningham, the son of the founder of PPS, was to be my guide and mentor for the duration of the fact-finding mission. He met me at the airport and we immediately embarked on a guided tour of San Francisco, which was just what I needed following a fourteen-hour flight. He did book me into a very decent hotel in Oakland just the same. In fact, the company's hospitality couldn't be faulted and during my five days in California, I never needed to put my hand in my pocket for a thing. Jim and I ate out at meal times, invariably in decent restaurants; or at the Cunningham's splendid family home. My programme included introductions to the sheriffs of various police precincts, a trip on a fire barge in San Francisco harbour, tours of Oakland and San Francisco and even a trip to watch an ice hockey match at San Jose. (For the record, San Jose Sharks beat the St Louis Blues 4-2.) It was all very pleasant, but I learnt the square root of nothing about the subject I'd travelled so far to bone up on. Jim wasn't interested in passing on his knowledge to an outsider and for all he taught me, other than to demonstrate he was a thoroughly spoilt brat, I may just as well have stayed back in Hong Kong.

My return flight to Hong Kong was via Los Angeles and I flew down to the sprawling city in the first class compartment of a United Airlines plane. Upgrades are the order of the day on internal flights within the USA for international business class ticket holders it appears. At Los Angeles International, I transferred to the aircraft bound for the Orient, took off my shoes, swallowed my first Valium tablet and waited for the 'fasten seatbelt' sign to be illuminated. First though, there was a message from the purser. Due to severe headwinds over the Pacific, they needed to reduce the plane's payload and wanted twenty volunteers to disembark and travel the following day. There would be an inducement: comprising a night in the Hilton, a generous meal allowance and $200 in cash slipped into one's back pocket. As a person who will use any ruse imaginable to get out of flying, I'd drained my champagne flute, pulled on my shoes and reached the purser before he'd finished his message. A friendly stewardess explained all about the unfavourable winds that blew at this time of the year, making this course of action a frequent occurrence.

Whilst flicking through several hundred channels on my Hilton Hotel TV, something occurred to me. Should the stratospheric winds continue to blow thus, I might be able to volunteer to disembark every day for weeks! This could turn out to be a nice little earner. Sadly, the winds died down overnight and I was required to endure more than fifteen hours aboard the next westbound 747. During the flight, I was attended by an inflexible and rather aged stewardess, who followed the regulations pertaining to passenger safety with the utmost rigour. I think she might previously have worked for Lufthansa although, given the number of wrinkles on her neck, possibly even the Luftwaffe. On the discipline of wearing a seat belt once the captain had switched on the sign, she was totally unbending. Finally, having been strapped into seat B3 for several hours with a bursting bladder, I was unprincipled enough to stand up and head for the lavatory whilst the sign was still illuminated. Her eagle-eye spotted me in a trice, whereupon she chastised me roundly for my sinful action. I'd had enough of this nonsense and informed her, in no uncertain terms, that unless she allowed me to relieve myself in the area designated for the purpose, then I would perform the deed in her galley. A crude ploy no doubt, but it did the trick.

Marginally better informed about body armour and other safety accoutrements following my trip to California, I did my level best to sell some of the stuff. It was an uphill battle though and sales were limited, to say the least. Some days I gave up the unequal challenge altogether and took a ferry to the islands, or went for a bus ride up to the New Territories. These excursions prevented me from going insane inside my cubby hole and sales were exactly the same as when I slaved away all day—negligible. My bosses didn't seem to give a hoot about sales and assured me they were perfectly content with my efforts. Could it have been they were actually looking for a loss making enterprise to offset against their tax bill? The singularly inept security equipment salesman battled on gamely against all the odds; kicked his heels and unashamedly dragged his money at the end of each month. Then, a stroke of good fortune befell me. No, I didn't sell anything, but the bosses thought it a worthwhile exercise to send their ace hawker up to Shanghai, to attend the city's inaugural Security Trade Fair.

Maximum Security Asia didn't actually have a stand booked at the show, but a business class seat on Dragonair and a room in the top hotel in town augured well for a pleasant few days. Stepping out of the hotel to sniff the chilly Shanghai night air shortly after unpacking, I was astonished to be approached by pimps offering 'Shanghai girls' for my delectation. Being rather tired and exceedingly cold, I did what any *News of the World* reporter would have done in the circumstances: I declined their offer and returned to my expensive hotel room to have a bash at the mini bar.

The Chinese are always on the lookout for something for nothing and, within an hour of the exhibition centre opening its doors, they had taken my entire stock of PPS catalogues. They would have put them to good use I'm sure; as kindling for the fire, or cut up into squares and stuck on a nail attached to the back of the lavatory door. It meant though, I had bugger all to do for the next three days; rather like the Singaporean based Indian Army brigadier of Parsee extraction and his lady friend, who had quickly given all of their brochures away too. The three of us spent our time together, drinking tea and fighting off both the inclement Shanghainese weather and our own abject boredom. It would have been difficult to argue that Maximum Security Asia saw a worthwhile return on the cost of sending me all the way up to Shanghai.

Unless accommodation expenses were included in your job package, then living on Hong Kong Island, or even in Kowloon, was beyond most expatriates' financial means. Those of us on modest salaries lived either in the farthest reaches of Kowloon, in the New Territories, on the drug takers' paradise of Lamma Island or, like many wasters of my ilk, on Lantau Island. My rented flat was conveniently situated for the Ferry Terminal and handy for the Tin Tin laundry, supermarket and betting shop, but as a place of residence, it had little to commend it. It was dirty, damp and had hot and cold running rats. My landlord was clearly charging far too much rent but, since my time and money had been spent in improving the ambiance of the hovel, I stayed put. To extract my pound of flesh from Hong Kong's Rachman style landlord; when finally leaving, I omitted to pay my last month's rent and utility bills.

The morning ferry from Mui Wo to Central usually carried a dozen of the Colony's financially challenged to their places of employment. We tended to gather around a few of the tables in the air-conditioned upper-deck lounge, although I avoided the table dedicated to early morning bridge like the plague and sat with the rest of the hangover sufferers. Whenever people are thrown together in this fashion, it invariably reveals a bizarre mix of talent, personalities and hang-ups. Our section of the air-conditioned lounge contained some very odd characters indeed:

Andrew Kennedy was an engineer of some description who had come to Hong Kong to forget a lost love. He claimed to have achieved his aim within an hour of arriving in the Colony, by successfully bedding a Chinese lady of dubious morals. There are some facts and figures around suggesting a man thinks of sex every six minutes. Kennedy certainly bucked this theory, by thinking of nothing but sex for every moment of his waking hours. This was a man who burnt the candle at both ends and in the middle too. He was intent on living the good life and relegating work to the status of a necessary evil; a means of earning sufficient funds to allow him to dedicate his time to drink and fornication. This suicidal social schedule notwithstanding, he somehow found time to live with Noelle, his Chinese fiancée and bane of his life. What an unlikely couple they made; him on the rebound from a girl in Peterborough and her from a German of unknown provenance. This scoundrel was involved in the planning and construction of the mighty bridge linking Kowloon to the new airport at Chek Lap Kok, on Lantau Island. I've been mightily apprehensive about crossing the bridge ever since because, if there was ever a man whose preoccupation with wine, women and song rendered him incapable of doing anything even moderately well, then it was Kennedy.

Dafyd the Magnificent was another lost soul looking for a fresh start. A broken marriage, an unfulfilled career as an accountant and a crap job in Hong Kong might have sunk a lesser man, but Dafyd had similarities to Mr Micawber. He believed himself to be an expert at everything, when he was, irrefutably, the master of none. Mind you, he was something special when it came to walking the hills and it took a good man to keep up with him when he was in full steam. Forever one to scorn the use of a map, compass or GPS, Dafyd knew his way around the Lantau Hills exceptionally well. He maintained his Buddhist faith enabled him to talk to the trees and rocks, thus ensuring sure–footedness and an immaculate sense of direction. Believe that and you'll believe anything! In my view, the bounder made clandestine walks along tracks we intended to tackle at a later date and was, therefore, merely going over routes he already knew.

The day dawned when Hong Kong's finance houses finally caught up with him and the Welshman made a rapid departure from the Colony. His last few dollars went on a single plane ticket, to Phnom Penh. There was no particular reason for him to choose Cambodia apparently, other than the fact nobody knew him there and the cost of the plane ticket was within his meagre budget. Dafyd was to appear in my life again some years later, this time over in the Philippines

Jackie Currie was from Northern Ireland and possessed an Ulster brogue as thick as a Belfast docker's cheese sandwich. It was an accent that rendered him all but unintelligible to anyone born outside of County Tyrone. His parents were well-heeled Ulster landowners it seems, but Jackie had no intention of following his father onto the farm, preferring to see what there was on the other side of the Sperrin Mountains. He was undoubtedly a very bright individual, although his academic excellence failed to pay dividends when it came to finding a job. His failures at interviews were numerous and finally he sought my counsel; desperation indeed! An honest, Protestant opinion as to why he was failing to land a job was required. This was a simple task:

"Firstly Jackie, consign your father's National Service de-mob suit, the one with the un-invisibly mended tear in the left knee, to the bin. Secondly, moderate your attractive, but confusing Ulster brogue and try to speak English instead."

Whether my advice did any good or not can't be verified, but I was on the ferry back to Devil's Island with him the day he landed his first job, in the financial sector. Even before I had left Hong Kong he was doing very nicely, speculating on the Japanese yen of all things.

Norman Norris was still breathing heavily when he arrived in Hong Kong, having escaped the clutches of some New Zealand bailiffs only by the skin of his teeth. His worldly possessions consisted of a plastic bag full of socks and underpants, a ghastly pin-striped suit and the contents of a 'borrowed' charity box. The escapee from Auckland spent the first two nights of his Hong Kong adventure sleeping rough in Statue Square and he might well have taken up permanent residence there, had an old acquaintance not happened upon him and offered a bed space in Mui Wo. Norman soon fitted in well with the rest of the losers and wasters on Lantau.

He wasn't averse to a glass of beer, wine or spirits; or all three at the same time for that matter and was to be found most evenings in Papa Doc's hostelry. This establishment, tucked behind the Welcome Supermarket, was run by a couple of football-loving cousins from Paisley, one of whom remained loyal to the local St Mirren team, whereas the other had committed the unforgivable sin of supporting Celtic. They employed a big-breasted barmaid from Rotorua in New Zealand to man the San Miguel and Sing Tao pumps and it was with this lady that Norman was to fall hopelessly in love. Now, while he remained hopelessly smitten by the lady, she soon tired of him and his outrageous pin-striped suit. He was given the bum's rush! Thereafter, life became difficult for Norman. He continued to use the only pub in the village and had to sit by impotently as she flirted with a succession of alternative suitors. Finally, the man confessed to being at the end of his tether and ready to do himself in.

The prospect of one of our number topping himself in a fit of alcoholically induced depression called for some form of positive action from the rest of the lads. There was no prospect of him reducing his intake of beer and whisky; he was under consideration for the British Olympic Drinking Team for goodness sake. There wasn't another boozer where he could keep up his training and so, at an emergency meeting of the Mui Wo Single Men's Welfare Committee, a decision of paramount importance was reached: Norman must move away from Mui Wo! He acceded to the committee's harsh but well-intentioned decision, albeit with the greatest reluctance. In the weeks prior his final departure, we deemed it prudent to set up 'Normwatch', to ensure one of us would be with him at all times, lest he consider doing something foolish.

He finally moved to Discovery Bay, where he met a rich bird, fell in love, married and moved back to the UK to live happily ever after—for a while.

Hereward. After several months of crossing the South China Sea on a daily basis, I noticed that one young Englishman always sat alone; a radio with a huge antenna invariably pressed against one ear. It occurred to me he might welcome an invitation to sit with the other destitute Brits and so I offered the hand of friendship. A few days of travelling in the company of Hereward revealed him to be a little restricted when it came to topics of conversation. Whilst his fellow travellers talked in ribald fashion about the going rate for a Wanchai whore, the outrageous cost of a pint of San Miguel draught or the prices in the Champagne Ballroom, Hereward preferred to talk about plane timetables.

He knew simply everything about every plane landing in, or departing from Kai Tak International Airport. This was impressive at first, but not when it was the sole topic of conversation and lasted throughout the journey. He was employed as a labourer at Ocean Park and seemingly spent a large part of his day in the bird cages, tending the exotic species. My decision to invite Hereward to join the rest of the team earned me no plaudits from my fellow travellers. Rather than endure daily monologues dedicated to plane arrival times, our team began to find alternative travel arrangements. Before long, the British contingent on the 0730 hrs boat was reduced to just two and one of them was getting somewhat bored of listening to matters aeronautic too. After a weekend spent working on a plausible excuse for jettisoning my travelling companion, I boarded the Monday morning ferry intent on breaking the news of my defection to an alternative vessel. Before I could deliver the ill tidings however, Hereward handed me an envelope. Inside were two free passes to Ocean Park; the two complimentary tickets he received from the company each year. Along with the tickets was a letter, penned in a childish hand saying, "To my best pal." How could I ever dump him after such a demonstration of friendship?

I ascertained from his parents that there had been complications during his birth, which had left him a little slow in some areas. Despite his obvious problems, there were times when Hereward would amaze me with his knowledge of certain subjects, albeit subjects connected with aviation. Sitting in front of us on the ferry one day were a couple of young Danish ladies and, when we disembarked, he asked me what language they were speaking.

"Danish, Hereward. They probably come from Copenhagen."

He thought about this for a moment.

"What do you think about the Danish Government's failure to vote in favour of ratifying the Treaty of Maastricht?" he asked, taking me back more than a little.

"How come you know about the Treaty of Maastricht?" I enquired.

"I don't know anything about it really. It's just that the most important aeroplane directional beacon in Europe is in Maastricht. When I saw the name in the paper, I read about it."

Hereward has become a good pal over the years and I'm still in touch with him. Yes, he still knows all about planes.

Trumpet John had played with Ted Heath and many other top dance bands during his long career as a musician and taught the trumpet to several clients around the colony. As a member of the London Palladium band, he had come into contact with every star worthy of the name and had some great stories to impart. Although his trumpeter's 'lip' was no longer as good as it had been in his prime, his memory about exactly who was having an affair with whom when the curtain came down was in no way impaired. His accolade for the nastiest person he had ever worked with went unequivocally to Tommy Cooper, with Norman Wisdom taking the runner-up berth. At the other end of the spectrum stood Harry Secombe who, according to John, was a perfect gentleman and probably the nicest personality he had encountered. Did the fact that Harry always stuffed a banknote down Trumpet John's instrument at the end of every performance influence the canny Yorkshireman's decision one wonders?

Ken the Alcoholic. A former engineer, Ken had dedicated his life to breaking all existing Skol lager drinking records and was well on the way to achieving his aim. He was yet another member of a large group of expatriates who had fallen for the guiles of a Filipina, only to suffer the financial consequences of undertaking such a liaison.

Luke the Poofter. Since advancing years had robbed him of the necessary muscle control, Luke the Poofter's career as a male prostitute had gone downhill. In fact, it had reached rock bottom! Once a popular guest at all the top homosexual gatherings in London, Paris and Rome; by now he was reduced to drinking local rice wine, or begging his drinks. Offering his 'Elephant and Castle' for hire these days didn't even bring him the wherewithal to pay his bills. He remained good company nevertheless and, provided he didn't touch me, I was prepared to buy him a few beers.

Tadger the All-Black. An emeritus professor of loquacity at Auckland University, Tadger immigrated to Hong Kong to take over the reins of the Silvermine Bay Boring Team. Against all the odds, he succeeded in taking them to the world championships and was subsequently elected to the Boring Hall of Fame. Upon espying Tadger coming in their direction, people have been known to fling themselves, fully-clothed, into the Silvermine River rather than be subjected to one of his riveting, one-way conversations.

Alexander Citröen-McNasty was the archetypal Scot; argumentative, nasty and smitten with a persecution complex. Like many of his countryman, he harboured an all-consuming hatred of the English. In his case, however, his character flaws were exacerbated by the fact his father was French. What an unfortunate *mélange*. He was a wiry individual and perfectly constructed for mountain walking, a discipline in which he claimed considerable experience. As a person who has walked every track and trail in Hong Kong however, I had my doubts about his alleged walking exploits. Having once announced my intention to ascend Sunset Peak from the west, he claimed to have walked the route only a couple of days previously. He designated the climb 'easy' and told those assembled at the Toilet Bar there were 136 steps to the top. To the best of my recollection, this was a particularly severe climb, with huge granite steps numbering in excess of two thousand. I was right of course. On another occasion, he refuted absolutely my assertion that a track led down from near the top of Sunset Peak to the village of Tung Chung. This time, he stated a willingness to bet money on the fact although, being a true Scot, he never coughed up when proved wrong. Whereas I had climbed Sunset Peak dozens of times, this braggart had certainly not.

Taffy the Mouth. Running Alexander a close second as Mui Wo's most obnoxious Celt was a Welshman whose name, mercifully, I have forgotten. He was yet another dimwit who had been cleaned out by a wily Filipina and had resorted to drinking himself to death. His disputed claim to fame was that he had boxed for Wales in the 1976 Commonwealth Games in Nigeria. Unless he had aged exceedingly prematurely, I calculated he would have been well into his forties at the time. When I pointed this out to him one evening in the Toilet Bar, the Swansea Mouth actually threatened violence. Given he was several years older than me, weighed in at featherweight and was too pissed to make a worthy assault on my person, I didn't take him seriously. The Commonwealth Games weren't held in 1976, nor have they ever been held in Nigeria. Some years later, this lost soul committed suicide by hanging himself, eliciting this comment from a long-time Mui Wo resident: "What a waste of good rope."

I resigned from MSA because I had no desire to be a salesman, but remained in Mui Wo for a while. Knowing the company's book-keeping system to be weak, it came as no surprise to discover they had paid me for the month following my departure. I withdrew the cash for my own use and suffered from pangs of conscience ever thereafter. Several years later I bumped into Joe Champagne at the Hong Kong Football Club and, excusing myself temporarily in order to scurry to the nearest ATM machine, gave him the money back. He'd long forgotten my underhand action, or perhaps was never even aware, but I felt better for settling the outstanding debt.

My next trip to the UK was to start me off on my African adventures.

Chapter 5

Mozambique

TRIPS TO THE UK in the hope of finding a decent job were becoming routine, as was the disappointment of failure. Here I was in Leicester once again, waiting for replies from a plethora of companies to whom I'd sent my CV and with ample time to address a few outstanding personal administrative matters.

A BUPA 'Wellness' medical set me back a king's ransom and revealed nothing amiss, other than the fact I was a stone and a half too heavy. Paying hundreds of pounds to ascertain I was overweight was hardly a cost effective undertaking; five pence in the weighing machine at the underground toilets at Leicester Market would have provided the same information. A friendly Gujarati dentist did the necessary in the oral department and, to tidy things up from a personal perspective, I decided to consult a lawyer regarding a divorce from my second wife. She had disappeared without trace several years previously, thank the Lord, and this seemed an opportune time to have the ill-advised liaison stricken from the record.

Despite carrying a surplus pound or two, my solicitor was an attractive lady to whom I gave my 'interesting squaddie back from the front' routine. Being a professional lady, she was required to display coolness and composure but, take it from me, this lady was mightily smitten by the bit of rough from the trenches. Our meeting went on for much longer than scheduled, as I regaled her with more than a few of my raunchier tales. When I gave her the chance to get a word in edgeways, she revealed her high standing in the ranks of the Leicestershire Ladies' Round Table. To her, it appeared, had fallen the responsibility of engaging a speaker for the following week's AGM. No less a personage than Lord Chief Justice Blenkinsop had accepted the invitation to address the region's top ladies, at a posh venue out in the county. That very morning however, the important man had been smitten by an ailment serious enough to render him incapable of fulfilling his engagement and my solicitor was in something of a quandary; top quality speakers not being readily available at the drop of a hat. How fortunate for her I'd decided to sort out my divorce at Chaucer, McSporran and Singh. Without any ado, I accepted her offer to top the bill at the annual bash.

I'd tucked into a couple of glasses of sherry, supped several pints of Stella Artois and shovelled down an entrée, fish course and a decent steak before my after-dinner services were called upon. A lie down on the settee would have been preferable at this juncture, but up I stood on my rear trotters to face several dozen posh tarts, all of whom would assuredly have preferred listening to the exploits of one of the country's premier judges. Still, when you've lectured a regiment of the Royal Green Jackets for two hours on the powers of arrest pertaining to troops in Northern Ireland, especially after they've been up all night on manoeuvres and are tired, hungry and mightily pissed off, then you can face any audience in the world in my view. The first sixty seconds of my soliloquy seemed to fall on deaf ears, as the ladies chatted on, supremely disinterested in anything I might have to impart. It was not until I mentioned a certain 'magic' word that they gave me the hush I craved.

"And so ladies, we must make a decision. Should I talk about my time as a resident in Edinburgh Castle Officers' Mess, or would you prefer to hear about the *fleshpots* of Hong Kong?"

"The fleshpots of Hong Kong!" they echoed to a woman.

From that moment on I had my audience by the balls, figuratively speaking. A speech scheduled to last for twenty minutes went on past the hour mark as the women, some of them attractive in an obscene sort of way, clung onto my every word. The more risqué my stories, the more rapt became their attention. I finally sat down to enthusiastic applause a full hour and twenty minutes after standing up.

I picked up a further speaking engagement immediately and a second from the lady who took me home in her Mercedes. She was brazen enough to enquire whether I was available to give private lectures; the saucy, upper echelon strumpet! She simply adored men dressed in uniform she confessed; what a good thing I'd hung onto my Mess Dress, Sam Browne and spurs! Perhaps I could have made a living telling ribald tales to lady audiences, or ladies on their own, but a chance telephone call from a fellow retired Royal Military Police officer was to change my life considerably.

The major was home on leave from Mozambique, where he was setting up a dockyard security team in the capital Maputo on behalf of the Organisation for Economic Co-operation and Development. He explained that following sixteen years of civil war, the rule of law didn't count for much in the former Portuguese Colony and any ship's captain foolhardy enough to put into Maputo harbour soon lost his cargo. The starving locals would set about the vessel and steal anything not welded to the deck. Confidence in the country as a trading nation could only be restored when a ship could load or discharge cargo without hordes of people descending from the hills to ransack its hold. The purpose of the major's mission was to train a body of armed men to guard the dockyard and any ships tied up alongside. Not that there were many vessels; the only ships to dock since the war had been humanitarian aid vessels from the USA, Australia and the UK. One of the OECD's team of three had thrown in the towel, thereby leaving a vacancy for an adventurous soul of my ilk to fill. As it transpired, the chap was seriously ill and died shortly afterwards. His wife, in a bout of depression brought about by her husband's demise I trust, wrote to my new employers to declare that Wally Payne was not a fit person to replace her recently departed spouse. She may have been right, but her crusade was a mite odd in my view, considering I'd never ever met the lady.

First though, my solicitor friend and I had an appointment at the County Court in Leicester. I thought she was bluffing when she told me the judge hearing my case owed her a big favour but, within twenty minutes of entering his chambers, she emerged waving a document at me. It was a decree nisi and I was divorced it seemed, only days after first setting eyes on the offices of Chaucer, McSporran and Singh and, furthermore, without ever facing the judge!

The major and I met up in London; our employers needed to cast their eyes over the new bloke, have me sign a contract, sort out my work permit and agree a departure date. The formalities completed, I invited the major to lunch at the Army and Navy Club, just off Pall Mall. This is an officers only establishment and, despite only ever having masqueraded as an officer, (I was always a corporal at heart, despite the three pips), I'd afforded myself the privilege of membership. This was my inaugural visit to the club and, although a stranger, as a former 4 Guards Brigade Group Provost Unit man, I had no problem sniffing out the bar. To my surprise, the major was already in position. At this early hour, we were the only two persons present and, when a formally attired steward approached, I imagined we had failed to conform to some secret rite. It transpired to be nothing of the kind; the flunkey was simply seeking a member for whom there was a telephone call. He approached the pair of us, coughed a diplomatic cough and enquired, "Excuse me, but are either of you two gentlemen General Sir Gordon Lennox?" We were both former corporals in the RMP and had been mistaken for a general; one of some renown at that!

The major, me and Colonel Rawson; our officer commanding when we had all served together in the Westfalian town Iserlohn, would meet for lunch in London whenever I was in the UK. The venue on one occasion was the Overseas League, the colonel's club. As we entered one of the establishment's splendid restaurants, the colonel was greeted like a long lost brother by the *maître'd* and Mr Limthong directed us to a superior table. Waiting for the drinks to be served, the colonel decided to introduce the major and me to the Thai *maître*.

"Limthong, may I introduce Major Toby Stratford MBE, an old friend of mine?"

Bowing low, he declared his obeisance.

"And this gentleman, Limthong, is Lord Walter of Leicester."

The Thai was quite overcome at the prospect of waiting on Lord Walter and bowed his deepest, most dignified bow; the sort he reserved for peers of the realm.

Word of a notable personage dining at table number seven was obviously passed down to the other waiters and, as the Moroccan responsible for dishing out the greens arrived at my side, the occasion proved just a little too much for him. He spilt the Brussels sprouts all over the place and, but for a splendid bit of slip fielding from the colonel, several might well have hit the floor. We kept up the pretence to the bitter end and I enjoyed the experience immensely. Why wasn't I born with a silver spoon in my mouth I wonder? Or was I switched at birth perhaps?

Within ten days of receiving my chance phone call from the major, here I was taking a beer in the bar of the celebrated Meikles Hotel in Harare. My abiding memory of the place was the row of people standing at the bar, each with a pistol stuffed down the back of their trousers. They clearly knew something I didn't. Next day a taxi delivered me to Harare airport, but not before the driver swerved off the road and into the bush, as a cavalcade of police cars and motor-cycles travelling in the opposite direction bullied all other vehicles off the highway. In an armoured limousine in the middle of the convoy sat a person I recognised; it was Robert Gabriel Mugabe and he never even stopped to say hello! A couple of hours after arriving at Harare International, I boarded an Air Zimbabwe aircraft bound for Maputo. The two-man crew at the front of the gaily-painted plane both bore a remarkable likeness to Idi Amin, something that did precious little to calm my pre-flight jitters. After a mercifully uneventful trip, I alighted at Maputo (formerly Laurenço Marques) and was greeted in the tumbledown arrivals area by the major and Colonel Paddy, the other member of the OECD team.

Paddy drove us to our apartment on the other side of the city in an exceedingly well-worn Volkswagen van. Despite its war-torn and badly run down appearance, there was something about Maputo which appealed to me immediately. In its colonial pomp, there's no doubt this would have been a fine looking city; with its wide avenues, splendid official buildings and carefully planted roadside trees. A note for keen horticulturalists: the trees were jacaranda, acacia and flame of the forest; selected so one variety bloomed, just as the other was on the wane. Thus, the city wore a purple, yellow or violent red look as the seasons progressed. My immediate attraction may conceivably have been attributable to the relief I felt upon discovering there were no longer any bullets flying around; well, not too many anyway!

Our accommodation was on the 9th floor of the CFM (Chemin de fer de Mozambique) Building, a lofty tower of surprising good quality residences, situated on an avenue named after one of the country's glorious revolutions. The flat was a little high for my liking: firstly because of my well-documented fear of heights and, secondly, because the lifts in the building were notoriously unreliable. More often than not, the residents had to walk up and down numerous flights of stairs. The chain smoking, but otherwise perfectly decent Paddy gave me a guided tour of the apartment, now occupied by three former British Army officers, none of whom would ever see fifty again. For me, the flat's *pièce de résistance* was its Sky TV facility. Nothing at all worked in this country, and yet we could watch the BBC news beamed in directly from the UK. Paddy switched on the set to show me how it functioned and, to my joy, a live soccer match from the UK was just about to be broadcast. As if that wasn't thrill enough, the match was between my Leicester City team and Manchester City. The 'Blues' ruined what ought to have been a perfect start to my new assignment, by snatching defeat from the jaws of victory and losing by the only goal of the match. The importance of a weekly live soccer match was lost on my flatmates, neither of whom had the slightest interest in the beautiful game.

By the time I'd unpacked and showered in lukewarm water, my companions were ready to show me the Impala Steakhouse, the nearby culinary hotspot. They warned me not to expect the highest standards. Since the dining area looked perfectly respectable and they served cold beer, what could possibly be wrong with the Impala? The major suggested I make a cursory visit to the kitchen on my way through to the apology for a lavatory. There were certainly imperfections in these areas that might concern a fussy Health & Safety man, but the Impala would do for me I decided. Slabs of steak were served, sizzling, on a red-hot stone and whether you wanted your meat rare, burnt to a tee or anywhere in between depended on precisely how long you cared to leave it on your slab of granite. I made a point of ordering fillet steak whenever dining there and always assumed it was beef, but in reality, it could have been anything. Elephant steak was on the menu and I wonder if I ever consumed a slice of pachyderm in lieu of Aberdeen Angus.

I remarked that the Impala served cold beer. Well, they served cold beer sometimes; provided the electricity supply was connected! Occasionally they ran out of alcohol altogether, although, for a few pence, one of the waiters would trawl other restaurants in the area to find a supply. Once, when I asked a waiter if he would be gracious enough to locate a bottle of 'throwing brandy' for me, he unusually and reluctantly refused the commission. Instead, he went into a backroom and returned with his only pair of shoes. He presented them for my inspection and the fact was, they were totally unserviceable; there wasn't another step left in them. Since he didn't have any footwear in which to walk Maputo's badly paved thoroughfares and with me being a man of compassion, I divested myself of my 'Cheney' brogues and presented them to him. A bottle of brandy appeared on our table in no time at all. I insisted upon the return of my shoes, but only until I'd negotiated the dog-shit covered pavements on the walk back to our flat; whereupon they became his property. Thereafter, he wore them proudly at all times and even polished them on a couple of occasions. To be honest, I really didn't fancy them any more anyway, not after he'd had his 'plates' in them. Next evening, the well-shod waiter arrived at the flat with a selection of young ladies in tow. By way of payment for the superior footwear, my task was simply to select whichever lady took my fancy and use her for my personal gratification. His gesture was appreciated, but I felt it necessary to feign a headache since my two companions were at home.

The major and Portuguese-speaking Paddy had been on the current contract for eight months and had lived in the CFM building from the outset. The flat lacked for nothing in the way of home comforts for, not only did we have a houseboy on hand, but a pair of Zulu handmaidens to help around the house too. Louisa was a tall, striking Amazon of a girl and the apartment was certainly a better place for her presence. In common with most Mozambican ladies under the age of twenty-five, she was possessed of a 'Laws of Gravity' defying bosom and scorned absolutely the use of a bra. One's breakfast certainly tasted all the better for having been served by Louisa, who would lean over your shoulder whilst delivering a fried egg to your plate. Her talent as a waitress remains an abiding memory of my time in Mozambique. The other regular female visitor to our flat was Lenore, who spoke neither English nor Portuguese, but could down a glass of gin and tonic with gusto. She was pleasing on the eye for sure, although having even the simplest of conversations with her was never a possibility, due to the lack of a lingua franca.

Our hard-working houseboy kept the place in excellent order. Despite only being the same age as me, Francisco was already an old man by Mozambican standards. He was a dear fellow, although undeniably stingy when it came to dishing out portions of food. To him, a solitary sausage or single slice of meat was more protein than he saw in a month and so, this was exactly what we were served at mealtimes. None of us had the courage to say anything about the insufficiency of meat and simply filled up on a slice or two of bread instead. Francisco was prone to illness however and probably only made it to work three days a week; thus the rationale for employing the two girls. We clubbed together to pay for his medical bills once it became apparent our general factotum wasn't in the most robust health. Finally, he was admitted to the foul smelling Maputo General Hospital and one of us called by each evening, to settle his account and take him something to eat. Mozambique was a place where you either paid for medical assistance, or you died.

On Saturday evening we called by as a team, but were surprised to see his bed empty. Assuming he'd recovered sufficiently to leave the hospital, we went to his home to wish him well. Alas, we discovered his family and neighbours engaged in a mammoth sackcloth and ashes session. Francisco was dead, at the venerable age of fifty-two! It transpired that the old rogue had a brace of wives, both of whom were trying to produce a more heart-rending wail than the other. Their main problem appeared to be the recovery of Francisco's body, which had been impounded until his final hospital bill had been settled. This presented the family with a conundrum; they had precisely nothing in the way of financial assets. We called the wives and brothers to conference and ascertained it would cost the princely sum of ten pounds to have his body released from the morgue. That problem swiftly resolved, we were able to enhance the family's reputation beyond their wildest dreams with another modest donation. Francisco's mortal remains were prepared for burial by the best funeral director in town and he was borne to the graveyard in a hearse drawn by a team of black horses with plumes. May the dear man's soul rest in the peace of the Lord?

The border crossing point between Mozambique and South Africa was within spitting distance of Maputo and, once a month, we took off for the provincial city of Nelspruit to enjoy a weekend's R&R. The journey across took us through a tortured, war-ravaged landscape, devoid of animals and with burnt out vehicles strewn along the sides of the badly maintained highway. Having negotiated the frontier, with its massive electrified fence designed to keep the Mozambicans on their own side, the transformation was stunning. Well-tended fields, full of fruit trees and vegetables, lined the smooth tarmac road for the entire sixty-miles to Nelspruit, the capital of Mpumalanga Province. After the austerity of Mozambique, eating and drinking whatever we wished alongside the Crocodile River was a rare treat indeed.

In between Maputo's mud huts and war-ravaged buildings stood the Polonia Hotel, incongruous in its opulence and grandeur. A night in this place would set you back what an average Mozambican earned in a year and yet there were still enough well-heeled locals to fill the place most evenings. Our visits to the hotel were restricted to Sunday lunchtimes, when the place did a reasonably priced fixed menu. Finding a parking space in the hotel's car park on Sunday mornings always presented a problem however. The place was invariably packed with Range Rovers and other expensive four-wheel drive jobs; all belonging to organisations like Oxfam, Médecins sans Frontières, Save the Children, Caritas and a throng of other do-gooder charities. The safari-suit bedecked employees and their families regularly thronged the hotel, believing they were doing their bit to alleviate Third World poverty presumably. To function effectively, large charitable organisations need to have sound infrastructure in place, but it was clear to me the management of some charity groups in Maputo abused the system and lived the Life of Reilly. It's my assertion that a large proportion of the money donated by benevolent folk back in the UK went to keep the Maputo upper echelons in a grand style; leaving the young volunteers to sweat it out in malaria-ridden mud huts out in the bush. I no longer give to any of these charities; a quid to a destitute guy lying at the side of the road seems to me an altogether better cause than keeping the flocks of pseudo philanthropists in luxury.

Our social life was somewhat restricted, as nowhere was particularly safe. The 'Piri-Piri' restaurant was a well patronized venue, catering to expatriates and the better off

71

locals; its popularity having much to do with the fact it was rather cleaner than most eating establishments in the beaten-up old city. My first visit came only a few days after the 'Piri-Piri Massacre', when a gang armed with AK47 rifles had entered the place late in the evening, intent on making off with the takings. The manager had fought back with his own weapon and something of a gunfight ensued. Several expatriates were killed, as well as the brave manager and several other locals. Apart from a few tell-tale holes in the walls, only two days later the Piri-Piri was functioning as if nothing had ever happened. Vendors flogging traditional wares to posh punters proliferated on the pavement outside the restaurant; the ubiquitous beggars scrounged leftovers and artists, who had apparently seen too much bloodshed, sold their accomplished, but tortured representations of Mozambican life. Several paintings still adorn the walls of my home.

Right at the end of the beach road, at the northern city limits of Maputo, stood a Greek restaurant. What were Greeks doing in this former Portuguese preserve I wondered? It was a fine establishment and another regular haunt of the well-heeled. Having eaten the fine seafood, notably prawns gathered from Maputo Bay, we would collect the shells together and give them to the ranks of urchins assembled to watch the privileged eat. It always made me feel terribly guilty to have so much, when the majority didn't have the price of a slice, never mind a loaf, of bread.

My second pair of expensive Cheney shoes came to grief at the *Faro Populare,* an area full of sideshows and seedy, prostitute-populated bars. Before the Portuguese had finally accepted Mozambique wasn't worth losing any further lives over, they embarked on a very effective method of sabotaging the infrastructure of what they were leaving behind. Every drain, cavity, hole, nook and cranny capable of taking quick drying cement was filled with the stuff. Consequently, there wasn't a lavatory in a public place that worked. The bogs in the *Faro* were particularly disgusting and only people of a particularly robust constitution would consider it worth braving the conditions. One evening, when a visit was deemed a priority, I showed courage above and beyond the call of duty, by making a sortie on an outstandingly disgusting toilet. In an attempt to disguise the smell, Teepol had been thrown around with gay abandon and a cloudy mixture of urine and disinfectant lapped over the welts of my shoes. By next morning, the stitching had rotted and the uppers had come away from the soles. There was nothing for it but to make a visit to the major's shoe repair man, the old cobbler who loitered for business outside our apartment block. This man had kept him well-shod for months, despite the desperate state of repair of his only pair of shoes. The cobbler actually cooed over my shoes, the quality of which I don't suppose he'd ever seen before in Maputo. The Teepol, though, had done its mischief and my shoes were never quite the same again.

Beggars proliferated in Maputo and, unless you were blind or missing at least one limb, competition for a hand-out must have been exceedingly fierce. The major had his special beneficiary, a man who was paralysed below the waist and incapable of speech. He lived in a hospice opposite our relatively palatial accommodation, although the 'Brides of Christ' dumped him at the side of the road, seemingly without sustenance, for long periods each day. He watched the passing traffic to while away the hours and did a little mute begging on the side. Thanks to the major's magnanimity, he never went without food, cigarettes or clothing during our stay. What happened to him after we had moved onto pastures new, heaven only knows. A young cripple who spoke very decent English became my private charity case, although my benevolence didn't extend to giving him a lift anywhere. To put in bluntly, he stank so badly it made me wretch. Running water is a rare commodity in Mozambique and it gets put to more important uses than washing and bathing.

Our other charity cases were a group of young ne'er-do-wells, who hung around the market where we bought our fruit and veggies. On the pretext of hiring them to guard our Volkswagen van, we gave them money to stand by the vehicle until we reappeared from the bustling market, our arms full of goods they could never hope to buy. Softies that we were, we gave them a fair proportion of our purchases too. What would have happened to the VW had we not been so generous doesn't bear thinking about.

The old van served us well. It helped us escape at high speed when under pressure from marauding bands of brigands, took us out socialising almost every evening and, in the cause of self-preservation, bumped the odd baddie out of the way.

I can't abide those Animal Right's people; they're misguided, generally unwashed and in severe need of both a dose of reality and a punch on the nose. To be honest, I'm not much bothered about animals either, with the exception of winning racehorses and greyhounds. Just the same, the major and I took pity on the captured wild birds crammed into home-made cages and offered for sale at the side of the main coast road in Maputo. We bought a quid's worth most days and released them back into the wild. So, militant Animal Rights' man with your silly stall in Leicester's Gallowtree Gate, don't get so shitty the next time I accidentally tip your pathetic little display over—I'm a bird lover.

It came as a great surprise to discover an Anglican Church in Maputo; right there on our street, the Avenue of the Glorious Revolution of the 24th July. The building appeared architecturally out of place in Mozambique and could have passed for a village church anywhere in England. On my first Sunday in the city, I wandered in for the morning service and found the place thronged with a congregation of diverse nationalities and a vicar who certainly knew how to make his audience sit up and take notice. Astonishingly, by the time the good Reverend Xavier N'Bongo presided over the English speaking service with such enthusiasm, he'd already taken a service in Portuguese and another in Shangaan. And it was still only 1030 hrs!

The first two rows of pews at the front left of the church were the preserve of the choir. Now, two whole rows might indicate a choir containing a good many voices, but this wasn't the case. The half-dozen Mozambican ladies, whose wonderful, strangely discordant harmonies cheered us considerably each Sunday morning, each had a bottom the size of a Shire horse! These ladies may not have had the numbers of the Huddersfield Choral Society, but their singing always sent a shiver down my spine. The fact they sang so well was all the more commendable, given they were seated directly behind John, the resident pianist at St Stephen and St Lawrence. I never went near enough to John to discover whether he was a leper, or whether he actually played the Steinway wearing boxing gloves, but this man was no Toscanini, that's for sure.

Reverend Xavier was a priest who found the constraints of *Hymns Ancient and Modern* rather too limiting for his musical taste, so he produced a booklet of the songs one could expect to hear at St Stephen and St Lawrence. Without it, singing along with the big-bottomed choir was virtually impossible and the publication saw brisk sales. Parsimonious I have never been, but neither had I ever been required to pay for my own hymnbook before. One wonders what the bishop of the diocese would have made of it—his name was Desmond Tutu!

Morning service in Maputo commenced with the good vicar and his entourage positioned at the church door, behind the congregation. After an opening address by the priest, they all moved forward towards the altar during the singing of the first hymn—standard Anglican procedure. My abiding memory of this church and the good Reverend Xavier N'Bongo will always be the day he selected an obscure Madagascan dirge as the processional hymn. The tune might have been known to the vicar, but certainly not to the choir or any of those assembled in the pews. Halfway down the aisle, the priest realised he was singing a solo.

"What's wrong my dear brothers and sisters, don't you know this tune?" asked the vicar plaintively.

There followed a great deal of confirmatory mumbling and head shaking.

"Well, never mind. Let's sing a tune we all know. John, number two hundred and ten in Ancient and Modern, number fourteen in the pamphlet, if you please."

John found his music, the choir struck up, the congregation sang with gusto and the wide bottomed entourage danced its way to the altar to the strains of "Rock of Ages."

November 11th fell on a Saturday and gave the three former British Tommies the opportunity of visiting the main cemetery in the centre of Maputo. We were looking to find any fallen Commonwealth soldiers to whom we might pay our respects, but there were none. Despite boasting a resident custodian, the graveyard was hideously overgrown and in a dangerously poor state of repair. His energies were certainly not channelled into tending the cemetery, although he showed some panache when it came to trying to elicit baksheesh from his British visitors. We discovered a Portuguese Military area and, since they are Great Britain's oldest allies, we dedicated our two minutes silence to these brave soldiers.

A wander around the necropolis revealed thousands of Portuguese dead, all laid to rest in hideous, over-elaborate tombs. In addition, there were the remains of people from diverse parts of the globe who hadn't made it any further than Maputo; including a couple of dozen Chinese, buried in simple graves, their memorials engraved with calligraphy. In the corner of the cemetery stood an impressive looking building, which was simply begging closer examination. It was a charnel house, full of desecrated coffins, all broken open in the search for anything worth stealing presumably. The coffins were stuffed full of lime, designed to make short work of the flesh of the bodies they still contained. The authorities would get around to interring them one fine day; but not just yet it seemed.

That I should know a single resident of Maputo wasn't conceivable. In fact, before my arrival, I'd needed to look up the location of Mozambique in an atlas. And yet, the well-dressed guy with whom I sometimes shared the lift had a familiar look about him. One morning, when just the two of us were descending together, he spoke to me for the first time.

"Your friends tell me you have a great interest in football," he said.

"Football is my life's passion," I confided.

"Then you may be pleased to know England defeated Switzerland 2-0 at Wembley Stadium yesterday evening."

It suddenly dawned on me; I'd seen this man playing football somewhere. I asked him whether he had ever played the game to a decent standard.

"If you would consider playing more than fifty times for Portugal and in the World Cup a decent standard, then yes," he said.

"Please tell me more."

"Did you ever see the semi-final match of the World Cup in 1966, between England and Portugal?"

"Of course."

"Can you remember the names of Portugal's attackers that day?" he asked.

"Indeed I can," I answered, "Torres, Eusebio and Colunna."

"I am Colunna."

"Bloody Hell! So you are."

This turned out to be a most opportune meeting, as Colunna's brother was none other than Mozambique's Chief of Police. So, instead of months of sweating over the preparation and implementation of tedious training programmes, a few hundred US dollars invested in the right place saw our recruits going through their paces at the Police Training School. Sipping cocktails under the palm trees at the Oasis suited me rather better than marching aspirant guards up and down a drill square.

The movement of ships in and out of the dockyards was presided over by a former sea captain from Birkenhead. His must have been the least stressful job in the world, seeing as Maputo had hardly seen a vessel in all of sixteen years. Then, out of the blue, came word of the imminent visit to the port of HRH, The Princess Royal. The sea captain promptly threw a wobbly, confirming he'd been doing nothing in the back of beyond for far too long. In the event, the event was a non-event. She arrived by car, boarded the only sea-worthy vessel in Mozambique for a sail around Maputo docks and then got back into her car again and went away.

There was hardly a soul around to witness the visit so, in an attempt to make it look as if there was loads of interest, we gathered together the pitifully small number of stevedores employed at the docks and drove the same guys around to the various vantage points. Then, each time the princess sailed past in the boat, the same guys waved at her. Very decent lady that she is, Anne waved back enthusiastically.

The dock workers at Maputo were hugely outnumbered by hundreds of illegal squatters, who lived underneath the dock itself, patiently waiting for a ship to berth so they could ransack it. We kept them well hidden during the royal visit; it would never do for any real facts to come out on a royal fact-finding mission!

With the men's training completed, it was time for them to be issued with their fine-looking uniforms. They were delighted, for none of them had ever worn such finely tailored garments before. A day later, on their first official night on duty in the dockyard, two of these proud men were murdered. A group of guards apprehended a man stealing from a container and were astonished to discover that he was none other than a police superintendent from Maputo. Stunned to find trained security guards in the area from where he had habitually stolen for years, he opened fire with his service pistol; killing two of our men. The superintendent disappeared, never to be seen again.

Shortly after the security force was established, the Organisation for Economic Co-operation and Development people pulled the plug on finances and we were withdrawn with the job only half done. We often wondered how the boys went on without us.

Chapter 6

The Moamba Ring

BEFORE THE TASK of training the Maputo Dock guard force was completed, the British Organisation for Economic Co-operation and Development announced that funds for the project had been exhausted. Consequently, the three musketeers were made redundant and I made my way back to spend Christmas and the New Year in the Philippines. I intended to start hunting for something else to occupy me after the holidays, but before there was even time to unpack my suitcase, my former employers sent a message via DHL. I was to phone them with all haste. Alas, a telephone in one's own home just wasn't an option for the inmates of Pacita Complex, the 'Dog Shit Capital of South-East Asia'. Instead, I had to cram myself into a tricycle; a mode of conveyance designed for light-boned Filipinos rather than British front row forwards and head for an office running a telephone service—of sorts. After a wait of thirty minutes, a mere blink of the eye to the ever patient Filipinos, but an infuriating length of time to wait when you're as impatient as me, I managed to get through to the company office in London.

"G'day Wally," said the operations manager, a New Zealander.

"G'day Phil."

"Have you ever done military operations mate?" he asked.

"Of course, hundreds of them," I replied truthfully.

"Can you run an Operations Room?"

"Yes, of course."

"Then we'd like you to get straight back to Mozambique to take up an operational role, with a couple of thousand dollars extra by way of remuneration. Paddy's running the show; liaise with him as soon as you arrive back."

Next day I was winging my way back to Maputo, via Hong Kong and Johannesburg. By massaging my CV in an outstandingly inventive fashion, my employers had managed to sell me to the United Nations as Operations Officer on their new project in Mozambique. Without ever interviewing me, an organisation of the stature of the UN appointed me, a person who thought mines were where coal came from and who had never seen an anti-personnel mine in his life, as their De-Mining Operations Officer for Mozambique. Such an astonishingly inept method of selection astounds me to this day!

An assortment of former British Army guys gathered under Paddy's command during the weekend and, on Monday morning, descended upon the UN camp in Maputo. We were a particularly motley crew and our number included a couple of really obnoxious bastards; both former warrant officers in the Royal Signals. They seemed intent on a little out of season RMP baiting and, under normal circumstances, I'd have been more than happy to rattle their teeth. There was too much at stake here though, so, by manifesting commendable and highly uncharacteristic self-restraint, I managed to keep my hands off their scrawny throats. The UN was pulling out and the master plan was for each of Paddy's dirty dozen to take over responsibility for a department of a military HQ from a soldier of the departing Aussie Army. After a fortnight's handover, our newly formed team would spend 12-months teaching Mozambicans the ropes and, a year later, we'd leave them to clear the millions of mines still left in the ground on their own.

I was replacing Don Allison, a major in the Australian Engineers, who sported not only the obligatory slouch hat but, ominously for me, the insignia of an ammunition technician. On Tuesday morning, despite protesting that my contract only required me to run the operations room, he whisked me off into the bush to view the Moamba Ring. This was a minefield, some twenty metres wide and twenty kilometres in circumference, which encircled the shabby village of Moamba down near the South African border. Major Don commanded the force of eight-hundred Mozambican de-miners responsible for clearing both the Moamba Ring and a smaller minefield encircling another village a few miles distant. Very shortly, these guys and the minefields would all be on my charge. The enormity of the task and the realisation of how easily I could drop a bollock filled me with absolute dread. There have been many times in my life when I've wondered exactly how I managed to land myself in such a dodgy predicament. Seldom was I ever so hopelessly out of my depth as in this instance however. It gave me cause to reflect on exactly why I'd left my nice, secure, safe career with Barclays Bank all those years previously. A bank clerk's life seemed infinitely more preferable to me at this moment. My mind wandered back:

After six months service, new entrants to Barclays were required to attend a course at the bank's training establishment, located on pre-Wombles Wimbledon Common. With the honour of St Stephen's Road Branch to uphold, I dutifully caught the Thames-Clyde Express from Leicester to St Pancras and made my way to Worcester Park in Surrey. "Vauxhall-Clapham Junction-Earlsfield-Wimbledon-Rayne's Park-Motspur Park-Worcester Park-Stoneleigh-Ewell West and Epsom," said a tinny voice at Waterloo, so I boarded a green carriage on platform nine. Bank managers from the London region with a room to spare could augment their salaries nicely, by putting up migrants from the provinces for the duration of these courses. Sharing a room with me in Worcester Park was a chap from York, called Noel Voice. The gods, it seemed, never intended our 'bank clerk bonding' to be a lengthy exercise.

At the time I was an acne-plagued, gauche, unconfident youth. A diet of 'chips with everything' couldn't possibly have helped my skin condition I suppose? My hair was a mess, thanks to the compulsion to add a dollop of Brylcreem to the rest of the grease each time I passed the bathroom. My wardrobe was cheap and looked it. One of my few redeeming qualities in those days was my ability as a footballer and I played for Brush Sports, in the Midland League. Noel, on the other hand, was horribly handsome; his hair was styled like Buddy Holly's, his skin annoyingly unblemished and he wore clothes crafted by a bespoke tailor. He was a former public schoolboy, spoke with a cultured accent and, to really kick me in the teeth, he was on the books of York City.

I disliked him from the outset, especially as he attempted to gain points from me at every turn. His first triumph occurred during our first evening in Worcester Park, when we sat down to dinner with our paid host, his wife and their fifteen-year old daughter. I was baffled by the array of cutlery on show and scored a quick own-goal, by eating my soup with a dessert spoon, the standing operating procedure where I came from. He bided his time and then sniggered knowingly at my ungainly attempt to dispatch jelly and evaporated milk with an enormous soup spoon. We travelled to Wimbledon Common together each day and I soon tired of his bragging and continued efforts to belittle me. The cocky bastard from York was treading on very thin ice.

After dinner on the first Friday evening, we were kicking a football around in our host's spacious garden when the daughter graced us with her presence. Voice immediately went into his 'bird pulling' mode and engaged her in conversation. I had no chance with the young lady and, rather than play gooseberry, elected to go and bang the football against the garage wall. Whether casually placing a foot on the ball was part of his 'cool' approach was never ascertained, but he took severe umbrage when I gently hooked the ball away from underneath his foot.

"Do that again and I'll thrash you within an inch of your life," he declared, seriously overestimating his physical ability.

I set about him with controlled fury, leaving him in need of rapid evacuation to the nearest hospital. He slept elsewhere that night and, next morning, failed to make it to school. I did, but was immediately summoned to the head instructor's office. He wanted to hear my version of the previous evening's incident. My fate was already sealed though; Barclay's regulations were quite specific—in the event of a punch-up, the son of a painter from a rough housing estate is automatically trumped by the son of a professional father with loads of money in the bank. They presented me with a train ticket back to Leicester and, after picking up my things from Worcester Park, I was back in time to spend Saturday evening honing my skills in Osborne's Snooker Parlour. I did have one last chance to see Voice before departing; he was lying in bed with sticking plaster and stitches aplenty adorning his no longer so beautiful face. I treated him to my victory smirk.

Mr Blackbourn, the manager of our branch, called me into his office on Monday morning and demanded an explanation. Having rendered my account of events, he sent me straight back to work on till number two. That same day, he sent his typed report to Barclay's Local Directors in Nottingham, to whom I was required to present myself for what turned out to be a very mild bollocking a few days later. Unbeknown to those in power, I had already seen a copy of the report concerning the naughty junior clerk. Carole, the typist, had given Mr Blackbourn a brand new piece of carbon paper when he typed his dispatch and, by holding it up to the light, it was simplicity itself to read his damning words. The bulk of the content of the report I have long since forgotten, but the opening gambit will always stay with me. Confirming Barclay's status at that time as a snobbish organisation of the highest order, the report started with the words: 'Walter Payne, son of a working-class family...'

I went back to Wimbledon Common on the next course and came top of the class. Mr Blackbourn was unimpressed.

It was a minor miracle that Barclay's put up with me for as long as they did, considering the number of howlers I committed. It was always me who gave out the wrong bank statement, or forgot to send one out at all, or tormented the female staff, or was disrespectful to customers. My real speciality though was forgetting keys and the bank opened twenty minutes late one Saturday morning thanks to me. Mr Blackbourn's demeanour was distinctly cool as he drove me home in his Rover to recover the keys to the strong room, which were lying safe and sound on our mantelpiece. Balancing my till could never be guaranteed and, one Friday evening after business, my till was £1,200 short; an immense amount of money in those days. No matter how many times it was checked, or by whom, it remained precisely £1,200 short. As this sum represented two year's salary to me, I spent a rather fraught weekend worrying about it. A gentleman by the name of Shipley Jayes came into the bank first thing on Monday morning.

"Did you miss this at all?" he asked, skimming the missing £1,200 over the counter.

It seems I'd given him three bundles of £500 in fivers, instead of three of £100. What a decent man.

Despite passing my banking examinations during my years at Barclay's, which entitle me to post-nominal letters incidentally, and making a name for myself by playing for their soccer side down in London, a job requiring diplomacy and politeness wasn't really for me. To the relief of many in positions of responsibility, I resigned. As I walked through the door for the last time, the Chief Clerk confirmed my status as a 'rum' lad; an expression I'd erroneously taken as a compliment for the first couple of years. Mr Blackbourn smiled widely, for the second time in a fortnight. Two weeks previously, Dick Peach Bourne had finally retired and this had filled the manager with uncharacteristic glee. In truth, Dick was a relic from the past; a man who really ought to have lived a hundred years earlier and whose only skill was to make ledger entries in the most beautiful copperplate handwriting, but at a speed that rendered his usefulness doubtful. I recall asking Mr Blackbourn who would be Mr Bourne's replacement. His reply summed him and Barclay's up perfectly:

"Mr Bourne will not be replaced. He didn't leave a vacancy."

I was just as well out of this uncaring organisation although, after a period performing a cruelly boring office job in a factory, life in the bank didn't seem so bad after all. Barclay's sensibly refused my overtures to return to the fold, but Martin's Bank in Charles Street weren't nearly as particular. My dubious banking talents were to be aired for a second time. Alas, Martin's too, would soon realise Wally Payne wasn't really cut out to be a bank clerk.

This branch was only the second bank in the country to have a 'drive-in' facility, although the designers certainly won no plaudits for their research into local weather conditions. They'd given no consideration whatsoever to the prevailing winds, which blasted down Free Lane and into Lower Free Lane, before hitting the main road at a speed comparable to the Roaring Forties. Once they'd bashed a hole through the bank to accommodate the drive-in, Lower Free Lane was rendered obsolete as a wind tunnel and the gales diverted through the drive-in instead.

In my view, wind conditions rendered the drive-in doomed from the outset, although the bank did place a heavy weight in the deposit tray, in a futile attempt to make the system work. Just the same, unless the drive-in customer put the weight onto his paying–in book immediately, cheques and cash were whisked out of the tray by the wind before the clerk could press the button to transfer everything into the bank. The pantomime of cheques and banknotes flying down the main road, hotly pursued by customers, bank staff and opportunists became a tourist attraction in Charles Street. So it was the designer's fault, rather than mine, when I occasionally forgot to remind customers to use the weight. The manager didn't see it that way though!

During one of my early days at the branch, the manager asked me to open the slide door at the back of the drive-in, in preparation for the start of the day's business. I duly unlocked the three securing bolts with the designated keys, but couldn't open the door for love nor money. I huffed, puffed and heaved with all my might—and succeeded in pulling out all the Rawlplugs securing the non-opening side of the door to the wall. How was I to know the door opened from the opposite end? Whilst displaying undoubted strength and determination, this had been an inauspicious start to my Martin's career.

It wasn't my fault either when it slipped my mind they'd fitted a silent alarm system connecting us to the main Police Station, located further up Charles Street. What a silly place to put the alarm activating device anyway—on the floor right under the counter. The police arrived with some regularity and, rather than accept the blame every time, in the end I used to zoom downstairs to the lavatory, feigning diarrhoea and innocence whenever I put my big foot on it by mistake. On reflection, the manager never liked me, especially not after my performance at the Christmas party. Lying on the floor, underneath the tap of an Everard's Crown Bitter barrel and drinking the dregs wasn't, it appears, the behaviour expected of a bank clerk. The girl I'd taken to the party wasn't impressed either and she refused to go out with me again.

Just in case you should ever get the question in a pub quiz; yes, it was me who set fire to Martin's Bank in Charles Street, Leicester. Old, unserviceable bank notes needed to be returned to the Bank of England on a regular basis, via the High Value Package department at the main post office. First, they needed to be packed into a stiff cardboard container, which was then tied with string and the knot sealed in wax with the branch's own unique seal. It wasn't brain surgeon's work; good reason for junior cashier Payne to be landed with the job on a particularly warm summer's afternoon. Once the bank was closed and my till balanced, it was time to get on with the mundane task. It was easy to ascertain where the spoilt notes originated: lumps of meat and blood indicated Dewhurst's the Butcher; a greasy stench the local fish and chip shop; oily streaks the car repair garage and, worst of all, the odd squashed maggot courtesy of the factory that prepared cowhides prior to being cured for making leather. The mucky and torn notes were piled on the public counter, separated from the rest of the bank by a tall, wooden screen. I liked the screen; it afforded sanctuary from the prying eyes of our officious manager. Things were going along pretty well and I'd just extinguished my fourth waxed taper, consigning it to the voluminous waste paper bin situated directly behind me and next to the screen. Shortly afterwards, I fancied it was getting warm and put it down to me being engaged in moderate physical labour, not something a bank clerk needs to bother himself with unduly under normal circumstances. It was becoming so warm I decided to chance my arm and the manager's wrath should he espy me, firstly by unloosening my tie and then by taking off my suit jacket. It didn't help and it was beginning to feel very warm indeed, especially from the rear. Glancing round, the reason for my excess bodily suppuration became instantly apparent. The plastic waste paper bin had melted and the screen was in flames, right up to the ceiling. The bank was on fire! It didn't take the fire brigade long to put the flames out; or for the manager to extinguish my banking aspirations, by offering to accept my resignation.

The branch had a guard with the most unusual Christian name—Marshall! I liked Marshall and listened to his war stories whenever there was an opportunity. He used to tell the most amazing tale about returning home at the end of the war in 1945, only to find a Canadian serviceman in bed with his unfaithful wife. He had taken summary action and dispatched the randy Canuk through the bedroom window. The Canadian had failed miserably in his attempt to fly and broke his neck when he hit the ground. Marshall was charged with murder, although an understanding judge sent him down for a desultory period of time.

It was Marshall who convinced me that banking wasn't the career for a chap like me; suggesting I give some thought to the police force instead. Rather than having a pint and sandwich in the Standard Arms next lunchtime, I made my way up to the Police HQ in Charles Street and sat the Police Entrance Exams. A month later, having served my notice at Martin's, I was marching up and down the drill square at the Police Training School at Ryton-on Dunsmore.

But back to the minefield:

During a two-week period, Don gamely attempted to pass on the knowledge it had taken him twenty years to assimilate. His technical literature was at my disposal, but it was impossible for a beginner like me to absorb such a weight of information in such a short period of time. In an attempt to raise my spirits as the date for the fateful handover drew ever nearer, he let me wear his slouch hat when I had my photo taken at the minefield. This was as near to being a de-mining operations officer as I was ever likely to become.

Part of my initiation was to take a trip out into the bush, to watch the rest of Don's Aussie de-miners 'making-safe' several thousand grenades and mines they had discovered in a subterranean cache. These munitions were hidden in the middle of nowhere and the only indication anything was hidden there at all, was a padlocked metal lid set into the sand. This lid opened to give access to a set of steps leading underground to an Aladdin's Cave of armaments. Row upon row of stored ammunition, weapons, mines and explosives, most of which was in a dangerous condition. It wasn't a spot where I felt particularly comfortable; in fact the place really put the wind up me. What the hell would I do with this enormous cache once the Aussies departed? Mercifully, the Antipodeans completed the hazardous task of making everything safe before packing their suitcases and heading homeward.

One of the missions Don and I undertook was a trip down to Nelspruit, just over the border in South Africa, to sort out medical evacuation procedures in the event of a serious accident. The result was mightily confidence building. Should anyone be seriously injured, a telephone message to a call centre in Nelspruit would result in a helicopter, staffed by a doctor and nurse, being flown directly to the scene of the accident. Within thirty minutes of an injured person being put aboard this aircraft, he could be on an operating theatre in a South African hospital. Prior to writing my Evacuation Procedures next day, I contacted UN Headquarters. I needed to know whether this excellent initiative extended to all personnel engaged on the de-mining project. Their response surprised, to say the least. They declared helicopter evacuation to be the right of expatriate employees only; injured Mozambicans would continue be loaded into the back of a Landrover ambulance and bumped over forty miles of rough tracks and roads back to Maputo. What a shabby state of affairs.

All too soon and long before I felt even remotely confident in the role, my mentor boarded a plane for Melbourne and left me to ponder just how I was going to bluff my way through this one. For certain Don would have scoured the Australian newspapers on a daily basis, fully expecting to see a headline along the lines of, "Dozens killed in Mozambican de-mining fiasco."

My evening trip to the Moamba Ring, to press a button and detonate the day's find of anti-personnel mines, was within my capabilities. Something serious was bound to happen though and, on only my third day in charge, it did!

The UN, presumably bound by political correctness, engaged several senior-ranking East German Army officers on the project. Accordingly, a gaggle of *Nationale Volksarmee* Old Contemptibles appeared one morning and, much to the chagrin of the New Zealand colonel from whom Paddy would eventually assume command, they were designated an area of responsibility. They were venerable old gentlemen of exceedingly high rank, although it's doubtful if any of them had donned combat uniform for a very long time. Methinks some of these blokes knew even less about mine clearance than I did and, as if the UN were trying to highlight my ineptitude, they placed these guys under my command! Thank goodness I could speak German, because this lot couldn't boast a single syllable of English between them. The ability to communicate with your peers wouldn't appear to be a prerequisite for employment with the United Nations. To satisfy the Germans and keep them busy, they were given a few Mozambican de-miners to play with inside their small area of responsibility. Their section of terrain lay outside of the Maomba Ring and contained no mines; at least it wasn't supposed to contain any mines. Twenty years of lying in soft sand; being buffeted by wind, rain and floods can move the bloody things considerable distances it appears. Conforming to Sod's Law, during their very first morning on the ground, two of the Mozambicans under Hun command managed to step on something. The explosions blew their legs off! One of them was conveyed to the Maputo General Hospital, where he died shortly afterwards. The other, fortunately for him, was shipped off to the Argentinean Field Hospital that was just about to cease operations and he pulled through. So, if you ever step on a mine in Mozambique, take the Field Hospital option.

My charges numbered eight hundred, all of whom seemed well motivated and keen to rid their beloved homeland of the accursed mines. They were sub-divided into four companies, each two hundred strong and commanded by a former Mozambican Army officer. As well as being attired in a smart uniform, each man was issued with a metal detector, headphones and some probes. For once in their young lives, they were doing something worthwhile and felt important. At the end of each day's de-mining, the offending munitions were linked together and the men would wait to see the fruit of their day's dangerous labour being made safe, before returning to barracks. They would clap loudly after I'd done the honours by pressing the button to detonate the mines. Only around fifty anti-personnel mines were uncovered each day, a rate at which it would take them several hundred years to clear the whole country. What was wrong with whizzing around the minefield on a tank fitted with flails I wondered? Then the lads could locate the remaining 10% with metal detectors at their own speed and in reasonable safety. It seemed the logical course of action to me; but what did I know about de-mining? I was only the De-mining Operations Officer after all.

The UN would never be able to convince me they were taking this job seriously and my best company commander felt the same way. Although Mozambican, he had served in the

Zimbabwean Army and attended several military courses in the UK. Consequently, his English was excellent and so was his appreciation of the political situation prevalent in his country.

"Tell me Mr Payne, now that you and the other Brits have taken over from the UN, how long will it be before you hand over responsibility for this task to our Government?" he enquired.

"In exactly a year's time," I replied.

"In that case, I'll start distributing my CV in six months' time."

"Why is that?"

"Because our useless Government will bugger this project up within a week of taking it over and we'll all be out of a job."

With the departure of Don, my Australian crutch, I made my visits into the Moamba minefield with great reluctance and no little trepidation. At least my Gurkha aide was still there. One morning though, the normally placid fellow began jumping up and down with apparent glee the moment he saw me dismount from my vehicle. This day was to become a defining period in my de-mining career.

"You're looking particularly pleased with life chum," I remarked.

"This is really a most auspicious day Mr Wally Sahib," he replied.

"Is it? Why?"

"Follow me Mr Wally Sahib and I will show you. Keep to the goat track though; we haven't cleared this section yet."

We set off along a barely discernable path, in the direction of whatever was exciting him so. It was all right for him, he weighed scarcely more than the average goat; I was carrying rather more overweight and therefore considerably more likely to detonate any hidden landmines than he was. Only a couple of days previously, a cow browsing in the supposedly safe area used by the de-miners for tea breaks, had lost its back legs in a bang and puff of smoke. It was steaks all round for the residents of Moamba that evening. This mine clearing business seemed to be too inexact a science to me and I wasn't exactly full of confidence as we approached an area where several de-miners were gathered. The Gurkha stopped and pointed at something inside the mined area.

"Can you see the cross on the top of that mine Mr. Wally?"

"Actually, I can't even see a mine," I confessed.

"Use my bins Mr Wally."

Through a pair of stolen British Army binoculars, I could actually make out three mines, all with a little cross on the top and all linked together by trip wires.

"What's so exciting about these mines, my friend?"

"They are ZZ52 Russian Bounding Fragmentation mines Mr Wally Sahib. It is a truly exciting find."

"What's the bottom line, Lambahadar?"

"Breathe on one of those little babies Mr Wally and it will jump out of the ground, killing anything within thirty metres."

Now, I've always had a decent turn of foot and this seemed an opportune time to put my sprinting ability to the test.

"Where are you going to Mr Wally?" enquired Lambahadar, as my speed out of the blocks caused the dust to rise from the goat track.

Without breaking stride, I turned and shouted, "Forty metres away initially and then back to Leicester at the earliest opportunity."

This was to be my last visit to the minefield; wild horses wouldn't have dragged me back.

Next morning, I left our base and headed in the direction of Moamba, but didn't turn off towards the minefield. Instead, I drove on to the South African border and, from there, to Nelspruit. Having booked into a decent hotel, I relaxed for the remainder of the day, had an evening of good food and wine and retired in preparation for the next morning's telephone call to my company in the UK. I thanked them wholeheartedly for dropping me in the shit and suggested they send someone to replace me as a matter of priority, before my incompetence had someone killed. A few days later, a suitably qualified guy arrived and I was on my way out of Africa, confident they'd never offer me another contract. At least one lesson was learnt during this escapade—de-miners are all certifiable!

Chapter 7

Algeria

TRYING TO FIND A JOB whilst based in the Philippines was a futile undertaking and so the decision was made to return to Hong Kong for a protracted period. Quite why I didn't book myself into a half-decent hotel from where my CV could be disseminated is inexplicable, given my normally cavalier approach to dispensing money. Occasionally however, I'm smitten by mysterious bouts of parsimony and it was presumably during such a period of stinginess that I chose to launch my job-seeking drive from a series of the most inappropriate lodgings.

In a moment of mutual drunkenness, Andy Kennedy proposed and I gratefully accepted an offer to stay with him in his flat on Peng Chau Island. Not that there was even as much as a hammock in his spare room, but for the price of a cheap mattress and some bed linen, I had a free billet. Two weeks of supping large quantities of San Miguel beer each evening with this bounder wasn't conducive to searching for a job though. It was time to move on.

Lin Hung Yee, my former RMP comrade and lifelong friend, introduced me to an American acquaintance, a physiotherapist by trade but, as I was to learn, a most peculiar man. In the USA, people in his line of work indulge in self-glorification by dubbing themselves 'doctor' which, in his case, was most certainly over the top. He occupied a flat in North Point and was willing to rent me a room for HK$5,000 a month, this sum being considerably more than he would have been required to pay for the entire apartment in my view.

Beggars can't be choosers however, so I accepted his offer and lugged my suitcases down to the inappropriately dubbed Healthy Building in Healthy Street. I couldn't believe the place when I saw it. It was located in one of the Hong Kong Government's Low Cost Housing schemes; areas constructed specifically to give the poorest Chinese a place to lay their heads. With so many disadvantaged locals living in sub-standard hovels anxiously awaiting the opportunity to occupy a flat in a public housing scheme, we had no right to be here at all. In fact, it was actually illegal for foreigners to rent premises of this sort and we were certainly the only *gwai-lo* occupying rooms there. The American did his best to blend in with the natives, by ensuring the flat was hot and dirty, and the pillow he gave me was undoubtedly the most disgusting bolster I've ever laid my head upon. With nowhere else to go, I stuck it out for just one night, before escaping to spend the next evening on the floor of my mate Gordon's small flat in Wanchai. Thereafter, still determined not to spend money on a hotel room, I accepted Lin's offer to stay at his home in Peng Chau. Rather than outstay my welcome, I only remained there for four days, before finally coming to my senses. I took a brand new flat at a sensible rent out at Tsun Mun, up in the New Territories. It was a long way from the centre of town for sure, but a splendid place to stay while I worked out my new strategy for gainful employment.

Whilst being shown around the apartment by the charming lady owner, she invited me to use the STD telephone, to confirm everything was in working order. I took the opportunity of calling my mother back in the UK, only to discover that the Foreign Office wanted to interview me about a job in Yugoslavia. Having explained my predicament to the owner, she reimbursed my rent deposit and wished me well—a most unusual course of action for a Chinese. So, using Virgin Atlantic for the first time, it was back to the UK once again, this time with the chance of landing a highly paid position in Zagreb.

At the Foreign Office, a quartet of inquisitors led by an objectionable lesbian subjected me to the most difficult interview of my life. I felt like the enemy. Unnervingly, they knew all about me; notably that I'd been divorced twice and had been suspended as an Army officer some years previously. Where do they get all their information from? One of their really testing posers was to ask my opinion about the political situation prevailing in Bosnia at the time. I recall telling them if Stoltenberg and Lord Young could make no progress during their six months on the case, then my sentiments could surely be of no relevance. I held up well enough under the grilling and considered it worthwhile staying in the UK for a couple of weeks, to discover whether I was about to earn a huge salary for standing at the side of a Yugoslavian motorway collecting lorry numbers. For whatever reason, the rotters turned me down.

Resolute in my quest to replenish the old bank balance, it was time to really put my shoulder to the wheel and so I took one of my old bosses out for a posh lunch at the Army and Navy Club. Alas, he could offer no solace on the work-front either. Then, twenty-four hours later, three job offers arrived in the same mail delivery. What a difference a day can make. To my considerable surprise, the company I'd walked out on in Mozambique contacted me, to see if I was interested in putting my life on the line for them in Algeria. A security outfit in London invited me down for an interview and then, just to confirm all good things come in threes, the Foreign Office decided I was the right man for Yugoslavia after all. What a conundrum! I decided to go for the Algerian option, simply because it offered a full year's contract, as opposed to the mere 3-months offered by the Foreign Office in Yugoslavia. I contacted the Londoners to decline their kind offer and, within days, was at Gatwick Airport, preparing to fly out and work for an American company laying a gas pipeline across the Algerian Sahara.

From Gatwick, an Air Algérie charter aircraft conveyed me and a crowd of Bakewell employees to Oran, on the north coast of what was, then, Africa's second largest country. (It became the largest when Sudan split into two in 2011.) The buff-liveried aircraft was clearly one of Boeing's earlier models and, from the state of the interior of the machine; little money had been spent on maintenance since it had become part of the Algerian national carrier's fleet. Before we embarked on our journey southwards, a stewardess went through the motions and carried out a safety briefing, of sorts.

"*Mesdames et Messieurs*, welcome aboard this Air Algérie charter flight to Oran. Prior to take-off, would you kindly put your seat back into the upright position, provided it will go into the upright position. Also, put the trays up into the seat backs, always assuming the catch isn't broken and, if there is a safety belt attached to your seat, kindly fasten it." She failed to mention avoiding the toilets, which were all blocked.

It was a non-alcoholic flight, as one might expect on an Arab airline, but they didn't provide anything to eat either, unless the boiled sweet offered before take-off constituted a meal. None of this seemed to bother the southern state American 'good old boys'. Previous experience of Air Algérie had taught them about self-sufficiency and they all carried an abundance of food and liquor in their hand-carry bags. The professionalism of the airline was confirmed when one of our transatlantic cousins, who was well into his quart of Jim Beam before we reached the Pyrenees, gave a rendition of 'I wish I was in Dixie' from the flight deck tannoy. I have never included Dixie among the places I'd particularly care to visit, but would have preferred being there than flying at 35,000 feet above Spain on a very dodgy aeroplane. Despite all my misgivings, the plane landed at Oran in one piece.

Oran airport didn't boast such niceties as a walkway, or even a bus and we needed to walk across the runway apron to the immigration hall. The first thing I noticed were the walls of the airport building; all pitted with bullet holes. Oran had obviously experienced rather more fraught days than this relatively quiet Monday afternoon. Having negotiated 'International Arrivals', we were required to walk through a public area to 'Algerian National Departures'. If anyone had a grudge against the capitalists from the west, then this would have been an opportune time and place to extract retribution. A few additional bullet marks in the walls would hardly have been noticed. We spent an interesting hour being documented by some less than proficient immigration officials and then having our hand baggage rummaged through by customs men on the take. We were then herded back onto the tarmac, where a mountain of suitcases confronted us. Once we had identified our own luggage, we put it onto a trolley and it was driven out to the self-same aircraft we had arrived on.

Had the pilot been inclined to fly in a straight line, the journey from Oran to Mecheria might have taken thirty minutes. For some reason however, he zigzagged along for a full hour, before descending at a rapid rate and bumping down onto the runway at an Algerian Air Force base. A former USAF man opined that the pilot had probably been trained by the Russians, as zigzagging thus and descending like a falling stone were classic Soviet tactics.

From Mecheria, a yellow American school bus took us out into the desert; stopping regularly to allow passengers to alight at various camps along the way. Camp Three was to be my home for the time being, so here I jumped off the bus and took in the view. Located a few miles from the fly-ridden town of Brezina, Camp Three was simply a compound containing a couple of dozen unostentatious portacabins. The view in every direction was of sand, right up to the stout barbed wire fence surrounding the enclosure. Then, outside the fence and as far as the eye could see, there was more sand.

Bakewell were an independent American company and world leaders in heavy engineering, for whom putting a gas pipeline into the ground from the Libyan border, across Algeria and into Morocco was bread and butter stuff. The skilled workforce on this immense project consisted almost entirely of Americans from the Southern States: Texas, Georgia, Alabama, Mississippi, Tennessee, Louisiana and the like. Rather like some British Army cavalry regiments, Bakewell was a family oriented outfit, with workers following their fathers and grandfathers into the company's employ. Whereas these men were experienced and absolutely expert in what they did, the mind-numbingly boring nature of their work didn't require them to be on the same cerebral plane as a Royal Military Police lance corporal. What I'm trying to say here is that the majority of them were as thick as pig shit and having a reasonable conversation proved a challenge indeed! None of them appeared keen to converse with a Briton in any case; a throwback to the War of Independence one assumes? Other employees included a sprinkling of Brits, a smattering of assorted Europeans, a platoon's worth of Turkish welders and loads of Algerians, to do the menial tasks.

A security detachment hadn't been a consideration when this project first started. Bakewell management had been criminally negligent in this regard and clearly hadn't read CIA briefings about working in this part of North Africa. Very early on in the operation a grave incident occurred; something which stirred the blood of the workers and made the managers rapidly rethink security policy.

One Thursday evening, a group of Americans went out into the town of Ouargla, probably looking for the nearest

McDonald's or somewhere to order a plate of fried chicken, grits and a mess of greens. They had undoubtedly been sucking on a bottle or two of something to lower the inhibitions, because they failed absolutely to take the sensibilities of the local population into consideration. Quite what they did to incur the wrath of the Moslems is obscure, but the subsequent revenge meted out by a group of vigilantes from Ouargla was well documented.

Next morning, Holy Day in the Islamic calendar, an armed Algerian group marched into the unguarded American camp accompanied by witnesses to whatever crimes were perceived to have been committed the previous day. Once the witnesses had pointed out those responsible, they were at liberty to leave. The punitive band then dragged those deemed guilty of offending Moslem law to an open area within the camp. The five Americans and solitary Scandinavian were shot through the legs and left lying in agony throughout the day. None of their kinsmen found the courage to come to their aid, for fear of meeting a similar fate presumably. Not a single Gary Cooper, John Wayne or Rambo was there to be found in the entire workforce. After Friday evening prayers, held at the scene of the shootings, the vigilantes summarily cut the throats of the wounded men. Not surprisingly, the remainder of the American employees were determined to head back to the States by the quickest means possible. With such a lucrative contract on offer however, the Bakewell management team quickly conceived a plan they hoped would encourage their artisans to stay in Algeria. They contacted my employers, who quickly had men on the ground to provide the physical protection the American personnel craved.

Under normal circumstances, a contingent of security men delegated by our company would have its own manager and chain of command. In their crisis management panic however, Bakewell had also engaged their own American security hierarchy, to whom the Brits would be subordinate. The security supremo was an inept Californian, known endearingly to us as Delray the Dipshit, whose empire had its hub at the Bakewell HQ in Camp One. Delray had seen a good many summers and was no longer as sharp as he might once have been. He had five fellow Americans in his command, one in charge of security at each of the five camps along the length of the pipeline. Each of them purported to be a former member of Delta Force, a band that would dearly love to be considered the transatlantic equivalent of our SAS. If this quintet was anything to go by, then their organization would come a very poor second to our famous regiment. The dopey Yank in charge of Camp Three was Scott Grasser, a man full of his own self-importance and seriously devoid of anything vaguely resembling a brain.

I had joined the PCL team at Camp Three some weeks after the rest of the crew and, despite me being the leader of the gang, they were the guys who already knew the ropes. A day after my arrival, Grasser disappeared for a couple of days and left me wondering if I'd said something to offend him. The remaining members of our security team, three tough ex-French Foreign Legionnaires, a former French soldier and a defrocked Canadian Mounted Policeman with a cowardly streak, assured me this was a regular occurrence and nothing to concern myself about. Grasser, it seems, was a Vietnam veteran who, convinced the camp was about to be attacked at any time by the Algerian equivalent of Vietcong gooks, was prone to creeping out into the desert in the middle of the night. He would dig-in and sit observing absolutely nothing for forty-eight hours, before returning with some improbable stories and highly dubious intelligence.

In addition to our alleged Delta Force dope, our task at Camp Three was further hampered by the presence of a squadron of Algerian Army Armour. With an ancient Russian tank dug in at each corner of the camp, their task was to guard the exterior of the compound. The Algerian troops were an absolute shower and provided scant comfort to proper, albeit retired, soldiers of our calibre. Our lives were in far more danger from the negligent discharges of their small arms than from any terrorist activity.

Listening to the conversation of a gang of former British soldiers, a casual bystander would be forgiven for assuming that a tour of duty with the SAS was a mandatory requirement for progression to the rank of lance corporal. Half the old soldiers one encounters will claim to have served with the SAS at some time during their service, the number rising in direct proportion to the amount of drink taken. Several years later, I was to work regularly with a genuine former SAS soldier. Upon revealing his regimental antecedents, he maintained that the first question people asked was, "Were you involved in the Balcombe Street Siege?" His response was always, "No, but I know several thousand who claim they were." There were only a dozen or so SAS men involved in this event. Presumably things are similar in the USA; because I'm convinced Grasser had never been anywhere near a Special Forces unit. I didn't want to lose this job though and so shrugged off Grasser's excesses, right up to the time of the riot in the Algerian compound.

As I came to know the rest of the Delta Force personnel working for Delray, they all gave me the same impression. Not one of them had the respect of our security teams; their stories were just too tall and their military skills all too limited. It's my conviction that these fellows were wannabees and had never been any closer to being members of the 1st Special Forces Operational Detachment-Delta than I had.

We worked what was, by any stretch of the imagination, a pretty severe shift pattern—fifty-six consecutive night duties from 1800-0600 hrs. Then, just to make life really tough, the consumption of alcohol was specifically forbidden by our contracts. To illustrate the harshness of life in Camp Three, my weight dropped twenty-five pounds during my first two month stint. Despite eating regally in the cordon bleu camp restaurant, the effect of temperance, walking all night in soft sand, nervous tension and suffering under Scott Grasser all combined to transform me back into a light-heavyweight for the first time in years. The guys working out on the pipeline had it even tougher than us; at least we suffered neither from the excessive daytime heat, nor from the unjustified excesses of slave-driving pipeline bosses.

As huts in the desert go, ours was pretty superior accommodation. We had both hot and cold running salty water, toilets that flushed hot and a daily laundry service. In addition, for a paltry number of dinars, the undiscerning could put the cleaning ladies to an alternative use. One really couldn't ask for much more in this godforsaken spot. Our exciting life of walking in soft sand, sleeping and eating was punctuated by long periods of doing nothing; we couldn't even lay claim to a short-wave radio to listen to the BBC World Service. In the same way as British soldiers do whenever they are really pissed off, former legionnaires pull on their boots and start running. Each evening, we set off around the camp's perimeter fence and ran ourselves ragged until, one day, our tame Frenchman produced a set of boules. Thereafter, we were to be seen throwing metal balls all over the place. It was occupational therapy at its most basic, but it served to maintain our sanity.

Local security guards were recruited from the nearly town of Brezina, although by recruiting chimpanzees we would have achieved the same results. They were bordering on useless, which was no real surprise given they were almost all former shepherds and, in almost every case, totally illiterate. To make matters worse, they had no equipment whatsoever and spent the nights staving off hypothermia rather than scouring the sand dunes for approaching terrorists. Brezina lay several thousand feet above sea level, up in the Grand Erg Occidental, and half of the poor buggers didn't have anything more substantial than a pair of flip-flops in the way of footwear. We had a couple of dozen of these guys strung out along the fence line, supposedly looking out into the desert around the camp for approaching baddies. As it was pitch black most nights, they wouldn't have been able to see much anyway, especially as they didn't even have a torch between them. Quite what they would have done had we come under attack is debatable; perhaps they would have followed me, by getting as far away from the place as possible.

We looked after the guards as best we could, by giving them our spare kit and slipping them food whenever none of the Bakewell personnel were watching. They still looked and acted like Fred Carno's Army though. One lucky chap experienced the charitable side of my nature, when I bequeathed him a radio on which I had never been able to get anything but Arab music. Just as an aside, if you are desirous of listening to the BBC whilst in the Sahara, then what you need is a shortwave set. The radio I gave away was only a Chinese assembled Gründig, but it gave Mohammed immense face to own a piece of equipment with such a prestigious trademark. His family responded to my perceived act of generosity with a gift no family should be without and, to this day, I still have a couple of hand-woven, woollen pillow cases.

Despite the way Arabs are viewed by many in the west, they can actually be disarmingly generous people. One black Algerian, with whom I conversed regularly, was about to travel home on leave to Tindouf, a town located in the far west of Algeria. Prior to his departure, he asked if he could bring me back a present. To decline would be considered an insult, so I asked for a small painting, or perhaps an ornament from his local area. He returned some weeks later and, with great ceremony, presented me with a brown paper bag. Inside was a large bottle of 'Head & Shoulders' shampoo, for normal hair; just what I'd always wanted. It's the thought that counts!

I went out of my way to talk to the guards, primarily in an effort to improve my French and then to give them a feeling of being appreciated for performing a truly crap job. Generally, the French they spoke was very poor anyway, so I'm not sure whether my time was fruitfully spent. At least my presence gave them someone to show their evening's collection of scorpions and snakes to. It was by talking to these guards I first began to realise that our job wasn't nearly as onerous as it might first have appeared. One of them asked me why we bothered to remain alert all night and make tedious rounds of the camp. Someone had to be ready to take action in the event of an attack by terrorists, I explained. He asked me to sit down, offered me a cup of vile Algerian coffee and explained the situation in his little town of Brezina. Apart from those who had gone away to work, there had been very little in the way of employment in the town since the salt-bearing camel trains had stopped calling, a hundred years previously. "You are paying us US$5 a day," he said, "which makes us rich men. Believe me, if the terrorists came within 100 km of this camp, the residents of our town would rush out and kill them. You are in no danger here monsieur."

We were suddenly blessed by an augmentation to our establishment table, as another alleged Delta Force nincompoop was posted in. He was senior to Grasser it appeared because, within a few days, he summoned us to a security meeting. The burning question on his mind was: what would we do if we were attacked by the enemy? With our weapons still held up in London awaiting a UK export licence, my immediate action drill would have been to hide as far away from the noise of gunfire as possible. In my view, self-preservation beats a medal for gallantry every time, especially if there's a chance the medal might be awarded posthumously. His master plan, designed to win him a deathbed Congressional Medal of Honour, involved us clambering up onto the top of a residential portacabin at the first sound of an attack. Here we would lie until the terrorists, armed to the teeth no doubt, conveniently manifest themselves in the vicinity of the portacabin on which we were lying. Then, we would jump down on them, shout 'boo', ask a terrorist if he'd be kind enough to hand over his AK47 and then kill 'em. Dead easy! Had there ever been an attack, I fancy he might have been a very lonely man sitting atop his cabin.

One of our Algerians came running into the guard hut to report a riot in the Algerian compound. Grasser was already there apparently and he wanted expatriate back-up with all haste. As the only person in the guard post, I locked the door behind me and followed the runner to the scene of the trouble. In the compound were two opposing groups, each comprising a dozen young Algerians, who were busily threatening and jostling one another. Although the odd glint of steel was discernable in the gloaming, nobody seemed keen to throw the first punch or thrust his knife between someone's ribs. Come to think, the glint could just as easily have been the gleam of a gold tooth. As with most altercations in this part of the world, the throng of spectators gathered to watch proceedings was of a proportion large enough to delight the accountants of any English lower division soccer team. I found Grasser in the company of three Algerian guards and was astonished when he announced he and I were going to wade in and stop the affray, which hadn't even started yet. Having spent a large proportion of my life sorting out the warring factions of many a British regiment, men indisputably tougher in every way than this rabble, I have developed a system of dealing expediently with such confrontations. It is not only effective, but ensures no mischief befalls yours truly. In English plain enough for even a thick Texan to understand, I told Grasser he was welcome to wade into the Arabs if he wished, but on his own.

"Let them knock the shit out of each other first and we can pick up the pieces at our leisure," I advised.

"Are y'all chicken?" he enquired.

"Indeed not, merely sensible. And furthermore, my transatlantic cousin, let me point something out to y'all. My experience in dealing with incidents of this nature is considerable; you would be well advised to heed my counsel."

There were too many hard words in those sentences for him to understand, so he elected to repeat his banal comment.

"Y'all are chicken!" he asserted, clearly enjoying the opportunity to practice the language of vituperation.

He turned to the Algerian guards and intimated, in his irritating Texan drawl, that the Englishman was a chicken and too scared to do battle. Very few of our Algerians spoke anything more than the most rudimentary English and no Texan whatsoever, so his comments fell on uncomprehending ears. Realising they had missed his point, he began to run around the compound making clucking noises and pointing at me.

"The Englishman is chicken," he announced to anyone who would listen.

This bizarre performance produced the most unexpected outcome. The warring factions found the spectacle of a manic infidel cavorting around the compound to be infinitely more entertaining than boring old stabbing and skull cracking. They shouldered arms at once, put away their knives and joined the audience. He continued to strut around, giving a very reasonable impersonation of a chicken if the truth be known, but making me very angry indeed. I don't take kindly to being ridiculed and, at this juncture, considered some kind of preventative action to be justified. Not being one to spurn the opportunity of performing in front of a large audience, I strode over to my tormentor and introduced him to my educated left hook. Two meaty punches were sufficient to leave him on the floor, spitting blood and sand. Declining autograph opportunities, I pushed my way through the ranks of my newly formed fan club and returned to the security post.

Ten minutes later, a much chastened Grasser appeared.

"I think y'all misunderstood me back there," he said.

"There was no misunderstanding chum and you got all you asked for. Try anything like that again and you'll be spending some time in intensive care. Do y'all understand?" I replied.

"Can we shake hands and forget the whole thing?" he enquired.

I shook the ridiculous man's hand.

There was precious little time to fall out with Grasser again. Shortly after the chicken incident, he was sacked for some other misdemeanour and went home to the west Texas town of El Paso.

With considerable relief, I went off on leave after my first two month stint. A Twin Otter plane flew a twice-weekly shuttle service between the camps and the Algerian Air Force base at Mecheria, from where a charter aircraft made the flight to Gatwick, via Oran. Rather than endure a bumpy ride in a Twin Otter, I elected to travel across the desert to Mecheria by vehicle. This decision was influenced in no small part by my lack of confidence in the pilot, a Yorkshireman whose party piece was to assure passengers that he adhered strictly to air safety regulations: by never smoking 24-hours before a flight and never drinking alcohol within fifty metres of the aircraft. I found the Tyke's play on words neither amusing, nor confidence inspiring. What's more, I remained highly sceptical about his ability as a plane driver.

Whilst away on my fortnight's leave, during which time I was put through my mother's famous 'ordeal by food' regimen, the guy in charge of our PCL operation in Algeria called it a day. He was a man whose experience in the security game was restricted to undercover work in Turkey; hardly ideal credentials for a project of this nature. Immediately upon my return therefore, I was summoned up to Camp One to take over his position as security co-ordinator. This badly upset the chap who had been second-in-command, as he had confidently expected to be elevated to the dizzy heights. He wasted no time in making it clear to me he wasn't a happy bunny. Whilst commiserating with the fellow, I made it equally clear I couldn't give a shit whether he was happy or not and offered him a seat on the next flight out if he felt so strongly about working for me. He stayed.

The American company's Algerian operation was controlled from within Camp One's barbed wire fence. It was a huge area of sand compared with Camp Three, but remained just another fly-bitten dump in the desert. I introduced myself to the Head of Security and was thoroughly 'underwhelmed' by the experience. Delray's recent charisma bypass operation had been an unreserved success.

I hadn't been on duty for longer than fifteen minutes on my first night shift at the camp, before a huge American Dodge pulled up outside our office.

"The General Manager wants to see y'all," announced the driver.

I clambered aboard the petrol-guzzling monster and was driven down to the operational headquarters. Sitting at a round table, reminiscent of King Arthur's knights, were a group of Bakewell bigwigs; the big cheese himself and several of his heads of department. The General Manager opened the batting.

"Do you think y'all could run the security of this operation without those dip-shit Americans?" he asked.

"Indubitably, irrefutably and indisputably," I replied, in my best BBC voice.

"In that case, get onto your people in London and as soon as you're ready to roll, I'll sack all these sons of bitches."

It seemed as if the management was as unimpressed with Delray and his Delta Force desperados as I was. Not wanting to let any grass grow under my feet, not that there was any grass for miles around, I sneaked away to feed the intelligence to my employers. There must have been a mole among the management group because, as word of the imminent overthrow of the American security team began to percolate, Delray confronted me with accusations of treachery.

Using my celebrated 'butter wouldn't melt in my mouth' ploy, a well-honed technique used to such good effect during a long Army career; he accepted my phoney explanation hook, line and sinker. My display of wounded innocence was of Oscar winning proportions and he apologised for ever having doubted my loyalty. In the event, there were contractual considerations to be settled and it wasn't until the end of the first phase of the operation that the Delta Force crew actually packed its bags and headed back to the Home of the Brave.

In the meantime it was business as usual, with the Security Manager doing precious little, the Delta Boys playing at soldiers and our gang working throughout the night to ensure the pipe-laying gangs could enjoy restful and terrorist-free slumber. We took it all very seriously initially, walking the perimeter fence throughout the night, eyes peeled and with infrared binoculars slung around our necks. Nothing happened and, as the weeks went by, nothing happened again. Then, out of the blue, the guns arrived and Delray assigned yours truly to assemble them. Had he been aware of my propensity to drop and lose small pieces of almost anything, he may have considered someone else for the task. Nevertheless, I actually managed to put them together, slowly admittedly, but each gun had all the bits attached it was supposed to have. Then, our men along the pipeline were presented with a Benelli shotgun and a Sig Sauer pistol apiece. Despite having served for many years in the Army and having earned my living since retirement in a semi-mercenary fashion, guns have never been my scene. To me, the Sig Sauer seemed a particularly comfortable weapon to handle just the same and it's talked about in glowing terms by the pistol packing fraternity. I've heard constant arguments about the provenance of the Sig; with Switzerland, Austria and Czechoslovakia taking roughly equal shares of the votes. The fact is they are manufactured in Eckernfoerde in Germany—take my word for it. The 'Sig' part of the name comes from a Swiss engineering company called Schweitzerische Industrie Gesellschaft—SIG. This company amalgamated with JP Sauer & Sohn in 1985 and it is the new company 'Sig Sauer' who make the pistols. We looked the part as mercenaries now, with a shotgun cradled in our arms, a bandolier around the chest and a pistol holstered at our sides. Two of our guys were such immense physical specimens that the bandoliers for carrying the shotgun cartridges wouldn't fit around their massive chests at all! I was delighted this pair was on our side; they would have made formidable adversaries.

One was Jim, who loved his beautiful frame and took legal food supplements, and possibly some illegal ones as well to retain his bulk. He was convinced garlic was good for him and there were few who would argue with the assertion, but I wonder if it was really necessary to eat a dozen raw cloves each evening with his dinner. I mention this, since it was my misfortune to share a room with him for a while.

The other, Simon, was an even bigger man and had been an RAF deserter when he joined the French Foreign Legion. Returning to the UK on completion of his time as a legionnaire, he had decided to settle the score by handing himself in, doing his porridge and starting life with a clean sheet. He told me of the time he went to the guardroom at RAF Hounslow to face the music. He spent the day in the sergeants' mess, drinking tea and eating his fill as his documentation was sorted out by a WRAF officer. He imagined this was the calm before the storm; or rather, the calm before several months in jail. During the course of the afternoon however, the officer reappeared with his discharge papers, a day's pay and her grateful thanks to him, for clearing the matter up. He was then at liberty to return home for tea as a free man.

Camp One was 5,000 feet up in the mountains and particularly cold at night. We had been issued with decent thermal underwear which, like all thermals, bore a maker's label cautioning against washing the garments in water at any temperature above tepid. Each morning, a bevy of laundresses appeared by bus from somewhere or other; their task being to attend to the laundry of the lost souls. Unable to read or write and accustomed to washing their dhobi by bashing it on a rock in the nearest wadi, they knew nothing of the niceties of low temperature washes. They put everything, regardless of colour; creed or manufacturer's recommended washing temperature into the boiler simultaneously. Within a week, our thermals wouldn't fit anything bigger than a 'Barbie' doll and dhobi that didn't shrink horribly disappeared at an alarming rate. If my journeys should ever take me back to the Grand Erg Occidental and I catch up with an Arab wearing my Leicester City jersey, then my solicitors—Mephastophiles, Shagnasty, Shagnasty and Spong—will be instructed without delay.

As I've already alluded, the ladies working in the camp did have their uses; proving my assertion that even in the middle of nowhere, it's always possible for a gentleman to find female company for a price, albeit sometimes company of non-league quality. One of our chaps availed himself of the services of the black woman in overall charge of the female workers. This liaison continued for several weeks until, with nothing better to say one day, he ventured to enquire about her marital status. It transpired she was single, but engaged to the Gendarme captain responsible for the region. Rather than push his luck, he transferred his allegiance to an alternative slut. I quite missed her!

The locally employed guards at Camp One were no better than those in Brezina and with this camp lying even higher above sea level, they suffered horribly in the bitter night-time cold. They lit huge fires each evening, made from the waste American organizations produce in unbelievable quantities. This had the effect of keeping them marginally warmer, on one side at least, but it blinded them from seeing anything going on outside the perimeter fence. In any case, they never seemed able to grasp that their attention should be centred on the exterior of the camp, rather than what was going on inside.

Bakewell insisted on the guards working 12-hour shifts, which was idiotic. In conditions such as these, a three-hour stint was the maximum period a guy could keep even vaguely alert. The person responsible for making such a crass decision had obviously never stood on guard himself. Without consulting Bakewell, Delray or his Delta Force nitwit, I initiated a system to give the guards a couple of hour-long break periods per night. It improved morale considerably, but didn't appear to make any discernable difference to the quality of their abysmal performance.

When I questioned these guards about the chances of a terrorist attack on Camp One, they responded by shaking their heads knowingly. They concurred absolutely with the guards working in Camp Three; there was no chance whatsoever of any attack happening at any location along the pipeline. As the weeks and months went by, we began to relax. We started riding around the area in vehicles rather than walking, started playing games and having quizzes to pass the long nights away until, finally, we locked our weapons in the armoury and never took them out again.

The job itself wasn't difficult, but managing to stick out fifty-six consecutive night duties in this godforsaken spot was. Again, without reference to the Americans, I began to allocate nights off to our team, making the drudgery a little easier to bear. Our contracts specifically forbade the consumption of alcohol, although I encouraged the boys to drink the odd beer in private. One of my guys however, tore the backside out of the privilege and drank to excess—there's always one who can't screw the bobbin! I turned a blind eye to the Brummie's transgressions, until he set about the Delta Force cowboy one evening and made a terrible mess of his beautiful American face. Despite applauding the splendid job he'd done on the Yank, I had no option but to put him on the plane home. Our only other casualty was a Welshman from Blaenau Ffestiniog. He found it all a bit too much, threw a wobbly and asked to be sent home.

At the very end of February, the weather really set in and it began to snow. With nothing better to do one night, several of us took out our 4x4 trucks and began to do handbrake turns in the deepening snow. It may have been a regular winter occurrence in these latitudes for all I know, but snow in the desert seemed a little incongruous to me. Tiring of the trick driving, I decided to call Nelia back in the Philippines. Her voice sounded as though it was coming via Houston and Uranus but, to my absolute delight, she announced she was pregnant. When we had finished congratulating each other, I decided to call my mum and break the glad tidings to her.

Thanks to the intransigence of the Roman Catholic Church in the Philippines, Nelia and I weren't technically married and, whilst dialling the UK, I couldn't help wondering whether my

Methodist Mam would condone me siring a child out of wedlock. When she answered, we chatted about all manner of things, but I decided to postpone the bombshell news until another time. She would have been absolutely delighted for us for sure, so why did I make such a wretchedly bad decision? It was something I'll never forgive myself for, because we were never to speak together again. Twenty-five minutes after I'd put the phone down to her, my mother was dead! It snowed heavily in the Sahara that night.

My brother had the unenviable task of informing me, although a call from him at 0200 hrs could only have meant one thing. The weekly bus from Camp One to Mecheria airport departed at dawn, with me aboard. I contacted my company from Gatwick and, to my considerable surprise, they showed great compassion; the company did have a heart after all. I went home to Leicester and, within eighteen-hours of my Mam succumbing to a heart attack; I was sitting alone in our lounge.

The funeral over, it was time to tackle the ridiculous administrative barriers associated with wrapping up a person's estate. There will probably be sound reasoning behind such complex regulations, but from my perspective at this time, they seemed specifically tailored to cause me maximum distress. My Mam didn't have much to bequeath for goodness sake and what little cash she did have was entrusted equally to Barclays and the Alliance & Leicester. These two organisations were most reluctant to release the funds. As I naively saw it, this was my mother's money, I was the eldest child, she was dead, so the money was mine and I wanted it—now! The manager at Barclay's quoted legislation about laws of probate, which, he was at pains to reveal, could easily be resolved should I care to hire one of their lawyers. It didn't take him long to realise that the demeanour of the big, angry-looking fellow who was foaming at the mouth, might prove injurious to both business and his features. Suddenly, he discovered a method of transferring the funds to the funeral director that involved neither a lawyer, nor any charge. I accepted this compromise.

My next opponents would be the Alliance & Leicester. Their head office in the city centre would be the scene of the next showdown. In me lurks a propensity for violence when I'm being mucked around for no good reason and these people were mucking me around for no good reason. I was breathing fire as I stormed into the public banking hall. Being considerably more level-headed than me, my brother realised fists might well fly and so took the precaution of forewarning the bank of my imminent arrival. The sneaky bastards sent out a manager to meet me; a heavily pregnant manager. She was all sweetness and light and, regardless of regulations pertaining to laws of probate, I left the bank some minutes later clutching a cheque.

There was nothing to be gained from staying in Leicester now everything had been done. I put the house up for sale, contacted my company and set off back for Algeria shortly afterwards.

I have scant recollection of the plane journey back to Algeria. Being deeply distressed and having espied a bottle of Wood's Over-proof Rum in the duty-free shop, I tucked into the contents with gusto once on board. I vaguely recall seeing the snow-clad Pyrenees, but there's not a flicker of recollection of events thereafter. As I reported for duty next evening, our Irish vehicle mechanic, who had been aboard the same flight, approached me for a chat.

"You were lucky there were no members of the senior management on the plane yesterday Walter to be sure, to be sure. Some of them have no sense of humour you know?"

"What do you mean?"

"Jesus you were in fine fettle, so you were."

"Oh dear! What happened? Did I do my George Formby impersonation? Did I smite anyone?"

"No, you were singing and keeping everyone amused just fine," he admitted.

"What was it then?"

"Can you remember who you were sitting next to?"

"No."

"You were next to that obnoxious French shite with the long hair."

"And?"

"As we were coming into land, you vomited all over him. Everyone loved it."

I sought out the little French shite and apologised profusely. He took it all very much in his stride; it was almost as if he'd been vomited on before! I kept a low profile for a couple of days.

This sector of the pipeline project was drawing to a close and Bakewell would soon move its operation to the east of the country. Next, they would construct a link from the Libyan border, to connect with the already completed section at a place called Hassi Massaoud. Meanwhile, Delray and his Merry Men departed without as much as a farewell wave; their presence wouldn't be required on the next leg.

A couple of days prior to my next leave there was a phone call from my boss at PCL. He thanked me heartily for my efforts on their behalf and confirmed that, thanks to my clandestine activities, the company had won the security contract for the second leg. He offered me the position of security manager for the remainder of the project, along with a very decent salary increase. I jumped at the offer. The details, he explained, would be discussed over lunch as soon as I arrived back in the UK.

On the forecourt at Victoria Station stood a uniformed chauffeur, holding aloft a board bearing my name. Never having seen my name on a chauffeur's board before, I was rather chuffed. He whisked me off to a restaurant, wherein sat two directors dressed in business suits. Their sartorial elegance put me at an immediate disadvantage, considering I was in the kind of scruff order recommended when travelling on Air Algérie. I ate with relish nevertheless, as they explained the plan for pipeline project GR2 and my part in the scheme of things. In a nutshell, I would return to Camp One upon completion of my leave and await instructions to travel south to Hassi Messaoud, where I'd assume control of the security contingent. As if to confirm my recently acquired importance, the company had the chauffeur meet me at St Pancras station on my way back from leave to convey me to Gatwick Airport.

My move down to Hassi Messaoud was scheduled to take place within forty-eight hours of my arrival back at Camp One, but there was no call from London. I waited a further twenty-four hours and rang them. My boss wasn't available. Each time I called over the next few days he remained unavailable—attending an important lunch meeting; holding a briefing or getting his leg over the receptionist. One began to smell a rat! Finally, after a week of waiting, the company saw fit to contact me early one morning. At the eleventh hour, they had decided to use a former SAS man for the new post, rather than me. This company had been formed by ex-SAS personnel and the old boy network counted for a lot. I have nothing against keeping it in the family and have been the unashamed beneficiary of more than a little nepotism myself on occasions. It was the underhand way in which they had handled the matter that pissed me off. To rub salt into the wounds, they offered me the position of second-in-command and, in a puny attempt to appease me, offered to pay me at the higher rate of salary when standing in for the new leader of the pack—how magnanimous of them! Before slamming down the phone with some force, I told them to stuff the job up their backsides and arrange to replace me at the earliest opportunity.

With that, I stormed out of the security office in a raging fury and ran straight into the General Manager of Bakewell and his arse-licking acolytes, out on their early morning jog. The manager noticed my troubled visage and brought the phalanx of joggers to a halt.

"What the hell's the matter with you, Wally Payne? I ain't never seen you before when y'all weren't smiling," he declared.

I gave him the full SP.

"That's one hell of a dirty stroke to pull on a guy. Hey, never mind those cock suckers, come and work for us instead. Y'all come and see me after breakfast."

It took him a mere thirty seconds to offer me a job as a camp coordinator on GR2 and specify a starting date. I gleefully accepted his offer. Under normal circumstances, PCL would have been within their contractual rights to prevent me from working directly for Bakewell. Since they had treated me so shabbily however, they agreed to let me transfer to the American company at my earliest convenience. First though, a confrontation with the SAS man who had stolen my job was necessary, just to leave him in no doubt about my feelings. I held nothing against him personally, but gave it to him from the hip. He clearly felt awkward in my company thereafter and, until my departure, I saw no reason to enter into conversation with him.

There was an opportunity to make a speedy return to the Philippines before taking up my job with Bakewell, during which time my new contract document arrived via DHL. The terms of the document met with my absolute approval, especially since the salary specified was considerably higher than the sum verbally agreed prior to me leaving Algeria. I was very pleased to append my signature and return the contract to Houston, along with no less than the stipulated forty-eight passport photos. Forty-eight photographs for goodness sake! What were they doing, papering the wall with the things?

At Bakewell's insistence, I was required to undergo a full medical. Aware of the chicanery prevalent in the Philippines, where doctors will certify anything if presented with a financial inducement, they insisted upon a European physician performing the examination. A friend recommended his GP and that's how I came to be in the surgery of Herr Doktor Varwig. The aged German medical practitioner was a legend in Manila; not only for his clinical excellence, but also for his homosexual tendencies. Tales of his unusual diagnostic methods abounded amongst the expatriate community for, no matter what ailment caused you to visit his surgery, he would require the patient to lower his trousers for a rectal examination. Every male patient leaving Dr Varwig's surgery did so confident that his prostate had been expertly examined and was in full working order.

A huge map of the Fatherland graced one side of his surgery wall and so I greeted him in German. He was delighted to discover I knew his homeland so well and we had a nice little chat. Having told him about my military service in his country, he reciprocated with some tales from his time with the Reichsfuehrer's mob. The wretched Sennelager Training Camp turned out to be a place known intimately to the pair of us.

"Did you serve with the occupation forces in Sennelager?" he asked.

"I served there briefly, although we were called the British Army of the Rhein by then."

"Did you ever know of a regiment called the Lancashire Fusiliers?"

"Yes indeed. In fact my father served with them during the war."

"Then perhaps you will know an officer in this regiment by the name of Major Smith?"

"I'm afraid not. The Lancashire Fusiliers disbanded years before I joined the Army you see."

"Ah so! I will never forget Major Smith. He took me prisoner of war in 1944."

"Doctor Varwig, I wasn't born until 1942."

"Mensch, die Jahre fliegen so schnell vorbei."

A full medical followed, during which the doctor ticked all the right boxes and confirmed my outstanding physical condition. I was just about to get dressed when he indicated towards the back room; my medical wasn't quite finished it appeared.

"Go into the back room and take off your pants," he instructed.

Just when I thought I'd got away with it!

"Lie on your left-hand side and bring up your right knee as far as it will go."

I complied.

"The tissues are on the bedside table," he said

"Tissues? What do I need tissues for?" I asked.

"You are about to find out," he sneered, before subjecting me to my first ever prostate examination and making my eyes water more than a little. Apparently my prostate was in the pink of condition too.

The job of Camp Coordinator with Bakewell on GR2 paid considerably more than PCL had considered me worth; and for doing a fraction of the work. Mind you, the location was in the middle of the Sahara and, during the daytime, it was bloody hot. Like the Americans working out on the pipeline, I arose before the sun and by 0545 hrs was in my office. On rare occasions someone would ask me to post a letter, or make a phone call on their behalf, but more often than not, I merely sat there in case someone required my services. At 0600 hrs the Americans would depart in convoy for the pipeline, where they would spend twelve mind-numbing hours in unbearably hot conditions. My duties were minimal; during the course of the day I might deliver incoming mail to the workers' rooms, check that the cleaners had been around with a duster and look in on the laundresses, to make sure they were shrinking our clothes properly. Even these mundane tasks weren't really my responsibility. I did this voluntary work on behalf of the American Camp Manager, who was bone idle and totally inept in every way. Quite why it was considered necessary to have the pair of us employed at the same location was a mystery, but I'll take anyone's money.

My first problem came, not because of any inability to perform a particular task, but because I had some difficulty understanding the Southern States' drawl. Early one morning, one of the Louisianan drivers called into my office. In an accent that presumably passed for English in those old cotton fields back home, but which proved almost unintelligible to me, he announced:

"Aa wanna draw-a."

"Sorry old bean, but I only play to win. I can meet with triumph and disaster and treat those two impostors just the same, but a draw is quite out of the question."

"Uh?"

"Oh, now I understand, you want a drawer. No problems old chap, does this one suit you?"

With that, I pulled out a desk draw and presented it to him.

"No! Y'all don't understand. Aa don't want a draw-a, aa wanna draw-a."

"Oh, I see, you wanna draw-a. Well, here's a piece of cartridge paper and a 2B pencil, sit over there by the window and fill your boots."

"Y'all still don't understand. Aa wanna draw-a. I wanna draw-a some money so aa can buy some beer and goobers tonight."

Problem solved, almost. I gave him the standard form to fill in, but he couldn't write. Having completed the form for him, he made his mark and, when he returned from his day's toil, I was able to cross his palm with greenbacks. Later, this dim but decent chap sought me out in the bar and, in gratitude for my unstinting efforts on his behalf, bought me a beer and gave me a plate full of goobers.

PCL had a security detachment at the camp, with an irritating Brummie as head honcho. He was a former French Foreign Legionnaire of course and, although his grasp of French was outstanding, I had forgotten more about the security business than he was ever likely to learn. To his credit though, he came and sought my advice whenever he needed to seek a pearl of wisdom. We were soon to have a serious conflict though—regarding the use of the camp's only satellite telephone, of which I had been appointed custodian.

It was Saturday afternoon and Leicester City were playing Crystal Palace in the First Division promotion play-off match. My chum Bob and the rest of our pub's 'Railway Crew' were down at Wembley and, at regular intervals during the course of the match, I called Bob to monitor progress. Then a minor administrative matter requiring Brummie's action arose, so I let him use the phone twice during half-time. As I was calling Bob during the crucial extra-time period however, the annoying Birmingham man strode into my office and demanded immediate use of the phone. Not being a football aficionado, the significance of extra-time in the play-off final was beyond his comprehension, as was his understanding of ancient Anglo-Saxon terminology. He wanted to use the phone immediately, if not sooner and even had the temerity to suggest his call constituted a priority, whereas mine was merely of a social nature. A call to ascertain the future of the Blues was a matter of national, if not international importance and this unpalatable fact was impressed upon him in no uncertain terms. His exceedingly boring administrative problem would simply need to wait until the referee had blown for full-time. Once Steve Claridge had scored to guarantee our first division future, I handed him the phone.

Some of the former French Foreign Legion blokes I've encountered have been rather peculiar, but this guy's behaviour following our little spat convinced me he wasn't all there. He took to staring at me, not for brief periods, but for minutes at a time. Well, I've been stared at by better men than him and was able to take it all with a pinch of salt. He then took the staring business up a notch, by sitting opposite me at the dinner table and gazing at me as I dined. This went on for a few days, until I deemed to break the impasse by talking to him.

"Are you mentally retarded?" I enquired.

"What do you mean?"

"Well, you've been staring at me at regular intervals for several days now and, in my view, it's hardly the action of a person possessed of all of his faculties."

"You prevented me from using the phone the other day when I needed to use it urgently. You made me angry and this is my way of offering you outside into the desert to settle our differences," he explained.

"How absurd," I replied.

"It's traditional in the Legion," he declared.

"Your silly legionnaires' traditions are supremely inconsequential to me old horse. If you should want to fight with me, then save yourself some time and simply take a swing. If you do decide upon such a course of action however, then be sure to put me down to stay because, if I get up, you will be hurt very badly indeed. You are outweighed by at least seventy pounds and you can be assured that, despite being very much older than you, I'm both nastier and tougher than you are. Take it from me young man; despite your undoubted youth in comparison with me, you are making a huge mistake and you will hurt for a very long time after I've walloped you. Now, before I get really angry and smite you down, either fuck off, or go and get two cups of tea. I don't take milk or sugar and prefer my tea on the weak side."

He elected to make some tea.

I never clapped eyes on the Brummie again after leaving the Sahara, although he subsequently did me an enormous favour. When PCL were desperately looking for a senior, grey-haired, French speaking person to send to Mali, Brummie happened to be in the company office at the time and suggested my name.

Nothing mattered on the pipeline, other than how many yards of gas pipe they could lay in a day. It seems Bakewell were exceptionally proficient in this regard, despite their plant operators being practically brain dead from years of boredom. They were rewarded for achieving performance targets with free beer and peanuts, rather like a winning racehorse being given an extra bag of oats. Then, with a few beers inside them, it was off to bed in preparation for another stimulating day sitting on a trench-digging machine. Although never one to refuse the offer of a decent salary, I found this unhealthy pursuit of the green back dollar rather sad. Several of the operators were actually dollar millionaires it was said, all from sitting next to holes in the ground in some of the world's most inhospitable spots.

Out of abject boredom, I took to deserting my post during the interminable days and accompanied a French Canadian engineer out to the pipeline. Staying in the office would surely have sent me around the bend. Quite what the camp medics would have done with a mental case I'm unsure, since when it came to first aid, they were a distinct danger to those they treated. There was one sad incident when the medics couldn't help at all; when an Algerian fell into the ditch-digging machine. There wasn't much left of him to piece together, although his demise gave me something to do for a couple of minutes. I took his name off the list of those living-in and added it to the deceased column.

When I'd discussed my contract with Bakewell's head administrator before starting work with them, we had agreed a salary and, to be honest, it had come as a considerable surprise to see a much higher figure specified in my written contract. I simply assumed they considered me worth more but, after working with them for several months, a phone call from the chief administrator up at the main camp scotched this supposition. There had been a mistake in the drafting of my contract, he explained, and my salary was 40% higher than it ought to have been. Someone back in Texas had assumed Wally Payne was an American and thus liable to pay tax on his earnings; whereas I was a Briton declared 'not ordinarily resident for tax purposes' by Her Majesty's Inspector of Taxes. My salary wasn't tax deductible. My contract, signed, sealed and delivered by Bakewell, offered me an agreed salary and I expected them to stick to their end of the bargain. The head administrator insisted on amending the document, by reducing my salary accordingly.

What really gripped me about the Americans was the assumption that every other nationality on the site was their inferior. Perhaps this xenophobic attitude is prevalent throughout the world, but here among the 'Good Old Boys' working on the GM2 contract, it was particularly evident. Americans made up the financial first division, American immigrants paying tax to Uncle Sam made up the second, Brits and other Europeans were in third spot, followed by the Turkish welders down in fourth place. Right at the bottom of the pile were the Algerians, who served two purposes: labouring and, as there were no Afro-Americans to kick around, the Americans were able to treat them as *Untermenschen* instead.

My case, I argued, constituted unmitigated racism and no self-respecting Englishman could conceivably accept such a slight on his nation's honour. I told the head man that, if he intended to reduce my salary, then he could find someone else to perform the mind-numbing task. My letter of resignation reached him later in the day and he called me once again. He agreed to let me leave, on the condition I stayed another fortnight until a replacement was found.

"You will need to find someone quicker than that," I declared.

"It'll take me two weeks," he retorted.

"I'll give you two days," I replied sharply.

"Remember y'all are stuck in the middle of the Sahara. What do you think you can do without my assistance? Like I said, you'll wait until a replacement is found."

"May I pose a question?" I asked, knowing full-well what the answer would be.

"Shoot."

"What do you do with personnel involved in fighting on site?"

"Kick their sorry arses right out of here," he replied.

"OK, stay right where you are. I'm driving down to your camp now to punch your lights out."

"Y'all are on tomorrow's flight from Hassi Messaoud."

Next day I was on the plane back to Gatwick, with the chief administrator sitting next to me the whole way. He was aware Bakewell didn't have a contractual leg to stand on. They paid me all my back salary at the higher rate, as well as a sum for holiday pay and then gave me a free business class flight back to the Philippines. I accepted their conciliatory gesture.

I'd made yet another acrimonious departure from my place of employment.

Chapter 8

Leicester

MY HOUSE was one of four properties in Leicester sold under a Forces scheme that provided military personnel with first choice when it came to purchasing surplus quarters. Because they were sold for give-away prices, competition was always keen and I was exceedingly lucky to have been offered the three-bedroom house in Blackbird Road. My primary reason for buying the place was to move my mother into a decent area of the city and away from the council house she had been occupying in a particularly awful part of the wretched New Parks Estate.

Her first next door neighbour had been an unsavoury hussy; an unmarried mother of two who entertained gentlemen, usually of the West Indian variety, for financial gain. On my first weekend visit to Pindar Road, the noise of reggae music was still booming out at 0300 hours and I asked my mother exactly what was going on. Being a gentle soul, she gave a plausible excuse for the mayhem. When I happened by for the second consecutive weekend and discovered the 'Best of Bob Marley' still rocking the foundations in the early hours, she confessed that this nonsense went almost every night of the week. It was time for some positive action, so I donned my Army boots and kicked on the door of Number 49. When a dreadlocked individual popped his head out to investigate, I entered without invitation. He and his Jamaican buddies, their demeanours seemingly tranquilised by the ganja, were summarily ejected without any repercussions. The Riot Act having then been read to Geraldine, the harlot tenant, I assumed the matter had been dealt with in a smart and soldier like fashion. Alas, this wasn't the case; she carried on plying her trade, perfectly unabashed by my remonstrations. Thereafter, I took to travelling up to Leicester on a regular basis, sometimes accompanied by some of the tougher corporals from my unit. Their remit was to help me to eject Caribbean customers from next door, lay complaints with the police and to pester the Council Housing Department. Nothing worked. In the eyes of the city's socialist council, the status of an unmarried mother prostitute apparently carried more clout than the standing of an Army RSM.

The resolution of my quandary was as swift as it was unexpected. Walking towards Colchester Garrison Headquarters one day, I espied a full colonel of my acquaintance dressed in civvies and proudly sporting his Royal Leicestershire Regiment tie. I felt compelled to comment on his outstanding neckwear and he was delighted that I should have recognised the grey, black and red diagonal stripes. What a fortunate meeting this turned out to be, for the colonel's brother it transpired, was head of the Leicester Council Housing Department. When I related the disgraceful story of my mother's predicament, he promised to contact his sibling with all haste. In less than a week, Geraldine had been re-housed at the top end of the giant estate. Unfortunately for her, the new abode was flanked on either side by properties that had been purchased by their former rent-paying tenants. Her new neighbours didn't take too kindly to a newcomer of her sort and the dwelling mysteriously burned down within days. I was brought up on the New Parks; it was a tough old area.

The new occupiers of the offending abode in Pindar Road were a family of ne'er-do-wells; the combined IQ of the six of them wouldn't have reached double figures! The antecedents of the new neighbours were alarming; parents with rap sheets as long as your arm, a daughter with convictions for prostitution, one son on remand for burglary and the other two guests of Her Majesty in Lincoln jail. My brother and I decided to pay the head of the family a visit. A brief introduction was followed by veiled threats as to what fate would befall him should my mother ever have cause for complaint. We then placed a tenner in his greasy paw and received his guarantee of undying friendship. Mum never had any cause for complaint thereafter. In his zeal to prove himself a good neighbour, he and two of his sons once accosted me at my own front door when mum was away. They didn't realise it was me they maintained. Mother ashamedly told the tale of a time the family from hell paid a social visit. Having commented about the age of both our gas fire and television set, they scorned mum's plan to purchase replacements in due course. Within a short space of time, a new fire and TV set appeared and were fitted free of charge. It didn't pay to enquire about the provenance of the items.

My mum had been supremely content in her house on Blackbird Road for several years but, since she was now dead and I was living permanently abroad, selling the property seemed the most sensible course of action. What a wretched mistake my decision proved to be, given the way house prices appreciated the moment I sold mine.

The semi-detached residences had originally been built for permanent staff members of a Territorial Army Centre occupying the land directly behind the houses. When the Army vacated the site, the Leicestershire Constabulary moved in and the dwellings, despite never having been occupied by custodians of the law, became known ever thereafter as the 'Police Houses'.

I served in the Leicester City Police for a while, before they amalgamated with the county force and before they invited me to resign. Cut down in my prime I was! Although my career as a boy in blue was brief and inglorious, some incidents amused me and the following vignettes are perhaps worth recounting:

St Peter's Lane ran parallel with High Street and to the rear of the shops located along the north side of the main thoroughfare. Most of the shops had gardens or storage areas abutting one side of the lane, whereas most of the dilapidated buildings on the other side had already been demolished. One building still standing was the Bethel Chapel, although it was also due to come down imminently. In preparation for razing the old chapel, the tombs in its graveyard had been opened, the bodies exhumed and taken away for burial elsewhere.

It was after 0200 hrs when I turned left into St Peter's Lane from the direction of the city centre. The chapel lay directly to my right and, as I passed by, it began to snow heavily. I plodded on, aware that my next 'point' was at 0215 hrs, down at the far end of the lane. Woe betide anyone missing a point when Inspector Goodman was the night shift boss. As it transpired, he didn't appear and so I turned back into St Peter's Lane to shake hands with a few more doorknobs. Retracing my steps, the footprints I'd made coming the other way were clear to see. The snowfall was getting heavier and, other than my hoof-marks, it lay deep and crisp and even. Reaching the Bethel Chapel, I was stopped in my tracks! Coming out of a recently excavated grave was a three-inch wide depression in the snow. It ran out onto the lane and continued its meandering route as far as the main road, where it was swallowed up by the tyre tracks of passing vehicles. I returned to examine the scene and ponder exactly what might have made such an impression. It looked like the tyre tracks of a bicycle, but was too wide and, in any case, it didn't overlap when it went around a corner. It was just like a wheelbarrow track, but who had pushed it? Could it have been a subterranean hot water pipe they had failed to disconnect? The snow had all melted when I walked down St Peter's Lane later in the morning and the mystery remains unexplained.

Spending a few minutes in a police box, getting away from the madding crowd or resting one's weary legs, was severely frowned upon by the bosses. Despite the severity of the consequences should you be caught, 'knocking it out' remained a popular pursuit amongst the lads, especially those on nights. So, there I was, knocking it out in the box located on the forecourt of Belgrave Road Railway Station, when there was a rap on the door. I replaced my helmet with all haste, took out my pocket book and pencil and hoped to give the inspector the illusion I was doing something worthwhile. Except the caller wasn't the inspector, but a Leicester City bus conductor. The last bus of the night was stationary by the traffic lights and aboard this bus was a passenger by the name of Patrick Anthony Finbar O'Shaugnessey. The Irishman, the conductor explained, was drunk, refusing to pay his fare, looking for a fight and refusing to get off the bus. Absolutely routine stuff; at least, it ought to have been.

Patrick was sitting on the top deck, along with thirty or so other drunken chain-smokers. I located him through the fog of Craven 'A' and Park Drive cigarette smoke and tapped him on the shoulder.

"Have you paid your fare?"

"No!"

"Pay your fare then, there's a good chap."

"I'm not paying any fare."

"Then get off the bus."

"I'm not getting of the bus."

"Well, you're going to do one or the other."

"I'm not doing neither," he declared.

I took him by the shoulders and lifted him up from his place, whereupon he grabbed hold of the curved metal bar on top of the seats. Despite my best efforts, he held on for all his worth and it required several meaty whacks to persuade him to submit and fall to the ground. I dragged him along the aisle to a chorus of abuse from his fellow passengers and threw him down the stairs. He landed on the ledge half-way down. As my opponent lay recovering his breath, I noted the particulars of the conductor and then booted Patrick down to street level. Having frogmarched him over the road to the police box, I called for the Black Maria, transported him to the station, charged him and showed him to his overnight accommodation. Just as the cell door was about to be slammed, he spoke for the first time since leaving the bus.

"You broke my fucking leg!" he exclaimed.

I slammed his cell door closed and went off to write my report. Patrick and I would meet in front of the magistrates next morning.

I arrived at Town Hall Magistrates in good time and booked in with the woman constable responsible for keeping the list of those appearing before Mr Frear that morning. Mr Frear was a well-respected magistrate, the owner of Leicester's most prestigious bakery and a leading light in the Methodist Church.

"PC273 versus Patrick Anthony Finbar O'Shaughnessy," I announced.

"Oh, it's you is it?"

"What do you mean?"

"Haven't you seen him?"

"Not since last night."

"He's there in the back room," she said, "Go and have a look."

Last night's opponent was lying on a stretcher, sporting a plaster cast from ankle to thigh. Goodness me, the man *had* broken his leg! As the court orderly called me in to give evidence, I felt somewhat apprehensive. There was no need for anxiety though—I wasn't required to say a word. As the charges were read, Patrick burst into a verbal tirade against the police constable who had arrested him.

"Do you see that bastard over there, he broke my fucking leg," he announced, pointing at PC273.

"How dare you utter blasphemous words in my court?" boomed the God-fearing magistrate.

"That fucking man broke my fucking leg!"

"Stop that foul language immediately!"

"Fuck you and fuck your fucking country," said the foolish Irishman.

"Mr O'Shaugnessey, how do you plead to the charges?"

"Guilty, but I can't pay any fine because I can't work. That bastard broke my fucking leg."

"Then you will go to jail for twenty-one days. Take him down."

"But your Worship, he broke my fucking leg!" bellowed Patrick, as he was manoeuvred down the well of the court on his stretcher. As the next case started, his pleas were still to be heard from the cells below. It must have been a slow news day, for the case made the front page of the *Leicester Mercury*, albeit tucked away in the corner next to an advertisement for Woodbine cigarettes.

A list of unoccupied houses on a particular beat was lodged in the nearest police box, although there were never very many, except during the Leicester Workers' Holiday Fortnight. During this period, half the population of the city disappeared in the direction of Skegness, Mablethorpe and Cleethorpes for their vacations. So many Leicester folk descended on the east coast resorts that it was even possible in Skegness to buy the *Leicester Mercury* from newspaper vendors. To the local Lincolnshire folk, visitors from Leicester were known as 'Chissits', resulting from the way all Leicester people intent on making a purchase would enquire, "Ow much issit?" This was my first time on the five-beat, so I made a note of the solitary unoccupied dwelling in Lower Willow Street and gave the flat a cursory glance when my perambulations took me in an easterly direction. There was a light on in the flat, so I rang the doorbell. The door was opened by a woman wearing an exceedingly low-cut top, which left precious little to the imagination. Admittedly this vamp wasn't in the first flush of youth, but she was definitely bedworthy. She spoke with a remarkably husky, Ertha Kitt type, voice:

"Yes, I've been away, but I'm back now."

"I'll have your name taken off the list then."

"You're most kind. Would you care to call round for a coffee sometime?"

"I could come in now if you like," I replied, sensing the chance of getting rather more than a cup of Nescafé.

"I can't invite you in now, I'm rather busy. However, if you have a few hours to spare tomorrow afternoon, why don't you visit me around two o'clock?"

"I will," I croaked, the words sticking in my throat.

Having changed my shift, I called at two o'clock as agreed and, by 1415 hrs, I'd supped my coffee and was rolling around the floor with the brazen hussy. Fancy taking advantage of a young policeman in that way! What's more, she took advantage of me regularly thereafter.

The winter of 1963 was bitterly cold and night duty was a real ordeal. Suitably attired for the Arctic conditions, I would have won no prizes for sartorial elegance as I turned the corner from Chancery Street and into Marble Street during the early hours. In addition to long johns and a pair of pyjama bottoms under my trousers, my torso was shielded against the Siberian temperatures by layer upon layer of clothing; even my old police cape had been mobilised into action. A combination of tiredness and the numbing cold had rendered me all but brain

dead, when a car pulled alongside. The rear window was
wound down a full inch and the duty inspector summoned me
over to speak to him. As I put my face to the window, the heat
and cigarette smoke made my eyes water. It must have been
tough on the inspector and crew of M2NT2, having to sit in a
warm car on such an inclement night; but someone had to do it
I suppose.

"All right lad?" said Inspector Goodman.

"All right sir," I lied.

"Define burglary boy!"

"Sir, in conditions like these, I'm hard pressed to remember
my name. Why don't you ask one of your crew inside the car
instead?" I replied insolently.

"Write the definition out twenty-five times before you
stand down in the morning," retorted the inspector.

Can you imagine a police officer being required to do that
in this day and age? Do you know though, I can still remember
the definition of burglary all these years later?

We went in for our forty-five minute meal break at 0100
hrs when we were on nights. My area of responsibility was
'beats one and two', the area around Leicester Cathedral in the
old part of the city. Knowing this, the older constables regaled
me with stories of the police inspector who, years before, had
committed suicide by hanging himself from a bell rope up in
the cathedral spire. They maintained the bell sometimes rang
mysteriously at precisely 0200 hrs, even though the cathedral
bells didn't strike the hour. The story was that the ghost of the
inspector would then appear from the path running alongside
the graveyard and ask you to record his visit in your notebook.
To show I was unaffected by their spooky story, I called their
bluff and agreed to make my 0200 hrs point at 'B-Bravo on the
2 Beat', at the junction directly opposite the cathedral porch.
Arriving five minutes before the appointed time, I pulled up

my coat collar to combat the cold wind whipping down New Street and awaited the possible arrival of our new inspector. My nerves may indeed have been affected by the old-timers' tale, as I was sure there were voices coming from the cathedral porch. The more I strained my ears, the more certain I became. My uneasiness grew as the minute hand of the huge clock crept, imperceptibly slowly, towards the perpendicular. With only seconds to go before the witching hour, the sound of giggling came from the porch and then, to my horror, an inspector's hat appeared, bobbing along atop the hedge bordering the path. The officer approached me. Was this the 'ghost of inspector past' in earthly form, or Peter Petcher, our new officer? Mercifully, it was the latter.

Emboldened by the presence of another member of the constabulary, I walked over to the cathedral yard to investigate the noise. There, on the stone bench inside the porch, was a couple engaged in a naughty activity. The inspector, a man with more degrees than an average thermometer and an expert when it came to obscure legislation, declared the couple in contravention of some long-forgotten section of the Ecclesiastical Courts Act. I noted their particulars and they were allowed to make a shame-faced exit. Under the instruction of the inspector, I wrote up a summons and they were later cautioned for their misdemeanour.

My shift mate Mick Wright had resigned and we were on the town, celebrating his appointment to the British South Africa Police, the force responsible for law and order in Southern Rhodesia. Next day, he would depart for a place called Wankie, a perfect spot for him in my view. Following a few pints in the rough pubs along Humberstone Gate, we repaired to the bowling alley in Lee Circle and selected lane 36, right at the end. As if able to recognize two off duty policemen, half a dozen yobs appeared on the adjacent lane and rather spoilt our game. Having been requested to desist from using my ball and to find an alternative projectile, one of the louts decided it would be a jolly jape to steal my ball and deposit it on lane number one, right at the far end of the alley. Witnessing his antisocial act, I confronted the perpetrator upon his return, gave him a good clout around the ear and made him recover my ball.

Scoring for the yobs was a well-behaved, well-built, immaculately dressed bloke who, having seen me dish out summary action to his pal, put down his pencil and approached me.

"You wouldn't have done that to me," he declared.

"If you'd done the same thing, then I would have," I retorted.

"No you wouldn't," he repeated.

Now, at that time, Leicester had a professional heavyweight boxer by the name of Mick Bastin, whose career had started encouragingly. I was about to drop an enormous clanger.

"Who do you think you are, Mick Bastin?" I was foolish enough to utter.

He took out his wallet and produced a Professional Boxer's Registration Card—in the name of Michael Bastin.

"And do you think that scares me?" enquired PC 273, full of false bravado.

"You've got a boxing ring at the Police Station," said Mick Bastin. "If you think you're tough, let's meet there tomorrow afternoon?"

"You're on! See you at two o'clock."

I foolishly shook hands on the deal and, next day, went to Northampton for a ride out. No sense in courting disaster.

"Excuse me constable, but I'm wondering if you could be graciously answering me a question? Is it permissible for me to be spitting on the footpath?" asked a turbaned gentleman.

"Afraid not squire; it's an offence against the Town Police Clauses Act 1847."

"Is it then permissible for me to be spitting on the roadway?"

"Afraid not squire."

"I will be explaining to you my dilemma. Every time I see a pretty girl, I feel the compulsion to spit. If I cannot spit on the path and I cannot spit on the roadway, am I therefore permitted to spit on the girl?"

"If you did that, she'd probably smack you around the ear and knock your turban off, which is exactly what I'll do if you don't bugger off."

Down in Halford Street, Mr Singh tried his silly ploy on another constable, coincidentally named Payne, and was given short shrift for a second time.

The man was clearly a few pence short of a pound, but not beyond marching up to Police HQ to lay a complaint. Mick Payne and I were called into the station where, after making a pathetic pun about 'pains in the neck', the duty inspector rebuked us mildly before sending us back out onto the beat. This was the first time I'd been subjected to a complaint; more were to follow, but I was out to gain revenge on the Sikh shit stirrer. A week later, I espied the complainant in the city centre, peering into Drage's shop window. A display of 'magnetic ladybirds' had taken his interest and, after a few minutes watching the toys spin around, he entered the shop to make his purchase. Coming out with a broad smile on his face, despite being half-a crown lighter, he took the ladybird from a brown paper bag to examine his new acquisition and discarded the bag. I had him by the arm before the paper bag had fluttered to the ground. I charged him with an offence against the 1958 Litter Act, but the Chief Constable decided not to proceed with the case.

The gods saw fit to grant compassion on this sore-footed constable on his seventh consecutive night shift. I was awarded a place in the front seat of the van, which the sergeant was driving. We were pootling along Asylum Street, later renamed Gateway Street out of political correctness, when we spotted a black chap, later renamed coloured out of political correctness, on a motorbike. West Indians didn't usually ride motorbikes in those days and the sergeant smelt a rat. He told me to slide the door open as we overtook the Norton and told me to instruct the driver to pull into the kerb.

"Pull in squire," I shouted.

He ignored me and drove on faster. We caught him up and I repeated my instruction. He ignored me again and drove on faster still. I looked at the sergeant, he nodded his head and, when we caught the speedster up for a third time, I put my foot on the motorbike and knocked him off.

The motorcyclist was not the least bit amused and a right carry-on ensued, during which time he was arrested for the suspected theft of the Norton. Unfortunately, whilst carrying out the arrest, I used one of my recently learned jujitsu holds and succeeded in dislocating several of his fingers. At the nick, we discovered he was, after all, the owner of the motor cycle and so no offence had been committed. Despite having his dislocated fingers relocated at Police expense, he was still bleating on when the CID superintendent happened into the charge office. He was taken away 'upstairs', returning twenty minutes later, craving forgiveness and having donated generously to the Policeman's Ball. I never did ascertain what they had on him up in the CID.

Meanwhile, back at Blackbird Road, my house had been on the market for many months without as much as a sniff from a potential buyer. Then, all of a sudden, three people came forward within a week. A lady from the Real Estate Agents called me with the glad tidings and I flew back to the UK from Manila at once. By the time I'd arrived back in England's green and pleasant land, one person had already lost interest and another had offered a sum so derisory that I instructed my people to tell him to take a running jump. That left Alexander Peacock Cant, who arrived with his two teenage children to view the Payne family pile late on Friday afternoon.

I'd never sold a house before and hadn't a clue what to expect from a potential purchaser. This Caledonian family group didn't strike me as the sort of people I'd care to meet socially but, by reminding myself that these ginger-haired Jocks might soon make me rather richer than I was at present, their rudeness was stoically born. I endured the banging of doors, stamping of feet on the stairs, running of taps and serial toilet flushing with as much grace as could be mustered, but their appalling manners began to grate badly. It was Cant minor who really got up my nose.

"Where's your ladder?" he shouted down the stairs.

"I haven't got a ladder," I confessed.

"How the hell do you expect to sell a house if people can't get up into the roof space?"

I didn't deign to reply.

Apart from taking umbrage at being talked to in such an abrasive fashion by a spotty Jock shit, I didn't follow his logic either. This wasn't, after all, a part of the house I'd ever had a compelling desire to visit. Cant the Younger clearly considered climbing through the inspection hatch and up into the roof space to be a priority and, without so much as a by your leave, he climbed onto a windowsill, swung himself up through the hole and left the imprint of a size 8 Doc Marten's boot on the wallpaper. Such outrageous behaviour peeved me no end and I went down to confer with the Estate Agent.

"Do all potential purchasers behave like this?" I enquired.

"Mr Payne, they are the rudest family I've ever seen during ten years in this business," she explained.

With that, the Caledonian Cants were ordered downstairs, I opened the front door and ushered them out.

"Bugger off!" I declared, "You're not having my mother's house."

"But we want to buy it," pleaded Cant senior.

"Well you can't have it! My mother was gloriously happy in this house and you ignorant bastards aren't going to destroy the ambiance of the place. Bugger off!"

They may have been somewhat surprised, especially as the newspapers were calling it a buyer's market. My brother suggested I was mentally retarded to travel so far and then dismiss potential purchasers thus, but they simply weren't having my Mam's house. Next day was a Saturday and I was waiting for my chum to arrive and drive me down to watch Leicester City play against the Arsenal. Stepping outside, I saw a couple taking down the housing agent's phone number from the 'For Sale' board. The vendor promptly waived the 'by appointment only' bit and invited them in for a look around. I put the kettle on, showed them where the coffee and biscuits were, handed them a bunch of keys and invited them to fill their boots. When I returned from the match, there was a letter waiting for me on the stairs. They loved the house and wanted to buy it. Very shortly afterwards, they were the new owners and my bank balance was swollen, temporarily, by a reasonable sum. Whenever my journeys take me back to Leicester, I call in at the house, just for old time's sake. They're a smashing couple, they still love the house and, what's more important, my Mam would have approved of them.

I shot off back to the Philippines, to pay the hospital bills following the premature birth of my daughter, Elizabeth. Rather later in life than is the norm, I became a doting father.

Almost immediately though, PCL asked me to return to the UK, to be briefed on a job down in Mozambique. On Monday morning, I called them to confirm my arrival in Leicester and announce my 'hot to trot' status. Without so much as a word of apology and certainly without any offer to cover my travel expenses, they told me they'd given the job to someone else. The bastards had screwed me yet again! There was nothing for it but to return to the Philippines. Emirates Airlines were becoming a very profitable company, largely at my expense.

Chapter 9

SE Asia with Jack

I WAS SITTING in my usual Philippines' inspired torpor when the phone rang. Nothing surprising about a phone ringing I hear you say, it happens all the time. Perhaps so, but not for me, not when I'm languishing in the wilds of Cavite Province. The caller was my cousin, a guy whose father had once said of him, "He'll either finish up a millionaire or doing ten years." Jack had made his fortune.

"I'm arriving in Manila on Friday. Can you fix a six-week holiday for the pair of us, to include a trip to Perth to see my parents and as many debauched spots in south-east Asia as we can manage? I've got a platinum card, so stick all the tickets down to me."

As employers weren't exactly queuing up for my dubious services, I had some time on my hands. Jack's proposition was too good an opportunity to miss it seemed to me, so I set about planning for his arrival. An exceedingly well-heeled pal of mine owned a splendid mansion in Tagaytay with a view overlooking Lake Taal and, as he spent the majority of his time in Hong Kong and rarely used the place, I asked if my cousin might stay there for a few days. He had no objections whatsoever; something to do with the rich man's Mafia perhaps?

Jack was delighted with his top-notch lodgings, especially since the fixtures and fittings included a live-in maid. I gave him a couple of days on his own to acclimatise, before arriving to pick him up for the first of our excursions; to outrageously naughty Angeles City in Pampanga Province, north of Manila.

"Best sex I've ever had," was his opening gambit, as I pulled up at the mansion.

"Excellent," said I to the cousin with a sparkle in his eye, "but exactly who have you been rogering?"

"The maid; best sex I've ever had."

Thereafter, he provided me with a ball by ball summary of the last couple of nights up on the volcano's rim.

The big houses in Tagaytay were built on the caldera of what must have been an immense volcano back in the days of the dinosaur. Today's diminutive Mt. Taal volcano stands on Taal Island, an islet in the lake formed in the ancient volcano's crater. It rises to a majestic 31m above sea level at its eastern rim. The volcano has had 34 recorded eruptions since 1572. In 1911, it killed a thousand islanders and there have been recent eruptions in 1968, 1969 and 2006. Nevertheless, there are still five thousand people living on the island.

Donald Stone was the owner of the mansion. He had come a very long way since; as impoverished soldiers back in the late sixties, he and I had shared the same run down room in the single man's accommodation in Kowloon's Osborn Barracks. His business ventures in the colony had flourished and, influenced undoubtedly by Chinese associates, he appeared to view life from a distinctly Asian perspective. Once, when I enquired at what point he would consider his coffers sufficiently replete, call it a day and spend his time wandering around the world, he replied: "Never in my lifetime." The Chinese, he explained, only gained face as rich men when they left behind huge fortunes for all to see. I know the Chinese do many things arse about face, but this philosophy was unfathomable to me.

When I went to live in the Philippines, Donald took to travelling over on occasional Fridays to have lunch with me. It was a hell of a distance to come for lunch! We would dine regally, drink a few glasses of wine and then, provided he hadn't supped too much stuff, he would board the plane back to Hong Kong. If we had tucked into the Bailey's with too much vigour, then he would book into a hotel. After a succession of Friday nights spent at the Inter Continental, the section of his brain dedicated to financial prudence activated. Why pay a hotel bill when you can buy a place and stay there for free? He promptly bought and furnished a splendid condominium in the very best part of Makati City. It was here in Ayala Avenue that we once shared the lift with Imelda Marcos, whose abode was up in the penthouse. I spent many a Friday afternoon in his apartment; drinking Bailey's, watching 'The Hill' time after time and looking at the exchange rates on Bloomberg.

Nearing Christmas one year, Donald and I were having lunch together at the Swiss Cottage in Manila, when the wine got the better of me. Emboldened by several glasses of an excellent Châteauneuf-du-Pape, I encroached upon the secretive domain of his private life, by enquiring whether his parents were still alive. His mother, it appeared, still occupied the same terraced house in London where he had been born. My next unwelcome question was designed to establish how many times he travelled back to see his Mum each year. He hadn't seen her in seven years! The Châteauneuf-du-Pape and I expressed our disgust at this shameful admission, whereupon he quickly changed the subject. My barbed comments must have found their target just the same because, on Christmas Eve, he called me from the airport. Donald was on his way home to see his Mum. On the twenty-eighth of the month, he called me again. Having enquired about the health of his Mum, I asked him how long he intended to stay in England.

"I'm already back in Hong Kong," he declared, "England was too dark, too cold and too expensive for me."

Whilst taking lunch some months later, Donald was encumbered with rolls of blueprints, which he lugged around from place to place. I didn't mention the plans; even though it was clear he wanted me to. "If you don't ask me about these blueprints soon, I'll scream," he said out of exasperation. They were for the house at Tagaytay. Having spent a fortune on altering and furnishing the place to his taste, he read a book about the volcano with the propensity of erupting and killing people. He confessed he would never have bought the place had he read the book first! He sold the property only a couple of years later, but not before my cousin had laid his head there.

Jack and I drove up to Angeles City, only to discover all the better hotels fully occupied. Instead, we selected the slightly run-down America Hotel as our lodgings. It was an establishment whose rooms bore out the town's reputation as the sex capital of the northern Philippines. Mine had suggestive pictures on the walls and mirrors set into the ceiling, whereas Jack's boasted not just mirrors and Playboy centrefolds, but a Jacuzzi to boot. We dumped our bags and set off for the bars almost immediately; we only had six weeks for the entire adventure after all. Jack, true to form, was smitten by a young thing working in the first bar we visited and our pub crawl ended there and then. He bought her out, returned to the hotel and didn't emerge until next morning. I went to an excellent Country & Western bar, where I discovered an excellent performer!

"Brilliant! The best sex I've ever had," he declared over breakfast.

The young harlot and Jack stayed together for a couple of days and, by all accounts, she continued to dispense the best sex he'd ever experienced. Forever the businessman and blessed with a shrewd eye when it came to getting value for money, he offered to sublet the young lady to me whenever he was in between screws. 'Two's up' never having been my thing, I felt compelled to decline. All good things must come to an end and having sated himself sexually, Jack crossed his

149

lady's palm with silver and bade her farewell. We headed back for one final night in Tagaytay, before setting off next day for the Thai capital.

Having booked into our very decent hotel, courtesy of the platinum card, we wasted no time in heading for the naughty Patpong district. The King's Castle was a tavern I'd frequented on previous visits to Bangkok and so I took Jack there for his first taste of Thai totty. He was suitably impressed by the goods on display and soon made his selection. The security guards at our 'posh' hotel were awkward though and required bribing with a good many baht before they'd allow the spoils of our evening's labour up to the rooms. Acceding to my cousin's quest for perfection on the female front, I agreed to a few days down in Pattaya, where the sex industry is the city's *raison d'être*. In my view, Pattaya is a squalid dump and has all the charm of the Reeperbahn in Hamburg, Soho and the Valetta Gut. The number and selection of practicing prostitutes leaves the aforementioned red-light areas languishing in Pattaya's wake however. We shared a room for the two days down on the coast, as a result of which I became very familiar with the hotel foyer while he set about sampling a cross-section of the local working girls, purely for research purposes of course. My time in the foyer, I felt, was a small price to pay for the advancement of science. Frankly, Pattaya wasn't an officers' resort; not even a retired officers' resort, and I was pleased to return to Bangkok. Next day, Maunday Thursday, we flew down to Perth in Western Australia.

Following one of Qantas' more bumpy descents, we arrived in Perth and moved in with Jack's parents, my aunt and uncle. I hadn't seen them for donkey's years, not since they moved to Australia decades previously, but was delighted to discover they'd eschewed the Aussie drawl and still spoke with broad Leicester accents. Next morning, having fulfilled family formalities and dispensed the duty frees, Jack decided to show me around Perth. I was happy to accompany him, but considered Good Friday morning hardly the time to see the city at its best.

"We're not going to town," he declared, "we're going to the best brothel in Perth."

"Are you sure such an establishment will be open on a Good Friday morning?" I enquired.

"Guaranteed."

"Then deal me in."

And a splendid bordello it was too!

We only had four days in Australia, but managed to take in several other interesting establishments in Perth just the same. Thereafter, we visited Freemantle, which I found attractive and a seaside resort in the south called Albany, which had too many similarities to Mablethorpe on a rainy day to commend it.

There's a town to the north of Perth called Geraldton. It was barely four inches directly up the coast on my map but, according to an old digger I encountered at the petrol station, it was a definite 6-stubby journey. (That was the number of bottles of beer he considered were necessary to sustain a person on the trip.) It took us almost six hours to get there in Uncle Ernie's ancient 'Ute'; so the old digger wasn't far wrong. The rationale for the trip was to visit Jack's brother, another of my cousins, who was still in short trousers the last time I'd set eyes on him. Bizarrely, he and his estranged wife reunited especially for the evening and hosted us at their home on the outskirts of the pleasant little town. Despite Victoria Bitter induced hangovers, next day the four of us made for the small town of Dongara, some forty miles to the south. The town was holding its annual horse racing event, an occasion not to be missed by all accounts. It must have been glaringly obvious to everyone gathered at Dongara Races that Jack and I were outsiders or, in a worst case scenario, Poms! Not only were we devoid of the mandatory vests, shorts and thongs, but neither of us could muster a khaki hat with corks suspended over the brim either. There was another dead giveaway; we weren't carrying a can a lager. At least we were able to rectify the latter deficiency.

Now, I know a thing or two about horses; or at least how to throw my money away on them. A glance at the beasts parading around the Dongara paddock for the first race revealed some very poor looking animals masquerading as race horses. The majority were only fit for dog meat and it wasn't difficult to spot the only two fit beasts in the field and select the winner, along with the second-placed horse to scoop the quinella. By adopting the same procedure before each race, I did something never previously achieved, by going through the card. The bookies were soundly punished at my hands and I considered it expedient to leave immediately after the sixth race, just in case the turf accountants' mafia ganged up to take me around the back of the sheep-shearing sheds.

Rather than suffer the never-ending concrete strip of the Brand Coastal Highway on the way back to Perth, we elected to take the road skirting an inland desert instead. We had been travelling through totally unpopulated countryside for a considerable period, when Jack announced he was seriously desirous of sustenance. Shortly afterwards, a road sign appeared: Arthur River was a mere 80km distant. We would stop there for some nosebag. Alas, Arthur River turned out to be just a river and a dried up river at that. The next sign announced that Three Springs was only an hour and a half's ride away; we would need to wait a while longer before sampling some local cuisine. Finally, Three Springs hove into view. A 'Welcome to our Town' sign told us the neighbourhood boasted a mere three hundred and seventy souls, but it did have a pub; one of those typical Aussie places with a balcony. We entered the bar and bade the other customers a cheery g'day. A couple of schooners of the publican's finest was our preference and, lest the natives weren't predisposed to a pair of Poms invading their watering hole, we stood the locals a tube of lager apiece. After an hour, an Aussie aficionado of diurnal drinking ventured our way, apparently intent on establishing our antecedents.

"Where you from mate?" he enquired.

"Leicester in England," I replied.

"Never heard of it."

"I'd never heard of Three Springs either, not until an hour ago."

"Nice one cobber."

As if our identical accents weren't clue enough, he turned his attention to my cousin and enquired from whence he hailed.

"I'm from Leicester as well," he replied, "but I live in Dorset now."

"I was shearing in Dorset last year," the black-vested Aussie revealed.

"Whereabouts?" Jack asked.

"Little place called Sixpenny Handley."

"Bugger me, that's just along the A354 from where I live."

"Where do you live then mate?"

"Milborne St Andrew."

"Sheared there as well."

"Who for?"

"A bloke called Tommy Connor."

"Bugger me! He's in my Freemasons' Lodge."

It's a very small world on occasions. What odds would Ladbrokes have given against such a coincidence I wonder?

I've never been one for letting people and especially companies get away with poor service, poor products or poor security. They can be sure of a tersely worded letter from me, demanding restitution should they fail to deliver decent service. These days, there are people to whom lodging complaints is a full-time occupation, but I've never been so inclined; I simply want my rights respected.

Whenever Jack was otherwise engaged, there was a casino in Perth where I would gamble away a few dollars. After my final trip to this splendid establishment, I was sitting all alone on the railway station, waiting for the train to take me the half dozen stops along the line to Kelmscott. The platform seats were made of metal, for maximum wear presumably, although some person intent on criminal damage had managed to prise up some of the metal struts forming my seat and render it a danger to anyone parking their rear end on it. As the train approached, I got up to the sound of tearing material and a large 'L' shape appeared in the back of my suit trousers. By putting my hands behind my back, I managed to hide my embarrassment, but the suit was irreparably damaged. I discovered the name of the company operating the trains and, once our trip was over, I wrote them a letter of complaint from the Philippines. Not only did they accept responsibility for the damage, but sent me a cheque to cover the cost of a new whistle, made out in Philippine pesos at that. What a decent gesture!

A similar thing had happened to me a year before, in the Shires Shopping Centre in Leicester. In the 'Shires' were a set a stairs with the worst designed handrails in the world, huge wooden things, jutting out from the steps like Rolls Royce Merlin engines. As I was striding up these steps, my suit pocket caught on the end of the handrail and tore the jacket very badly. I sought out a security guard with the intention of reporting the incident, although that was a waste of time. The shabby individual wasn't equipped with a pen or notebook and didn't seem to have much enthusiasm about having to investigate anything. Perhaps he'd been a former corporal in the RMP! By providing him with a pen and an old envelope, at least he made a note of my name and address. Not wishing to leave the matter in his inept hands, I wrote a concise letter to the manager of the mall and received a very snotty reply. He suggested there must have been some kind of tomfoolery afoot and that the damage had probably been caused by me 'bounding' up the steps. In my reply to him I revealed my age, declaring that my ability to 'bound' anywhere was no longer a physical possibility. My plea fell on deaf ears.

I simply couldn't have been the first person to damage an item of clothing on these badly designed handrails. The mall manager, however, clearly wasn't inclined to pay out any compensation; presumably in case it opened the floodgates to hordes of other worthy complainants. Several letters of an increasingly acrimonious nature went hither and thither, until he finally put the matter in the hands of the mall's insurers.

The lady from the insurers proved to be a woman possessed of an even less magnanimous attitude towards honest complainants than the Shires' manager was. We exchanged numerous letters, but she wouldn't budge. By this time, the cost of defending their case must have exceeded the sum I was asking for tenfold, but they remained resolute. Finally, they simply closed their file on the case. I'd been screwed.

Amazing, an opportunity arose whereby I was able to extract a modicum of revenge from the insurance company. Shortly afterwards, whilst driving down to visit a friend in East Sussex, I was overwhelmed by the need to ease my bladder. It was after midnight and there was nobody around when I espied a dark industrial area. It appeared a perfect location for the clandestine voiding of urine, so I drove up an access road and swung into a large car park. To my astonishment, my headlights picked out the name of the head office of the unhelpful insurance company! Their letter box was set at a convenient height for a man of my proportions and I took great pleasure in moistening their foyer. My action may have tarnished my honour, but it was worth more to me than any payment they might have made.

After Australia, Jack and I enjoyed stays in Hong Kong and Macau, where he experienced some of the "Best sex he'd ever had." Then it was back to the volcano side, where he was content to spend the remainder of his time with the housekeeper.

As soon as Jack departed for the UK, I went down to the Australian Embassy in Manila. I'd been much taken by the land down under and wanted to investigate the possibility of emigrating. The Aussies operated a points system for immigrants, based on a series of personal characteristics, financial position and skills, with a score of more than a hundred points being required for the process to get over the first hurdle. The first category on the weighty pro forma dealt with age and I failed to trouble the scoreboard. My financial means were nothing to write home about; I had no skills worth mentioning and possessed neither a university degree, nor any technical qualifications. To be honest, I scored hardly any points at all. My interview with an embassy official was brief; I'd scored far too few points to be considered a serious contender. He was a man with a big heart just the same and, once he was made aware of my ability to sing all the words to Walzing Matilda, he generously awarded me an extra half a mark. It didn't help.

Chapter 10

Mali

Part 1
Finding my feet

A **PURPORTEDLY** '**HIGH-PROFILE**' **COMPANY** placed an advertisement in the situations vacant pages of the *Leicester Mercury*, offering experienced security personnel top wages to man their prestigious premises in Leicester. My CV went off by first-class post and, three days later, I received a reply from the high-profile company with the prestigious premises—Leicester City Football Club. Presumably the Trade Descriptions Act doesn't extend to football clubs? A couple of days later, a person of indeterminate sexual leanings interviewed me, appointed me and passed me on to the club's administration manager. The administration man presented me with my Club tie and a pair of shoes with steel toecaps, both obligatory items of attire apparently, before briefing me on my duties. So, by Monday morning, I was working for my favourite football team, but for a salary one could hardly describe as top dollar.

Having earned some overtime by enduring a reserve match on Tuesday evening, I presented myself for work again next morning. The day was to prove inauspicious in the annals of Leicester City Football Club for, ere the clock had struck twelve times, I was to leave their employ.

Each Wednesday morning, Hilda the cleaner was required to give the CCTV room a going over and it befell me to unlock the door and watch over her as she set to work with her trusty

Hoover. In the corner of the room stood a kettle and all the makings so, like any good soldier would, I made myself a cup of tea. I was barely halfway down the mug, when the administration manager happened by. The sight of me sipping my elevenses didn't seem to please him in the least.

"I thought you were supposed to be the consummate professional? What are you doing drinking tea when you're supposed to be supervising the cleaner?"

"I fail to see how having a cup of tea affects my professional status and having a 'brew' is hardly an impediment to me watching over Hilda. Would you care for a cup yourself?" I replied.

"Don't get cocky with me!"

"Well, don't you be so pedantic."

"In my opinion you are conducting yourself in an unprofessional manner," he whined.

"There's only one person in this room lacking professionalism and managerial skills chum, and it's neither Hilda nor me."

Before he could add to the conversation, I ripped off my tie, suggested a suitable place for him to stick it and strode out of Filbert Street, never to return. Well, not until the next home match anyway, but I paid for my ticket like any other fan this time. Thus, another employer was added to the long, long list of people for whom I have laboured and failed.

I made my way back to my chum Bob Fisher's house and contemplated my navel. Almost a year without a job and I'd thrown the towel in after only three days; perhaps I should have bitten my lip? There was a solitary fiver remaining in my wallet, so I strode out for Ladbrokes, to invest my cash on a sure thing running in the first race at Newbury. It came second but, fortunately for me, there was another cert running in the next race. I went up the road to the bank, pushed my cash card into the dispenser and entered my PIN number. The machine wasn't playing. After half a dozen attempts and with me getting progressively more agitated, a guy passing on his bike put me out of my misery.

"The bank closed down last Friday mate. If you want any cash, you have to go all the way down to Narborough Road."

Of course my fancy won the second race, without me troubling the bookmaker and, as I came out of the betting shop, it began to pour with rain. I scurried back to Bob's house, cursing my luck. No job, no money, no umbrella and a good soaking to compound my misery. The phone was ringing as I opened the door so, in Bob's absence, I picked it up.

"Bob Fisher's."

"G'day. I'm trying to track down a guy by the name of Wally Payne. He left this number as a contact," said a voice I recognised immediately.

"This is Wally. Is that you Phil?" I enquired.

"Wotcha Wal. Are you doing anything mate?"

"In between jobs," I declared.

"How's your French Wal?"

"Magnifique!"

"Do you want to go to Mali?"

"Sure."

"Interview here on Monday at noon, in French. We'll take it from there."

"See you on Monday."

I put the phone down and, having glanced at the atlas to see exactly where Mali was, reached for the yellow pages and found the number for Salzmann's Language School in Market Bosworth. I arranged a series of one-on-one lessons with a Belgian lady teacher, starting first thing next morning. This fine teacher understood that my interest didn't lie in learning the past pluperfect of irregular verbs, but in cramming in a series of sentences to get me through the interview. That's how ever useful phrases like, 'I didn't realise French was a prerequisite for the job' and 'My French is a little rusty, but I'll soon have it back up to scratch' entered my vocabulary. As linguistically well prepared as it was possible to be, on Monday morning I set off for London and my interview, in French.

The chap who interviewed me could have used a few lessons at Salzmann's himself, for he was certainly no linguist. In any case, I didn't give him a chance to say very much before launching into my well-practiced phrases. After ten minutes he brought the interview to a close declaring, to my considerable relief, my French to be better than his.

Thanks to Air Afrique, a mere forty-eight hours later I was in Bamako, the capital of the Republic of Mali. Having spent a night in the capital's Tennessee Hotel, an establishment that neither had nor merited any stars, I reluctantly hopped aboard a small Cessna and landed in Sadiola a couple of hours later. We would have been quicker but for the Estonian Administration Manager, who wanted the pilot to swoop down over the Manakali Lake to get some pictures for his album. He might have been proud to show his pictures around, but I never forgave him for putting me through an extra half hour of flying.

The mine village was several miles away from the airfield, along a rare stretch of tarmac; the only surface of its kind for many miles around. The road ran past the mine itself and gave me my first view of the place I'd be working in for the next four years. The home of SEMOS (*La Société d'Exploitation des mines d'or de Sadiola*) didn't look like much at first sight.

The mine village had the appearance of a concentration camp, with high wire fences very evident around its three-mile perimeter. Inside though, was an array of very decent detached bungalows, the residences of the expats and upper echelon Malians. Considering the mine was in the middle of nowhere, the quality of the house to which I was shown was of the highest order. An engineer and two pilots shared the spacious abode, although for most of the time I was left to occupy the place alone.

The villa was looked after by an elegant Senegalese lady— a woman with the bearing of someone whose station in life ought surely to have been above that of a humble housemaid. This statuesque creature was tall, proudly breasted, immaculately attired and possessed of a deep, mysterious air. It soon occurred to me that, given the dearth of available Caucasian bits on the side, she might well come in handy. The opportunity to test the water presented itself when I returned to the house from the mine one morning. When she enquired about my health, I was brazen enough to make it clear that some female company would be a boon. She didn't bat an eyelid and wasted no time in informing me, "*Je suis toujours là pour toi.*" How comforting. It remained only to discuss a fee for her services, which never failed to satisfy.

On the other side of the divide, some smaller, less swanky looking houses had been constructed for the local employees. A local's house, whilst basic by European standards, constituted a veritable mansion to those with the good fortune to have been allocated such a dwelling. These were, after all, people who had come from very modest homes and, in many cases, from one of the mud huts evident throughout Mali. We had a splendid club, which boasted a fine swimming pool, tennis courts, a squash court and a restaurant swerving *cordon bleu* fodder, courtesy of a high calibre Moroccan chef. The village also had a supermarket, selling all the stuff expatriates hanker after when away from home. Unfortunately, imported goods were frightfully expensive thanks to transportation costs and the punitive 100% import duty imposed by the Malian Government. These products were financially out of the reach of locals and, had I not been so splendidly remunerated, the prices would have made me baulk too. It was embarrassing to do a week's shopping all at once, since I'd spend more on my items than the local standing behind me in the queue with his loaf of bread and a tin of sardines earned in a month. I began to shop on a daily basis, to save myself embarrassment and the possible resentment of the Malians.

The fortress-like appearance of the village had been the brainchild of Conroy, the person from whom I was taking over. He was a man possessed of a hubristic nature, who harboured an exceedingly high opinion of himself. It was instantly apparent that his ideas on how to run a security operation were at severe variance with mine. In fact, if there was any truth in the rumours, it would appear he was at variance with most people in Sadiola on most subjects. Following spats with the Governor of Kayes Province, wherein the mine was located, Government officials and the local Police Chief, he was being required to leave Mali as quickly as his ex-Parachute Regiment officer's legs would carry him. Later I was to discover that he did possess an undoubted talent when it came to training guards, but he was neither honest nor honourable and, most of all, he wasn't Africa-wise. He had treated his second-in-command, a retired Malian Army officer, in a disgraceful manner and it was this unwarranted action that had brought about his downfall.

He had demoted the long-suffering Captain Sanogo, on the grounds of the Malian's inability to speak more than rudimentary English; thus rendering him incapable of fulfilling the requirements of his job description. It was undeniable Sanogo's grasp of the Queen's English wasn't up to much, but my subsequent inspection of his job specification revealed there was no mention of a requirement for him to speak the language. Conroy had compounded the decent fellow's misery, by having him and his family removed from their splendid manager's bungalow and into local style accommodation. Written warning orders had followed and, finally, the sack. Captain Sanogo had taken his persecution like a man and prepared to set off on the long journey back to his home in Sikasso, in the extreme south of the country. He had spent the first night of his journey in Kayes, the regional capital, from whence he would take the train home early next morning.

Conveniently, Captain Sanogo's long-time friend and brother army officer lived in Kayes and he was invited to spend the night at his home. Now, Sanogo's friend just happened to be a Malian Army colonel and no less a personage than the Governor of Kayes Province! When he heard of his chum's woes, he was aghast; sufficiently aghast to telephone the general manager of SEMOS early next morning. It was made clear to the GM in no uncertain terms that, if he wanted to dig for gold in the Kayes region, then Sanogo was to be reinstated immediately. Furthermore, he declared Conroy *persona non grata* in his country. He was to leave within a fortnight. It was a clear victory for nepotism at its most blatant.

Sanogo was reinstated immediately and instead, it was a crestfallen former British parachute regiment officer who was required to pack his bags and leave. Prattle-bag Conroy never made me privy to the reason for his enforced departure, but since his downfall was my good fortune, I really didn't give a hoot. Much later, the Governor confided in me that he had been waiting for an opportunity to drum Conroy out of Mali. As the inspecting officer at a SEMOS guards' passing out parade, he had been startled to find Conroy's men better trained and equipped than his Army's elite special forces. This was also the reason he had refused permission for the SEMOS guards to be armed, as Conroy had so vigorously advocated. From my perspective, there was no reason whatsoever for our guards to sport AK47s and I never broached the subject with the Governor.

I still had to endure a five-day handover from Conroy; the self-assured bastard. It seemed to last an eternity. When I finally bade him farewell, he left behind a deflated band of security men and a Serbian assistant in sore need of psychiatric help. This former French Foreign Legionnaire was Vlad, one of the strangest people I've ever encountered. He seemed to survive without food, drink or sleep and, in my view, he'd left most of his marbles down in Sidi-bel-Abbès. He had some barmy Conroy induced ideas about how a security unit ought to function and when I changed the system without consulting him, he took the severest umbrage. Then, when I promoted a man on the advice of Captain Sanogo whom he didn't consider worthy of elevation, he sent me to Coventry and never spoke to me again until he left several weeks later.

He did send me a written invitation to his farewell party however; a function that turned out to be odd, to say the least. There were just three of us present; Vlad, me and Eva, the general manager's secretary and arguably the rudest human being ever to walk the earth. She remains the only Sudetenland German I've ever met and, if the rest are like her, then I'm in no rush to meet any others. Since nobody would have wanted Eva's company at a funeral, one can only presume they were drawn together by some odd antisocial bond, or perhaps he had been giving the old bitch a bit on the side. The evening consisted of a dinner at which scarcely a word was uttered, followed by a couple of drinks taken in silence. It came as a blessed relief when the little hand finally reached ten and I could decently take my leave of the odd couple.

Settling into the job and finally getting to the bottom of the in-tray, I unearthed a long outstanding disciplinary matter requiring action. One of our men had been charged with careless driving and Conroy had been sitting on the disciplinary case for a couple of months. There was no need for him to have tarried for so long; there was a set procedure for such matters for goodness sake. In my view, there were two reasons for his inertia. Firstly, he simply didn't know what to do and was too pompous to ask for advice and, secondly, he was scared to face the mines' militant trade union organization, which would be guaranteed to defend the case with vigour.

I arranged a hearing, listening to the evidence in the presence of our Human Resources manager and the Trade Union Leader, Mamadou Macalou. The case was perfectly straightforward in my view; the driver was guilty of causing a traffic accident and of carrying an unauthorized passenger, a woman hitch-hiker. I found him guilty, but restricted his punishment to a verbal warning. The guy had been left hanging on for weeks, all the time wondering whether he was about to lose his precious job. He had undoubtedly been punished sufficiently already. This turned out to be a particularly wise decision on my part, as Mamadou Macalou had considerable clout amongst the locals. To his fellow trade union members he pronounced me *un homme sage*, which was to hold me in good stead for the duration of my stay in Sadiola. Thereafter, whenever there was a case to be tried, I held court as speedily as practicable. My judgements at hearings invariably erred on the side of magnanimity and my men were only subjected to financial loss if they had been really naughty.

When it came to leading a band of Francophone Malians, my linguistic ability just about saw me through. When a summons to appear before the Governor of the Province of Kayes arrived however, I was forced into confronting some self-doubt. It was still only six weeks since my arrival and although I was studying hard to improve my French, a meeting at this level would undoubtedly expose my linguistic deficiencies. He probably only wanted to run his eye over me, to confirm I wasn't likely to conduct myself in the same arrogant manner as my predecessor. Nevertheless, I flapped. On the day prior to the meeting, I decided to bare my soul and went to see the stand-in General Manager. My job description required me to be bilingual and I fell short of this requirement.

"That doesn't matter. We like you. Take Victor to interpret," said the big, quietly spoken Boer.

So, with Victor, the French speaking Estonian by my side, I set off for Kayes and my 'ordeal by governor'. The important man was busy when we arrived, this being the day he set aside for listening to disputes and ruling over them with Solomon-like wisdom. Finally though, in between the alleged theft of a goat and a case of 'throwing insults', he found a slot for me. By this time, Victor had grown bored and departed for a nearby restaurant, to order lunch for the pair of us. The bugger had deserted me in my hour of need! Oozing bonhomie, tempered with just the right amount of servility required when speaking to an autocrat in this part of the world, the GCE 'O' level French speaker launched into his opening gambit. Managing to conceal any howling deficiencies in the linguistic department, I didn't do too badly and succeeded in getting my point across pretty well. Whether tiring of listening to me massacring his adopted tongue, or simply because he was a man of compassion, halfway through the meeting the governor put me out of my misery. Still speaking in French, he first asked if I wanted a cup of coffee and then enquired whether we might continue our chat in English, since he hadn't had the opportunity to practice speaking our language for a considerable length of time. I was happy to accede to his request and he opened the batting:

"Firstly, may I congratulate you on your truly excellent French, Mr Payne. I also want you to know what a great pleasure it has been to make your acquaintance this morning," he said, in an accent as cultured as any BBC newsreader and with more than a touch of mendacity.

"Many thanks for your compliments Monsieur le Gouverneur," I replied.

"Furthermore Mr Payne, I wonder if you would be gracious enough to allow me to converse in English whenever we meet again to discuss security matters?"

"I'd be delighted to speak English with you at any time, but tell me, where on earth did you learn to speak our language to such a high standard?" I was compelled to ask.

"Oh, it's perfectly simple really old chap. One's pater was the Malian Ambassador in the United Kingdom for many years and, consequently, I grew up in London. After prep school, I was educated at Charterhouse and Harrow, before taking my degree at Trinity College in Oxford."

We were both exceedingly busy men in our respective ways and I never had the pleasure of meeting him again. Although he always denied the fact, I'm convinced Captain Sanogo called his friend the Governor to ensure our meeting went cordially.

Captain Sanogo was one of life's unlucky souls. Not only had Conroy made his life a misery, but he had also been treated singularly shabbily by the Malian Ministry of Defence. In 1985, there was a war between Mali and its eastern neighbour, Burkina Faso. Known as the War of the Agacher Strip, it started on Christmas Day in 1985 and, following two failed cease fires, hostilities terminated five days later. A mere five days, during which the death toll was officially declared to be between 59-300 persons. Hardly precise accounting! At the end of the fight, Captain Sanogo's tank lay irreparably broken-down on the front line and, before he could make arrangements to have the Russian-made monster recovered, orders were given for troops to pull back. Sanogo had no means at his disposal to move sixty-tons of armour and so left it where it was, falling back with his crew on foot. The tank remained in its location, with the knowledge of the Burkinabe authorities obviously and on the understanding it would be returned to its rightful owners in due course.

The war had been a draw and, some weeks later, the Burkinabe Government held a 'peace parade' in its capital Ouagadougou, an event to which the President of Mali and his ministers were invited. Imagine the chagrin of the Malian leader when, included in the parade for all to see, was Sanogo's 'captured' tank. The President of Mali didn't see the funny side of the jolly jape, but identified Sanogo as a convenient scapegoat for his loss of face. He ordered the good captain's immediate dismissal from the service.

Someone in a position of power had seen fit to redress the Draconian and patently unfair punishment meted out to Sanago, by wangling him the post of head Malian in the SEMOS Security Department. As my second-in-command, his responsibilities included the discipline, administration and performance of our ninety guards and I couldn't have wished for a better person to fill the role. Not only was the loyal and decent fellow now back in gainful employment, but earning a salary several times higher than that of a tank commander in the Malian Armoured Corps.

With two notable exceptions: Mohamed's Skin, Bone, Gristle and Sinew Restaurant in Farabakouta and the Sewa Restaurant in Jinguilu, there wasn't a decent watering hole within a hundred kilometres of the mine. Yet, right there in the middle of the bush, stood the Sadiola Club. With its bar, quality restaurant and every sporting facility you could wish, it could easily have been mistaken for a sporting facility for the well-heeled in Surrey. Membership was restricted to whites, South African coloureds and Malians of high rank. The South Africans found sharing with 'blacks' hard to swallow and nothing cleared the much used swimming pool of Boers quicker than the sight of a Malian coming down from the 10m diving board. I was to find the attitude of many of the Boers very difficult to take.

Some of the senior Afrikaners were vastly experienced in the gold mining game and may well have been good at their jobs but, to me, a large proportion of them seemed rather average at what they were doing. This assertion might smack of arrogance, given I knew precisely nothing about the business, but I had an ally in this regard. Our British Quartermaster often said the SEMOS Mine was too successful for its own good, in that several inept characters kept their jobs simply because the gold was coming out of the ground in record quantities and at record-low production costs. Considering our expatriate strength numbered barely fifty-five souls, a monthly gold production of around 1.5 tonnes meant Sadiola was considered the template for small mines in the AngloGold group.

Home leave was taken after 100 days and I contacted my employers back in the UK to arrange for someone to replace me for three weeks. The man they sent was a New Zealand Maori and former French Foreign Legionnaire by the name of Kotiata. I took an instant dislike to the man and disliked him even more when, returning from leave, discovered he had replaced my 'Leicester City for Ever' screen saver with something extolling the virtues of the All Blacks. I must hand it to Kotiata though, he was an honest individual and, before he departed, he spilled the beans about the remit he'd been given by PCL's Africa Chief, Dastardly Dave Clott.

Dastardly Dave had instructed Kotiata to see how much 'black' he could find on Wally Payne. He had also encouraged him to circulate a rumour suggesting I drank to excess and kept a stock of whisky in an office drawer. Anyone knowing me would have scoffed at this fabrication, as I have never touched a drop of whisky since getting horrible drunk on the stuff in

1963 and finishing up asleep in the gutter of a Scottish village lane. In addition, he had been told to approach SEMOS management and tell them PCL considered the standard of security operations to have fallen since my arrival. Kotiata hadn't seen fit to carry out these tasks.

As PCL was founded by former SAS personnel; it wasn't surprising they employed their *Kamaraden* whenever possible. I was only too well aware that had a grey-haired, French speaking SAS man been available to replace Conroy at short notice, then I would never have been approached in the first place. Since my appointment however, PCL had suffered a body blow. The Angolan Government had cancelled a security contract in their country at short notice, thus rendering a host of DSL's finest men redundant. Now there were loads of unemployed former SAS men looking for work and what better place to send one of them, than to Mali? All they had to do was find a plausible reason to get rid of Wally Payne. Conroy and mad Vlad had obviously done their damnedest to blacken my name on their return to London and, to compound my problem, Conroy and Dastardly had been brother officers in the same regiment!

Kotiata's revelation infuriated me and I called London to confront Dastardly Dave, who was allegedly out of his office. Instead, the PCL Managing Director was told precisely what I thought of their underhand methods of trying to unseat me. My next stop was the office of the SEMOS General Manager in Sadiola, where I revealed the whole seamy saga. A genuine man in every way, the GM was almost as angry as me and phoned PCL to tell them he was perfectly content with his Security Manager. Having me replaced was out of the question, he declared. The fact I was the general manager's table tennis doubles partner had no bearing on his decision.

Thereafter, there was no further contact between the company and me and Dastardly Dave failed to make his planned trip to visit Mali—a prudent move on his behalf. My guys could see I was an angry man and word soon got around about Clott's shitty performance. Passing the garages one day, my man on guard ran over to ask if he could talk to me on behalf of the lads. I joined him for a coffee and was able to assure him there was no chance of me leaving Mali. Then he quizzed me about Dastardly. How old was he? How tall? What did he weigh? Was he married? How many kids did he have? Where did he work? I had no idea why he wanted to know these things, but told him anyway. When it came to divulging the address and telephone number of PCL however, I felt compelled to draw the line. There was nothing to be gained by having the African guards phoning PCL; I was well able to fight my own corner. My man was quick to point out that they had no intention of contacting my company; they simply needed all the information they could garner in order to present it to the witch doctor. They intended to put a curse on the man and, frankly, I hope some of his bits dropped off.

In May, our Administration Manager Victor Genulaitis asked whether I knew who to contact at PCL in order to discuss the renewal of the Security Manager's contract. It was due to expire in June and he had been singularly unsuccessful in getting any sense out of their administration department. In legal terms, the PCL/SEMOS contract had actually expired the year previously and there was good reason for my employers to hang back. Under Malian employment law, they were required to have a registered office in Bamako, despite employing only one person in the Republic. In other words, they wanted to carry on making a few quid out of me, without having to go through the rigmarole of opening an office in the capital and thereby losing money on the Malian operation. Anyway, since they had treated me so despicably, I had no intention whatsoever of speaking to them.

A couple of weeks later, Victor gave up the unequal struggle and presented them with a *fait accompli*. Since they had failed to renew their contract the previous year and since no solution had been proposed again this year, SEMOS felt justified in cancelling the contract. Under normal circumstances, security companies include a clause in contracts preventing employees from jumping ship and working directly for a company to whom they have been sub-contracted. This clause prevents a return within a year of leaving the security companies employ. In my case however, I had never worked under a *bona fide* contract since my arrival and SEMOS were at liberty to offer me terms of employment. So they did. The GM called me one morning to ask what I was earning. I told him, whereupon he offered me an immediate 40% salary increase and married/accompanied status. This even extended to schooling for my daughter; BUPA health cover and three business class return trips from Bamako to Manila each year. Talk about falling on one's feet! The only imposition he placed upon me was to establish and edit a Mine magazine, which was right down my street. It was thus that the *Sahel Baro* was born and continued to be published throughout my stay. (Sahel is the name of the area of north-west Africa where we operated and 'baro' is the local Bambara dialect word for 'chatter'.) PCL continued to provide me with a leave replacement, until I objected to the name of their nominee on one occasion. They still weren't talking to me, but Dastardly Dave had the brass neck to write me a snotty e-mail, demanding to know why I had refused to accept his proposed nominee. He received an even snottier letter back, impressing upon him that things had changed somewhat since he last tried to poke me in the eye. I was now the customer and him, merely a service provider. If he was unable to supply me with a man of the required standard, I was at pains to point out there were plenty of other security companies who could. He sent someone else; a former French

Foreign Legionnaire with a Cockney accent, poor French and tattoos all over his body.

By the time my next leave came around, I had convinced the GM that paying through the nose for another sub-standard PCL replacement, just so he could sit on his backside for three weeks doing bugger all until I returned to pick up the pieces, wasn't really a cost effective option. Captain Sanogo could do 'bugger all' equally well and at a fraction of the cost. Show me a GM who won't go for financial savings! He afforded me the pleasure of writing one final letter to my former employers, thanking them for their previous service, but regretting we would no longer require their assistance. I went on to work in Mali for almost four years and proved that he who laughs last, laughs best. Game, set and match to Wally Payne.

Although well able to bluff my way as a security manager, I knew precious little about the gold business. A fact-finding mission to South Africa, the home of gold mining, would prove beneficial both to SEMOS and to me, I concluded. There was sufficient money in my judiciously managed budget to support the cost and so, off I jolly well trotted. At the time, South African Airlines had just started operating a new route between Johannesburg and Dakar, in Senegal. This had proved wildly popular with our Boers, as it saved them risking life and limb travelling home on less safety conscious African airlines. The only other option for them was to fly north to Brussels and then all the way back down again, over the entire length of the African continent, to Johannesburg. Alas, the Jo'burg—Dakar venture proved a financial disaster for South African Airlines and was short-lived. Fortunately, I was able to take advantage of their service while it lasted.

Our Cessna could manage the distance between Sadiola and Dakar without needing to refuel and our little airstrip was duly designated an International Airport. This pleased the Gendarme chief particularly, as he was issued with a rubber stamp by the immigration authorities and gained immense 'face' each time he branded an expat's passport.

Eight of us travelled on the day I departed for Johannesburg and, despite my doubts about small planes and especially our exceedingly youthful pilots, we made it safely to Dakar. We booked in at the SAA desk and waited for our connection. Due to an aborted take-off from Jan Smuts Airport however, the plane from Johannesburg was several hours late arriving. Seemingly, the passengers and crew had all exited the plane by sliding down the emergency chutes! The fault identified, the same plane finally made it, although so far behind schedule we needed to spend the night in Dakar and fly early next morning. At least this gave me the chance to have a look around the Senegalese capital, a vibrant and bustling city.

As we taxied along the apron towards the main runway next day, the pilot decided to test his brakes. The aircraft responded by shuddering violently, before coming to a halt. After trying this manoeuvre three times, the pilot made an announcement: "Ladies and Gentlemen. As you 'ave probably noticed, there's something 'orribly wrong with this aircraft. There's no way I'm going up in this thing." The plane returned to our stand and we all trooped off for a free lunch. With the brakes adjusted, the plane was finally deemed airworthy and we made the trip to Johannesburg without further ado.

AngloGold, the parent company of SEMOS, had reserved me a room in a splendid hotel in the Sandton area of Johannesburg and my arrival couldn't have been better timed. As I was sipping my post 'booking-in' beer in the bar, what should come on the TV but a live English soccer match. It was a splendid game, although my viewing was spoilt momentarily when a stunningly attractive black girl approached my table and offered her services. I was forced to decline of course, on the grounds of her poor timing. "Good grief woman," I said, "it's not even half-time yet!" Ignorance being bliss, later in the evening I embarked upon a promenade around Sandton, without a care in the world and certainly not cognizant of the fact muggers wandered these parts in battalion sized gangs. During my walk, I espied a church building with a sign outside proclaiming the place of worship to be the 'Union Church of Sandton'. A member of the Union Church of Manila when in the Philippines, I planned to attend their service next morning, until I spotted a small sign screwed to the bottom of the notice board. This informed the world that the Sandton church building had proved too small for the size of the congregation and had moved a couple of years previously, to a new location in Sandown, a few miles along the road. Next morning a taxi took me to Sandown, where an impressive avenue of trees led down to the church entrance. Standing in the foyer, handing out hymn books and greeting visitors, was a guy about my age. He welcomed me in his clipped South African accent and I, in turn, introduced myself.

"Wally Payne, spending a few days in South Africa with my company," I declared.

"Wally Payne from Leicester, judging by the accent," he replied.

"How astonishing! How come you recognise a Leicester accent, especially since mine isn't particularly marked?"

"Not so clever really; my wife and I lived in Leicester for several years you see."

"Were you working in the city?"

"Yes, at the AEI on Blackbird Road."

"Good grief! I used to live just over the road, opposite the Blackbird pub."

And so it went on. His wife had taught at my brother's school, we had the same dentist and he was a regular at Filbert Street football ground. What a small world!

The AngloGold Asset Protection Manager picked me up on Monday morning and we spent a few days together, looking at gold mines in places whose names were totally unfamiliar to me. I saw mines in Carltonville, Klerksdorp and Orkney, as well as Western Deep Levels and three mines in a place called Welkom. They all looked the same to me. There was a nasty surprise in store for me at Western Deep Levels, the deepest gold mine in the world. They planned to take me down 2.33 miles, to the very bottom of the shafts. Since I'd flown only a couple of days previously however, they wouldn't allow me to descend on medical grounds. How very unfortunate!

The security manager at Western Deep Levels was English. He had left Blighty's shores many years previously and joined the British South Africa Police, the custodians of law and order in Southern Rhodesia. He gave me the rundown on life as an expatriate policeman in those parts and told me he had finished his service in the rank of chief superintendent. For the want of something better to say, I asked about his pension, whereupon he pulled an envelope from his inside pocket.

"It just so happens my pension cheque arrived this morning. I'd like you to have it as a souvenir," he said.

"That's most generous of you chum, but I really couldn't take your hard earned pension off you," I retorted.

"You'd be taking bugger all. The currency in Zimbabwe has devalued so badly, my cheque wouldn't buy you a pint of beer."

Fancy working all your life and have nothing to show for it.

My grand tour of the goldfields ended with an invitation to the AGM of the AngloGold security managers. The conference served to convince me that security managers are the same the world over: mostly inept, bored and bluffing their way.

Chapter 10

Part 2

Crime & Punishment

'TAILINGS' are the huge volumes of noxious sludge and liquid created as a by-product of gold production. They are deposited in a designated area known as a Tailings Storage Facility and ours was located in a natural valley, plugged at the lower end by a huge earthen barrier and situated only a mile away from the mine. What would have happened if the dam had ever given way was too dire to contemplate. This facility was referred to by the Afrikaners as the 'sleimsdam' and, throughout this chapter, I will use their terminology when referring to the area. As production went along, the lake of water, acid, cyanide and other nasty substances would rise until it became a hill, the likes of which are to be seen all over South Africa. The life expectancy of animals drinking the deadly cocktail contained in the sleimsdam was distinctly limited and to prevent any precious domestic beasts dying thus, the whole area was fenced off by ten miles of a lofty, high quality and exceedingly expensive wire barrier. Before my arrival, there had been a succession of unsolved thefts of sections of perimeter fence and, sure enough, the very first offence to occur during my reign was the removal of several hundred metres of the stuff.

There must have been a thriving market for top quality fencing in the Sadiola area because, over the next few weeks, the 'Phantom Fencing Filcher' struck with alarming regularity. Our felon made his fatal mistake when a section of rolled-up wire, not yet picked up by the thief, was discovered hidden in some long grass. I had a group of our guys dig in nearby and, when he finally returned with a borrowed lorry to collect his booty, he was nabbed. I had the pleasure of escorting him down to the 'Pink Palace', the gaudily painted and exceedingly insanitary buildings located on the outskirts of Sadiola that served as police station, jail and married quarters for the gendarmes.

Gendarmes in Mali receive a pauper's stipend and ours were certainly not averse to boosting their incomes by accepting financial considerations. In the British Army vernacular, they were 'as bent as nine-bob notes'. Although SEMOS were unbending when it came to paying bribes of any description, the General Manager allowed me to give them a monthly donation out of my budget. My relatively modest gift had the effect of doubling the salary of the Adjutant Chef and his eleven men. Consequently, Monsieur Wally's every wish was their command.

The chief was delighted to see me arrive at the Gendarmerie with 'Sadiola's Most Wanted' clapped in irons and, without further ado, he had him strip down to his underpants. He was then given a terrible hiding by several of the gendarmes, before being locked up in the Pink Palace Hilton. This cell was not a place where one would care to spend too much time; it was unbearably hot, indescribably filthy and room service wasn't of a particularly high standard. I presented the chief with my file on the case and drank a cup of disgusting Malian coffee with him. The caffeine did something to him, because he went into the cell and gave the miscreant another sound beating for good measure. I left the case in the good hands of the Adjutant Chef and had nothing further to do with the matter, other than to make a short statement for the Prosecution Service in Kayes. The judiciary in Kayes, aware of the importance of the mine to the district, were out to give a warning to would-be miscreants and the wire thief was sentenced to no less than five years in the slammer.

Having made my mark as an uncompromising security chief early on, a second incident occurred, the outcome of which would convince the locals of one thing—Monsieur Wally was not a man to be trifled with. Water is a scarce and precious commodity in this part of the world and the citizens of Sadiola were delighted when the company piped running water into the village. With a stand-pipe on most street corners, it was a major public relations success. You can't please all of the people all of the time though and there was a dissenter in the ranks. He considered the white man's magic to be evil and unilaterally set about the water pipes with a pick-axe. Over the course of three nights he managed to drive all the villagers back to using artesian wells, before being collared by his own people and handed over to me. He turned out to be an old man and so, at the Pink Palace, he was allowed to forgo the traditional thumping and was simply conveyed to Kayes to appear before the judge. Once again, I insisted on the maximum punishment and, as 'anti-social behaviour to the detriment of the public good' is seriously frowned upon in Mali, the old fellow was sentenced to six years. I wondered whether he would survive to see the end of his sentence in the notorious Kayes jail, but had no qualms about sending him down.

I was sheriff inside the Mine Village too, where crime figures were very moderate. Expats were only too well aware of company policy: committing any offence meant immediate repatriation. Locals earned salaries five or six times the national average and enjoyed *de luxe* accommodation by

Malian standards; they would have been foolish in the extreme to jeopardize these benefits by stealing. Apart from the odd loaf of bread going walkabout from the supermarket, very few thefts worthy of the name occurred in the village during my four years in Sadiola. The first semi-serious offence happened when the teenage son of a senior Malian employee stole a video camera from the house in which a baptismal party was being held. He was caught 'bang to rights' by my guards and, next day, I played a blinder. The Malian chief surveyor had made the trip to Mecca on no less than three occasions and such a pedigree was highly revered amongst the locals. As this was the first crime worthy of the name ever recorded inside the village, I decided to consult him on the matter. Playing to his vanity, he was asked whether, given his high standing amongst fellow Moslems, he might wish to deal with the young offender personally. The facts could then be withheld from the Gendarmes, the judgement would be common knowledge amongst the village residents and justice would be done just the same. He was very keen to take on the responsibility and I considered the incident closed.

Next morning, there was a knock on my office door and in walked the chief surveyor. He wanted to thank me for allowing him to deal with the previous day's misdemeanour in the time-honoured Malian fashion. The young man, who had been soundly lashed on the back with electrical cable, stood meekly to his side. On a word of command spoken in Bambara, the young man fell to his knees, crawled over the office floor towards me and grabbed me around the thighs. I was a little unsure what he might attempt next, but he merely thanked me wholeheartedly for allowing him to be punished in the traditional way. I assured him the pleasure was all mine, whereupon we all shook hands and the matter ended there.

Self-respecting thieves anywhere in the world would shake their heads in disbelief at the antics of the pathetic, petty-pilferers pervading Sadiola. Ignoring items we would consider valuable, they generally concentrated their larcenous efforts on pinching stuff we considered to be rubbish: bits of wire, rope, string, plastic containers and the like. Our chief accountant Philippe Berten, my Sunday morning bush-walking colleague made an unprecedented visit to my office, to report a theft from his home. His houseboy had failed to report for work for three days and, at the time of his last appearance at the Berten's bungalow, a radio, tape recorder and sum of cash had disappeared. Nothing very earth shattering there and the list of suspects was hardly likely to prove expansive. It was the circumstances surrounding the guilty fellow's arrest which proved rather interesting.

Along with my trusty assistant, Sissoko Fily Mady, I made my way down to the village of Alamoutalia, where the suspect had his mud hut. It was always good protocol to call on the village chief in such circumstances and mandatory if you intended to haul one of his men before the Gendarmes. I went to the chief's hut and was surprised to find him attired in his best grand boubou, as if he was about to attend an important function. He was. The funeral of one of his villagers was about to take place. Malians are nothing if not hospitable and, before having the thief and the stolen goods handed over to me on a plate, I attended a Moslem burial service and subsequent funeral party.

Knocking on Berten's door with his suitably repentant houseboy cowering at my side, I was to be surprised for the second time in one evening. The officious accountant and scourge of his subordinates displayed a hitherto unknown benevolent side to his nature. He forgave the miscreant houseboy and ordered him to start work again in the morning. All my efforts had been in vain.

Some other offences committed within the village were reported to me by our South African doctor. In the space of a week, there had been an epidemic of Malian wives admitted to the clinic, all suffering from injuries consistent with having been physically abused. One woman required a dozen sutures after her husband had stuck a broken bottle in her face. Another needed four stitches after her husband had stabbed her in the back, while a third sustained several broken fingers, a result of her spouse stamping on her hand. I spoke to the three husbands, all of whom insisted the Koran allowed them to assault their wives in this way. That may have been the case, but I wasn't having that kind of behaviour on my patch and decided to seek some words of wisdom from the Gendarme chief. As far as he was concerned, they were talking rubbish and he promptly arrested the three of them for committing serious offences against the Malian Criminal Code. By arrangement, they all stewed in Kayes prison until I returned from three weeks' leave, whereupon I made a statement asking the judge to throw the book at them. At this juncture, a quaint piece of Malian law came into operation. The three assailants went before a reconciliation board and, in the presence of their wives; they each swore on the Koran to be better husbands in future. Their pledges having been noted by a scribe in his leather bound ledger, the judge released them without charge. It wasn't quite how it would have been dealt with in Her Majesty's Courts, but at least the incidence of assaults on wives ceased forthwith.

Having demonstrated my zero tolerance policy during the early months, I was able to sit back and send a 'nil' crime statistic return to the AngloGold Asset Protection Manager for month after month. I'm not naive enough to believe Sadiola was a 'theft free' zone; on the contrary, a multitude of unreported minor thefts most certainly occurred at SEMOS. In almost every case though, the aggrieved invited theft through carelessness and negligence. Rather than be made the subject of a scathing report from me, the majority of those who had stuff taken chose to keep stumm and write off their losses. There was one exceedingly serious incident in the mining village during my stay, but it happened at the very end of my time in Mali.

No matter how all-encompassing the standing operating procedures, how efficient the Security and Health & Safety managers' guidelines or how rigorously departmental heads strive to ward off serious incidents, they will happen nevertheless. Just when the Health & Safety man was preening himself and accepting tenders for the production of tee shirts bearing the logo 'Zero Serious Injury Accidents', we had two deaths to deal with inside a week. One of the fatalities was tragic; the other a simple cardiac arrest that turned into an international incident.

It was normal practice to bring in subcontractors whenever short-term specialist tasks needed performing and, for this reason, we had half a dozen Australians living in a hotel in Kayes and working somewhere out in the bush. As they worked and played many miles away from the mine, very few people even knew they were engaged on the project. One morning though, the doctor and I were called to their hotel in the regional capital at the behest of a flustered Aussie foreman. One of his men had failed to respond to his early morning call and, once the remainder of his team had driven away into the bush, the foreman had stayed behind to investigate. On forcing open the missing man's room after there was no response to his knocking, he had found his chum lying stiff and still on the floor. He had called the SEMOS office as required, but had omitted to inform either the hotel manager, or the local police.

Doctor Andre and I arrived at the scene and met the foreman. We put the hotel manager in the picture, had him contact the local Gendarmerie and took a walk down to the dead man's chalet. He'd been dead since the previous evening and had most probably died of a heart attack, declared our able physician. A senior gendarme officer arrived from Kayes to carry out an investigation and, once the police surgeon confirmed the cause of death, he told us we could have the body. No post mortem requirement here it appeared, so we zipped him up in a bag and took him back to our morgue. It's amazing how many people turn up for a shufti at a stiff, and equally amazing how quickly they disappear when volunteers are required to pick the body up. Mali was no different to anywhere else it seemed. Up to this point, everything had gone without a hitch, but a farce of mammoth proportions was about to begin.

Malian regulations require bodies of deceased expatriates to be embalmed and placed in a zinc-lined coffin before repatriation can take place. This was a Moslem country though, where the dead are wrapped in burial cloths and laid to rest the same day. If there were any coffins available, then they might have been obtainable down in Bamako, but as for a zinc-lined model? Our Head Administrator must have had some previous experience of repatriating bodies because, before you could say *rigor mortis*, an embalmer arrived from South Africa. His baggage included a coffin conforming to the required specifications. Once Mr Gilfellan had done the necessary with the mortal remains of the former Aussie, it was time for a multitude of officials to descend upon the mortuary. In accordance with the laws pertaining to such matters in Mali, the ritual closing of the lid needed to be witnessed by every Tom, Dick and Mamadou remotely involved in the unfortunate business. From Kayes came the doctor who had certified him dead, the Aussie foreman, the police chief, his honour the mayor and the town clerk. Then, from Sadiola, there was the mortician, Dr Andre and me; our mayor, town clerk and police chief and, unless I'm mistaken, there was a butcher, baker and candlestick maker in there for good measure. Once we had all signed the form confirming that the coffin contained a dead Aussie, Mr Gilfellan screwed it shut and set off to Bamako in the company Cessna, along with his excess baggage.

The master plan was for Gilfellan and the deceased to travel in our plane as far as Bamako. From the Malian capital, he would take a scheduled flight to Dakar, whereupon he and the cargo would transfer to a SAA flight bound for Johannesburg. Once in South Africa, other arrangements would be made to forward the Aussie's remains to his homeland. Gilfellan called me from Dakar as planned. He had arrived in the Senegalese capital, but the coffin hadn't.

Seemingly, whilst unloading the coffin at Bamarko, the baggage handlers had found it so heavy, they felt it necessary to inform their supervisor they considered something was amiss. He agreed with his men and jumped to the idiotic conclusion that SEMOS were attempting to smuggle gold out of the country in the sarcophagus, which was impounded for further investigations. This improbable story even found its way into the local newspapers and TV broadcasts. The real reason for the abnormal weight was perfectly simple; an oak coffin, lined with zinc and containing a particularly corpulent corpse tends to be on the heavy side.

There appeared to be no simple solution to the dilemma; there never is in Africa unless you are prepared to grease the wheels of progress. All those who had signed when the coffin was sealed in Sadiola were required to reassemble in Bamako, for a grand reopening ceremony. The majority of us gathered a couple of days later when, to the consternation of our accusers, the only thing they found inside the box was the late Aussie. Everyone signed again, the coffin was screwed down again and

Gilfellan went off again, this time with his cargo. By the time the unfortunate Antipodean reached Melbourne, he'd already been dead for eleven days!

I'd seen the new geologist a few times, although never for long enough to give him more than a passing nod. As I was leaving work on Friday evening however, Ben Roux, a stocky Afrikaner with a sporting look about him, was at the main gate. I stopped to introduce myself and spent half an hour chatting with him and his pretty fiancée, also a geologist. Next evening, Ben was reported missing.

Ignoring the established procedures for booking-out at the village guard post, Ben and some other South Africans had gone to the banks of the River Senegal, to have a 'braai' and do a little swimming. Their chosen venue was a spot called the *Chutes de Félou,* where the mighty river had once been blocked by a huge basalt plug. Millions of years of raging flood water had eroded the rock, leaving pools and channels that made ideal swimming areas. Ben had last been seen when he came up after diving into the narrow channel nearest the shore, but the current had taken him over a waterfall leading down to a wider expanse of river. His companions made a frantic search for him in the fading light, but there was no sign of the big man.

A solemn group comprising me, our South African doctor, the Gendarme Adjutant Chef and a couple of the previous evening's revellers, made its way to the riverside location early next morning. After a futile search of the river bank, the gendarme suggested we talk with the chief of the nearby village. The chief listened to the tale and enquired exactly where Ben had gone over the waterfall and into the river. Then he pointed his stick towards a large rock, a hundred yards downstream. Ben's body would be underneath it, he declared. I wondered how he could possibly be so certain and asked the gendarme to enquire. All people and animals drowned at this time of the year were taken there by the flow of the river, the old chief explained.

The River Senegal was reasonably shallow at this point and when a crowd of villagers constructed a barrier to stem the flow of water, Ben's arms became visible, flailing in the current. The locals went in and recovered the badly-battered body, which we took off to the mortuary in Kayes. The wheels of the convoluted administrative requirements of Mali I'd experienced following the death of the Australian began to turn once again and Gilfellan needed to make a second trip to Sadiola. This time the repatriation of the body went without a hitch and a post mortem carried out in South Africa revealed the cause of death to have been a broken neck.

Just one last death for good measure!

The Malian National Route Number One ran from the capital Bamako to the border with Senegal and was, for the most part, in a deplorable state of neglect. During the rainy season, water-filled potholes of indeterminate depth often made the road impassable. The section of road between Sadiola and Kayes was maintained by SEMOS and, whilst not metalled, was kept in an excellent state of repair. This largesse had nothing to do with the magnanimity of the South African company, but was done to ensure tankers carrying fuel to the diesel-guzzling gold mine generators could get through in all weathers. This was a sparsely populated part of the world and few people owned private cars; consequently, traffic was very light. As if in defiance of statistics though, the number of traffic accidents was staggering. As drivers, Malians are uniformly reckless and blighted with a compulsion to travel on the wrong side of the road. Safe driving wasn't helped by the uniform ridges that appear, as if by magic, on laterite roads.

I heard the desperate radio message as I sat in my office in the early afternoon.

"Mate, is there anybody listening out there?"

I recognised the voice; it was our man-mountain Australian driller.

"Hello Shorty! What's the problem cobber?" I answered.

"Christ mate, there's been a really bad accident. I was coming around the curve at Kourouketo and hit a local taxi coming the other way. He was on the wrong side of the bloody road. There are people lying all over the bloody place mate. Can you get out here with the doctor as quickly as possible?"

"No problem Shorty. Keep calm and we'll be there just as quickly as we can."

"It wasn't my fault mate; the silly bastard was on the wrong side of the road."

"I'm sure it wasn't your fault chum. Keep listening on the radio and we'll be with you before long."

"Good on yer Wal."

In no time at all, I mobilized a response team and off we sped for Kourouketo, some 15 miles away.

The sight greeting us was just as Shorty had described, with upwards of twenty people lying in various states of distress on and at the side of the road. Naturally, there was no sign of the local constabulary. Shorty's vehicle was a huge, specialist trench-digging machine and it had collided with a Nissan pick-up, the model favoured by Malians as taxis. By using packing methods perfected by witchdoctors through the ages, the Malians were able to stuff unbelievable numbers of passengers into these vans. The vehicles were, of course, under maintained and patently unsuitable for the purpose to which they were put. The Ausdrill truck was scarcely damaged, but the Nissan had been torn apart by the collision, throwing its payload of people and packages all over Route Nationale 1. Strictly speaking, we were under no obligation to give medical assistance to these unfortunates, but unless we did, they would receive no aid whatsoever. Doctor Andre Willemse hadn't been with the company long and spoke no French, so I accompanied him on his rounds of the wounded. We had to decide which passengers had injuries meriting a trip to the mine clinic at Sadiola and which of them were malingering. A dozen walking wounded were packed into a Landrover and conveyed to the clinic, whilst Andre tended those with more serious injuries. Finally, six stretcher cases were put into the ambulance and the back of Landrovers before our work at the scene was finished. For my part, quite how so many passengers were able to squeeze into such a small Nissan will always remain a mystery.

By next morning, the doctors and medical staff had treated and released all but one patient. This man had very nearly failed muster the previous day, as he had no obvious injuries and didn't respond to any of the good doctor's probing and questioning. Furthermore, he had been covered by a blanket and was lying on a stretcher, neither seeming conducive with having just been involved in a horrific accident. Doctor Andre and I did consider the possibility of him having been someone from the local village, who had been brought out opportunistically for the chance of treatment by the white medicine man.

Andre was a worried physician. Despite his best efforts, this patient wasn't responding to treatment and furthermore, his problems were in no way related to the accident. The old man was suffering from cerebral meningitis. Procedures required us to send this man to the Government Hospital in Kayes, but Andre was aware that even if he survived the journey, the medics there would have neither the drugs nor the expertise to save his life. He asked for my opinion and I suggested we send the patient to the Government Hospital as regulations demanded. He died shortly after being admitted at Kayes.

Apparently, this man and his son had left their home village in the south of Mali to pan for gold in Tabakoto in the west of the country, near the Senegalese border. He had taken seriously ill and, aware he wasn't long for this world, had asked his son to take him home to die. This explained the blanket and stretcher, but the poor sod never made it to his native ground to take his last breath. What a shame.

Chapter 10

Part 3

Yarpies

PRIOR TO ARRIVING in Sadiola, I'd only ever seen one Afrikaner and then only from a considerable distance. I was in the cheap seats at Wembley Arena when a South African heavyweight, by the name of Gerry Coetzee, took on Frank Bruno for the Commonwealth title. So distant was my seat from the action that, as the bell sounded for the start of the first round, I needed to bend down to pick up my binoculars. By the time they were focused in, Botha was lying on his back and the referee was counting him out. Whilst not thinking too much of Mr Coetzee, I was willing to take his kinsmen in Sadiola at face value.

As a young man, I was often guilty of generalising when it came to peoples and nationalities. This failing dissipated the more I travelled around the world and discovered there were good and bad in all nations. Almost to a man however, the Afrikaners in Sadiola were not the kind of people I'd care to socialise with. Perhaps gold miners need to be rough, tough characters in order to survive the rigours of a harsh method of earning a living; in which case I'd need to reconsider my philosophy about generalisations. Although Nelson Mandela had been elected as President of the Republic of South Africa and apartheid declared dead and buried, SEMOS employees had, seemingly, not been made privy to the information. The

191

way they treated local employees was disgraceful and the boorish manner they adopted when talking to the English security manager wasn't any more acceptable. The Boer Wars, or the Anglo-Boer Wars as Afrikaners insist on calling the conflicts, have never been forgotten. There were even times, especially when South Africa lost at rugby, when I was held personally responsible for the wars. Well, me and Winston Churchill.

If ever there was a classic case of 'the pot calling the kettle black', then it was perpetrated by a chap called Henning. He and I watched the South Africa v Australia rugby union international together in the bar, a match which the Aussies won. He was suitably gloomy afterwards and said, in all seriousness, "The trouble with the Australians is, they're so bloody arrogant." That was rich coming from a Yarpie.

On an isolated industrial site, the security manager is the whipping boy. He represents authority and, in lieu of a policeman to abuse, he has to shoulder the blame for any number of spurious complaints. Whether I was popular with the men from the former Union was a matter of supreme indifference to me and I sometimes went out of my way to irritate them. Here were a few of my security rules they found inconvenient:

a.   An Afrikaner could speak in his strange tongue to his heart's content, but any attempt to speak Afrikaans in my office rendered the miscreant liable to summary and forcible ejection. Only the mellifluous tones of 'English as she is spoken' were tolerated on my patch, along with the French spoken by the Malians, of course. This punitive course of action was carried out regardless of how tough the offender considered himself to be, or how many times he had purportedly played rugby for the Transvaal.

b.   Expatriate personnel were not permitted to enter the mine without a company badge. They couldn't do it anywhere in South Africa, so why should this mine be any different? To their fury, those arriving for work without their company badge were required to obtain a visitor's badge from my guards. This would only be issued if they were polite to my black security men, which was something they found very difficult to stomach.

c.   Any person treating a Malian as an inferior species was taken to task in a brusque fashion.

d.   Pet dogs barking with an Afrikaans accent and thereby annoying village inhabitants were summarily executed. Under duress, the doctor would inject them with something noxious; otherwise, the security manager would be only too pleased to have them shot.

This story concerns a man with truly wretched antecedents. He was half-South African, half-Italian and a 100% pain in the backside. One morning, the Administration Department hired a group of casual labourers to mend an internal fence in the office compound. I was loath to provide casual workers with badges, since they never returned them when a job was finished. A SEMOS badge not only represented something of a status symbol amongst the locals, but it also gave them access to the mine buses. There were times when genuine workers were hard-pressed to find a place on a shuttle bus, as freeloaders enjoyed free excursions hither and thither. This misuse continued until, finally, I was forced to provide guards on buses to prevent access to the 'chancers'. So, instead of badges, companies providing short term labour would present me with a list of names and I would issue a *laissez-passer* to facilitate entry to the relevant site. Even then, it was an inexact science. Few of the labourers had a national ID card, many went under a pseudonym, few could write their names and every company employed half a dozen blokes called Camara Mohamed.

Dominico the Spic chose this day to forget his identity card and, him being an odious, obnoxious and nasty individual, I instructed my lads to be extra zealous before issuing him with a visitor's card. Having undergone an 'ordeal by black man' that went very much against the grain, the Italian went berserk when he discovered a score of Malians working inside the administration enclosure, without a single badge between them.

The *laissez-passer* system being beyond his comprehension, he burst into my office and confronted me with an accusation of pandering to the blacks. What he actually said was, "pendering to the bleks." He went on to censure me for persecuting the whites; committing reverse discrimination in effect. How absurd! Had this little spic been anything other than a rampant racist, or had he matched me in size or intelligence, then I might have treated him to a debate on the subject. As it was, I took him by the front of his shirt and threw him out; with the express instruction that he was never to darken my doorstep, or even speak to me, again. Although we sat in adjoining offices for a couple of years after this incident and really needed to talk, most of our business thereafter was conducted by memo.

The South Africans all worked in departments containing fellow landsmen or western expatriates; so they had someone to talk to. My fellow workers consisted of a throng of big, black Malians and any conversations needed to be carried out in Bambara, of which I had nothing but a very rudimentary grasp, or French. To get the best out of my guys, it behove me to become one of them. So, to facilitate this aim, I greeted my blokes each day in the same way as they greeted each other, by giving them a half-hearted kiss on both cheeks. Similarly, when walking around the site, I would hold hands with them, as was their disposition. My conduct was deemed sacrilegious by many South Africans; they would have died before touching one of the locals. Actually, holding hands with another man made me feel terribly uncomfortable, especially when it was the giant gendarme chief; a serial hand-holder and kisser of his fellow man.

For unfathomable reasons, traffic accidents involving SEMOS personnel were investigated by the Health and Safety wallah, rather than the Security Manager. Now, while I have little doubt about Denis' efficacy as an HSE man, he most certainly knew bugger all about traffic accident enquiries. In any case, the legal validity of his investigations was severely compromised, since he refused point-blank to give evidence in traffic accident cases should the driver plead not guilty. The rationale behind his reluctance being: "I will never submit to 'aving my evidence questioned by a blek." Did that not smack just a teensy-weensy bit of racism? Furthermore, he never saw fit to hold a hearing at all should the driver be white! When the General Manager pranged his Range Rover, an incident witnessed by the Security Manager, there was a cover-up of Watergate proportions. Apartheid was alive and well in the HSE Department in Sadiola.

Since he confirmed he wouldn't appear to be questioned at my hearings, I dismissed all my traffic accident cases within seconds. My personal driver admitted to driving too fast when he crashed and wrote off my old Landrover, but I instructed him to plead not guilty, on the grounds he wanted to question the HSE investigator. Denis was informed but failed to put in an appearance, so I found my man not guilty when he was patently culpable. To really rub Denis' nose in the dirt, the company presented me with a shiny new replacement vehicle.

The AngloGold directors were holding their Annual General Meeting in Sadiola and departmental heads were expected to give a presentation to the board. In the General Manager's absence on leave, his German deputy left me a message outlining the subject on which I was to address the directors. In a Gothic hand he had penned, "1999 Incentives." I couldn't question him any further, as he had departed for South Africa to meet and travel back with the directors. It was a strange topic for the security manager in my view, but I laboured away and produced a speech designed to enthral my public. It was only fifteen minutes before the meeting that I finally saw the German again.

"Have you your presentation prepared, Walter?" he enquired.

"Ja wohl Werner! *1999 Incentives*, in twenty exciting minutes."

"Verdammt nochmal! Didn't I say *1998 Incidents*?"

"No!"

"Oh hell! Can you talk on incidents for twenty minutes?"

I work well under pressure and scribbled down enough facts and figures to confuse Einstein. After listening to hours of technical bumph, none of which was comprehensible to me, it was finally my turn to perform. As I strode to the podium, the 'big cheese' spoke to me.

"Wally, we're running terribly late. Could you restrict your presentation to five minutes? Thirty seconds would be even better, or perhaps you can just leave it until another occasion."

I'll do anything to oblige.

Chapter 10

Part 4

Malians

IN THE EARLY DAYS, I was passing the main guard post one morning and greeted the security man controlling the barrier restricting access to the office compound. Continuing my conversion with a Malian geologist accompanying me to the main plant, I was suddenly stuck for a particular word in French and struggled to find the correct expression. On my way back to the office, my guard whispered in my ear in almost flawless English:

"Mister Payne, if you ever have any difficulties with your French, then please don't hesitate to ask for my assistance; in the strictest confidence naturally."

"My goodness, your English is exceptional. Where did you learn to speak the language to such a standard?" I enquired.

"Initially at school and then I read English at university."

"Can't you find a job commensurate with the obvious talents?"

"Most certainly; in fact I was Professor of English at Timbuktu University prior to coming here to Sadiola," he explained.

"Why on earth would you leave such a prestigious position in favour of becoming a security guard and lifting a barrier in a gold mine?"

"A salary several times higher than a university professor can earn," he explained.

Shortly afterwards, I appointed him as my assistant. Over the next few years, the exceptionally talented Sissoko Fily Mady became my friend, confidant and advisor on both Malian affairs and life in general. I negotiated several pay rises for him during this time, but he was still worth more. Three years after I left Sadiola, SEMOS decided to dispense with an expatriate in the post of Asset Protection Manager and appoint a local instead. They were wise enough to select Mady. A year as 'Asset Protection Manager under Instruction' ended with his elevation to the post of APM and he phoned me whilst I was in Algeria to break the joyous news. I expressed my absolute delight.

"Do you know what thrilled me most though?" he asked.

"What was that my friend?"

"To be allotted your old house as my family's new home."

According to the pilots who used the Sadiola airstrip, the laterite surface was as good as any to be found in the Republic of Mali. Nevertheless, the inspectors from the Malian air traffic control department descended to take a look. Apart from a slightly bumpy section towards the end that was never used, there was absolutely nothing wrong with the *piste* and they ought to have given us a clean bill of health. In countries like this though, airport operation licences and airworthiness certificates are not issued for the standard of the surface and other amenities, but on how much money you're willing to slip the inspectors. They submitted a ridiculous report, requiring us to 'grade' the bumpy bit and then made another stunning observation: our windsock didn't meet Malian specifications. It was probably the only windsock in existence outside of Bamako International Airport for goodness sake! They allowed us to continue flying, but threatened to withdraw our licence and close the airport unless we acted upon their observations within three months.

SEMOS didn't pay bribes and, rather than give the scoundrel inspectors a penny piece, a huge amount of money went on resurfacing the whole runway. We even had a couple of bespoke windsocks constructed, to comply exactly with specifications laid down under Malian Air Transportation regulations. When the inspectors arrived to look at the airport a second time, they were most disappointed to find everything in perfect condition. They grudgingly issued a licence and departed without the £120 equivalent bribe they had demanded and without as much as a cup of my imported German coffee.

Camara Mohamed was always one of my favourite guards and I liked him even more when he won us the cup, by slotting home the winner during the penalty shoot-out. He was always a deep, private lad, but there was never anything in his demeanour to suggest he would go mad. Working a boring, twelve-hour shift in extreme temperatures would have been mind-numbing for sure, but these guys were earning many times the Malian national wage and surely this would be the incentive to keep a bloke going. He'd been to see Captain Sanogo a time or two, complaining about tiredness, although he was never too tired to turn out for the soccer team. It was when he started to report late for shifts and then miss them altogether that Sanogo brought the matter to my attention. I had him in for a chat and was stunned to discover the extent of his mental problems. He was convinced everyone was talking about him behind his back; thought people were following him and believed there was a conspiracy to have him sacked. Despite my assurances to the contrary, he called me a liar. In fact, he accused me of being the main conspirator and threatened to kill me if I didn't stop following him. Mohamed was a very big, powerful fellow and having him as an unhinged enemy wasn't a situation to relish.

I consulted Doctor Andre Willemse, who was of the unshakeable opinion we had a paranoid schizophrenic on our hands. Getting Mohamed down to Bamako, where the country's only mental hospital was located, was simple enough. Getting him to turn up for an appointment with the psychiatrist was a different matter altogether. Convinced the whole world was conspiring against him, he refused to go anywhere near the hospital. Finally, for his own good, I sent four of his best friends down to his parents' home in Bamako and had him dragged along to see the shrink. Over the next few months, poor old Mohamed was in and out of the mental institution. Occasionally he would show up back at Sadiola, having sweet-talked his way onto the company plane and seemingly in full control of his faculties. Sometimes he would even work a few shifts, but the respite was always short-lived and the doctor would arrange yet another appointment with the psychiatrist.

The Human Resources Manager wanted to pay him off with a couple of month's salary and give him his cards, but I wasn't having any of that. Any SEMOS employee injured or taken ill in the course of his work received the very best medical treatment and, should he be unable to return to work, he would be adequately compensated. For some reason, psychiatric patients were treated differently. It would have been all too easy to say, "Camara Mohamed? He's a nut case, let's get rid of him." That would have made me popular with the personnel people, but Mohamed had taken ill during the course of his duties and I insisted on having him treated in the same way as every other injured employee. I made sure the powerful trade union were on my side and won their applause for taking up the fight on behalf of a local.

He was finally taken off my establishment and became the responsibility of the Human Resources Department. My regular demands for progress reports on my former charge probably annoyed them considerably, but somebody had to ensure he was getting a fair deal. I made sure the General Manager was kept in the picture too; he was a humanist and agreed Mohamed should receive treatment at the company's expense for as long as it took. Amazingly, someone was still letting a madman onto the plane at Bamako, because he continued to turn up to see his mates. He wasn't really any better though and I really wished there had been better psychiatric facilities in Mali.

The General Manager and I left Sadiola for good around the same time, whereupon the Human Resources Department wasted no time in striking the unfortunate Mohamed off the company's books.

As the opencast pit grew deeper, wider and longer, the geologists discovered considerable deposits of the yellow stuff under the villages of Sadiola and Farabakouta. No matter that the localities had been inhabited by the Bambara people for thousands of years, the mighty dollar was to win the day and the villages would have to be relocated. It was a mightily convoluted business, but plans were finally agreed with the village chiefs and the process of building New Sadiola and New Farabakouta began. The locals were onto a winner in reality; the two new locations were only a couple of kilometres from the original villages and they were to be given brick houses, rather than the mud huts they and their forbears had constructed and lived in since time immemorial. It was calculated that a million large bricks would be required, to be made locally, out of mud, straw, cowpats and some poor quality concrete. To the men of Farabakouta was afforded the opportunity of proper jobs, though it came with the travail of making bricks by hand in temperatures often rising above forty degrees Centigrade in the shade.

Their village was seven kilometres from the worksite and, each morning and evening; it was possible to see a file of thirty or forty Farabakoutans going o and from their place of hard labour. I once stopped to pick up a few workers in my Landrover, only to discover it was possible to get the entire male population of the village into the back, on top, on the bonnet and hanging from the side of a three-quarter tonner! After that, I only applied the brakes when there were less than ten of them in a group. The only exception to this rule was when Waly Macalou was on the road, whereupon I would stop regardless. Waly was the younger brother of Mamadou Macalou, the Trade Union boss, and a terrible cripple. His disablement notwithstanding, he made it to and from work every day, albeit at his own pace. He had my profound admiration.

As the boys began to earn money, it became a status symbol to have a bicycle. In Malian terms, this equated to owning a Rolls Royce. Soon, the only person to be seen making the daily pilgrimage on foot was Waly, whose legs were too buckled to manage a bike. I encouraged the other non-South African whites to pick him up too and, by the time the job came to an end many months later, Waly had a lift more often than not. On occasions, Mamadou Macalou would call into my office to thank me for helping his brother and, a few months after the job finished, he called in to see me once again.

"I've come to see you about Waly," he said.

"Oh yes, how is he? I haven't seen him for ages," I replied.

"He died last night," he said, choking back a tear.

"I'm so very sorry Mamadou."

"He liked you very much Monsieur Wally and I thought you should know. In any case, you're the only white man who would care."

"How old was he?"

"Twenty-seven."

"What did he die from, Mamadou?"

"Who knows Monsieur Wally? Here in Mali we don't have doctors, or post mortems, or registrars of births, deaths and marriages. It could have been a virus or a fever, or anything."

I hadn't been so choked up since Leicester lost 1-0 to Manchester City in the 1969 Cup Final.

"Mamadou, I'm not a Muslim, but I wonder if you would give me the opportunity to show my respect, by letting me attend his funeral?"

"We buried him under the big tree at the edge of the village last night," he declared and left to grieve, his duty done.

If the locals working for SEMOS were anything to go by, then Malians are prolific when it comes to producing sons and heirs. Scarcely a week went by without an invitation to a baptism landing on my desk and, always keen to experience local custom, I invariably went along. Baptismal ceremonies conducted in the Moslem tradition were nothing like those celebrated in the Christian Church. For a start, they took place at 0600 hrs and were strictly a male-only preserve. Once all the members of the congregation had taken their places, anything up to half an hour late, the Imam and his acolytes would chant and pray in Arabic for ten minutes and then it was all over. All that remained to be done was to drop a sum of money on the Imam's carpet, slaughter a goat in preparation for the evening feast and head off to work. Since my salary was fifty times greater than any of these guys, I was probably overgenerous with my financial offerings. Forever the sceptic, I often wondered if this was the reason they invited me in the first place but, since no other whites ever appeared at a baptism, perhaps not.

The only time females were seen was before and after the service, when they came around with the coffee and bread they had been busily preparing. The men did the important job of sitting on their arses. Even stranger, only on infrequent occasions did the baby ever feature at its own baptism. I always made a point of seeking out the mother later, to tell her how beautiful her child was. This probably went against all accepted behaviour, but I was never challenged in this regard.

Unlike the South Africans, who had been brought up differently to me, I wasn't averse to giving locals a ride in my vehicle. As anyone who has ever spent time in Africa will know, no matter how isolated the place you're driving through, you will always find an African walking somewhere and hoping for a lift. Most villagers in our area used their paltry water ration for drinking and cooking; precious little could be allocated to washing and frankly, they stank, particularly when they were inside a vehicle. There were grounds, therefore, for drivers to be selective when picking up a hitchhiker. Strictly speaking, giving lifts was against company policy in any case; for insurance purposes presumably.

On the day of my family's inaugural trip in our new Landrover, we decided to travel along the fifty kilometres of bumpy track to Diamou. This track was the service road for the underground pipe carrying water from the River Senegal to the Mine. I made this journey on a weekly basis, on the pretext of visiting the half-dozen security men stationed in the village to guard the water pumping facility. In reality, it was simply a pleasant ride out for me and my family. We had gone only three or four miles when we saw a black chap walking, none too fluently, up a hill on the Diamou road. Despite avowing to ignore hitch-hikers in order to preserve the 'new' smell of our recently acquired machine, Nelia saw me looking at the limping man and pre-empted my thoughts.

"I wonder where he's going?" she said.

"Let's stop and ask," I suggested.

We pulled alongside the fellow whose limp, I was pleased to see, was caused by nothing more serious than a broken flip-flop and asked him in French where he was going.

"I only speak English sir," he declared.

He was Ghanaian and had walked from his home in Accra to Sadiola, in the hope of finding work at the gold mine. This was an immense distance, approaching a thousand miles by my calculations. Unfortunately for him, the mine was only permitted to employ indigenous Malians and so he was now walking to Kayes, in the hope of meeting up with some fellow countrymen. I told him he was taking a particularly circuitous route, but then he had all the time in the world. It didn't seem to matter to him if he was embarking on a sixty-mile hike, with only one serviceable flip-flop. We couldn't see the poor chap spending two days walking to Diamou when we would be there in a couple of hours so, smell or no smell, he became our first passenger. The poor chap didn't have a penny piece to his name and the plastic bag he was carrying contained nothing more substantial than a pair of underpants, a spare shirt and an enormous sponge. We had little in the way of alms to offer him either, although he made short work of the apples, coke and water we were carrying.

As it happens, the trans-Mali train stops at Diamou before moving on to the regional capital of Kayes, some forty miles further down the line. It would have been criminal to let our newly found charity case walk all the way, when a couple of pounds would have secured him a ticket. With not a sou in my pocket, I had to travel down to the house where my guys lodged and borrow the equivalent of a tenner in CFA, the local currency. With this, we bought our Ghanaian a ticket to Kayes and shoved the remainder in his pocket to buy some food. Then we drove off in the direction of the magnificent and yet seldom visited *Gouina* waterfalls, our original destination. On the way, we were suddenly overcome with compassion for this poor chap and returned to Diamou, with the intention of taking him back to Sadiola with us. I could probably have found him a job as a gardener and could most definitely have given him a bed for a few nights, as well as augmenting his meagre wardrobe. When we arrived back, there he was sitting in an armchair under the shade of a large tree. The next train didn't leave until the following morning it appeared and, in the meantime, he had hired an armchair to sleep in and would later buy some food. Despite my offer, he declined to accompany us to Sadiola. Our charitable actions were, he declared, the most overwhelming act of kindness he had ever experienced. He didn't want to impose upon us further. I often wonder what happened to him.

On a subsequent trip to Gouina Falls with Fily Mady, I elected to jump over a deep hole, scoured into the rock in a perfectly cylindrical formation by water erosion. In mid-flight, my eye was taken by something moving at the bottom of the hole and I went back to investigate. Peering over the top of the aperture, I espied a huge cobra trapped at the bottom. He was looking back at me, hissing, spitting and rearing up with his hood spread. The serpent gave the distinct impression he would sooner have been elsewhere. My guide, Mady, picked up a piece of rock and, like some modern day David (of Goliath fame), killed the snake with a single shot.

In the event of a foreign invasion, coup d'état or riot, the security manager of an expatriate company is the person responsible for producing an escape plan; hopefully a workable plan. Our plan at Sadiola was as good as any, although I doubt whether we would have got very far if the airstrip had been secured by baddies. Whilst in the process of rewriting this document, I began to ponder just how our locally employed workers would react towards the whites if things got out of hand. Our Malians were charming people on the whole, but then so are most Africans until something happens to make the hackles rise, whereupon out come the machetes and rubber tyres. I took the opportunity to consult my good pal, Sissoko Fily Mady, about what we might expect should the natives turn nasty. What he said made me feel very humble and, at the same time, glad I'd always done my bit for the locals:

"Monsieur Wally, there are some white men here who would surely be killed. There are also some Malians of high rank who would also be killed. In the case of you and your family however, nothing would ever happen to you. You have many friends here who would protect you to the end." How very reassuring.

Our single men were accommodated in a building previously used to house the mine stores. Puny plywood panelling had been erected to give each inmate a modicum of privacy, but without air-conditioning or windows, the place was oppressively hot and the majority of them chose to sleep outside in the open. The only hope of getting a through flow of cooling air was to open the wide doors located at either end of the building, but this only resulted in clouds of choking dust entering each time a vehicle passed along the adjacent Sadiola to Kayes road. To compound their misery, all the waste water from the ablutions and lavatories went into a cesspit located directly outside their billet. This shit-pit may have been adequate when six storemen used the facilities, but it couldn't cope with the waste of thirty blokes. It overflowed regularly and stank appallingly all the time. Occasionally a tanker arrived to suck out the sludge, but not regularly enough. I considered our block to be the place most likely to see the next outbreak of bubonic plague.

The engineer ultimately responsible for real estate was Dominico, the South African/Italian midget, who despised me with a passion. I despised him back, only more so. This made having improvements carried out at the Black Hole of Sadiola difficult to achieve, as the poison dwarf went out of his way to be difficult. I carried out an administrative assault of his repair budget on a daily basis just the same. A few bits of cosmetic cobbling and patching were addressed, perhaps because he was on a firm promise that, if the cesspit overflowed one more time, I'd drag him down there and throw him in. All this negotiation was done by means of memo notes, as we were still not talking.

All went reasonably for a while, until the lads really dropped me in the mire. The dwarf had actually gone down to the Black Hole at my behest, with the intention of finally spending some money on major repairs, only to discover one of the rooms occupied by a battery of French hens the lads were fattening up for eating. He flatly refused to dispense funds on improving the lot of poultry, and rightly so. Thereafter, he spent money only when safety was a consideration and even the shit sucker's visits became less and less frequent.

The situation took a dramatic turn for the better, when the directors of AngloGold came for their annual visit. The big boss himself appeared in my office, by mistake I'll warrant, as those not directly involved with the production process were seldom graced with such an honour. He tarried awhile nevertheless and walked straight onto a sucker punch, by asking if I had any major problems. He was rewarded with a volley straight from the hip and, after lunch, an entourage of important people paraded for the purpose of inspecting the Black Hole. It was a murderously hot day and the temperature inside the building made it almost impossible to breathe. The cesspit was suppurating beautifully, with the overflow extending beyond the fence marking the company's boundary and onto the main road. The big cheese was stunned, the General Manager embarrassed and the Poison Dwarf turned purple with rage. I'd nailed the little bastard. Within a week, a happy group of Asset Protection personnel gleefully moved into single, air-conditioned rooms, the standard of which exceeded their wildest dreams. The French for a cesspit is *la fosse septique,* which is a phrase I'm never likely to forget.

Life was sweet in Sadiola and it would take something, or someone pretty obnoxious to piss me off. It was a 'someone' who won the day; an arrogant, conceited, American school headmaster. My daughter was just three years old, but entitled to start kindergarten at the village school nevertheless. The school, which was run under the auspices of the 'American School' set up, had one teacher and a grand total of six pupils on a busy day. SEMOS was graced by a visit from the headmaster of the American School in Bamako, who would interview parents and the three infants wishing to join the classes.

When it was our turn, we entered the interview room to discover an obese, bearded individual waiting to interrogate us. He was sporting a badly wrinkled safari suit with huge sweat stains under the arms. His loud voice and aggressive attitude was enough to put me off and must have scared my three-year old out of her wits. Worse was to come. He insisted on interviewing the little ones without either parent being present! My daughter lasted barely a minute with the ogre, running back to us with tears streaming down her face. I was ready to clout the perverted bastard at this point, but was held back by my wife. Then, I really lost my temper when he declared he was not allowing her to join the school, on the grounds of her lack of maturity. How mature was a three-year old expected to be for goodness sake! The fat slob came precariously close to getting a hiding and the incident left me mightily angry.

Next morning I did something totally out of character, by complaining to the GM about this American shit. My complaint was the straw to break the camel's back it seemed, for the two other fathers had already been in to bend his ear about the despicable man. Shortly afterwards, to my unalloyed delight, this clown was relieved of his post.

Chapter 10

Part 5

Gold (Wally went to Ougadougou)

WE DISPATCHED GOLD on the same day each week. I won't disclose which day, as the mine is still operational and they may sue me if I do. Insurance regulations stipulated the product must reach the refinery in South Africa without ever stopping off in any other African country. Consequently, the gold went by Cessna from Sadiola to Bamako and then on Sabena Airlines up to Brussels, thence to Switzerland and finally, on a non-stop flight down to Johannesburg. Nothing ever went wrong and the gold always arrived at the right place at the right time. It was time for some leave and, by chance, we were booked onto Sabena instead of Air France. Our departure coincided with the gold run and so, for the first time, I was able to travel on the same aircraft as our valuable cargo. As the plane gained some height out of Bamako, I couldn't help noticing the sun. It simply wasn't in the right place! This plane wasn't heading for Brussels and the north, but to some undisclosed destination to the east, with my family and my gold on board. After a short period of time in the air, the plane began to descend and touched down at Ouagadougou, in Burkina Faso! I summoned the purser, to ascertain whether this detour had ever been made before. Imagine my horror when he revealed the service had been stopping at Ouagadougou for almost twelve months.

The fact that the Sabena planes now stopped in Burkina Faso would most definitely have invalidated the insurance cover for the safe carriage of several million US dollars' worth of the gold each week. SEMOS certainly wasn't aware of Sabena's change of schedule, neither were the purchasers, insurers or smelters in Johannesburg. My leave period was undoubtedly going to prove an anxious time for me; I would be duty-bound to report the facts to the GM upon my return and forced to tender my resignation. The fabled Payne good fortune was to manifest itself once again before the information could leak out however. On my second day back in the Philippines, I bought a copy of *The Inquirer* newspaper. Imagine my relief when the front page headline read, "SABENA GOES BUST." During my absence, Sabena's demise had become common knowledge and the company had transferred the business of shifting the gold to Air France. The subject of our bullion making an illegitimate stop in Ouagadougou for a year was never even raised.

No matter how much money a big company is making, the quest for savings is always ongoing. Combined with this parsimonious philosophy is the popular misapprehension that the jobs of the Security manager and the Health & Safety manager are interchangeable. They most certainly aren't; not if you want the jobs doing properly. When the H&S man went on leave, someone at SEMOS considered the cost of bringing a replacement up from South Africa to be excessive and nominated me to stand in for the three-week period instead. This pleased me no end!

As all the inspections and requirements for the following three weeks had been completed prior to Dennis' departure, there would be precious little for me to do—or so I was reliably informed. Dennis couldn't have been more than half-way back to his home in the Western Cape, before there was a huge fire in Sadiola Village. We weren't responsible for civilian firefighting of course, but since the nearest fire engine was stationed 50 miles away, a moral obligation fell on the company. On this occasion, the best efforts of the newly ordained fire chief were to no avail, as flames devoured half of the village.

The Mine Superintendent knocked on my door next morning. There was an urgent requirement to check the cyanide towers; they needed to be certified safe before the gold making process could start. All this involved was for me to don a protective suit and oxygen gear, climb up the inside of the towers, take samples of the cyanide and certify the area safe. This was a task Dennis had overlooked presumably. Well, there was as much chance of me performing this life-threatening procedure as Leicester City have of winning the Premiership. I refused the Mine Superintendent's request and miffed him considerably. His gold making process couldn't begin without a confirmatory certificate, signed by me and I refused point-blank to sign one. He told me he would need to suspend production and explain the position to the General Manager. I told him to go ahead; better the sack than a death certificate in my view. In the event, they fiddled the dates of the inspections and carried on regardless, until Dennis returned.

The Mining Engineer came into my office with a red-hot snippet of information to impart. During his morning walkabout, he had overheard a South African bragging about having seen some pieces of gold displayed in the bar the previous evening. Since gold in a solid state could only occur in the Mining Engineer's area of responsibility, he was understandably worried about the rumour and asked me to investigate.

The rumourmonger was a South African subcontractor, engaged on repairs to the sleimsdam retaining barrier. I found him up to his knees in sludge and, not wishing to soil my immaculate garb, required him to wade out through the morass to speak to me. This didn't please the objectionable individual one little bit and he refused absolutely to say anything about what he had witnessed the previous evening. Thirty seconds in his presence, however, was sufficient to convince me he knew everything about the display of gold and probably the names of the perpetrators too. In this obscure part of Mali, where the Gendarme chief and I had an understanding, compliance with bothersome Rules of Evidence, Prisoners' Rights and Judges' Rules weren't a requirement. Furthermore, as there had never been a reported theft of gold in the mine to date, it was imperative to get to the bottom of the matter without delay. I proffered the Boer a little advice:

"Let me point something out to you Mr van der Kerkof. You're not back on the Veld now; you're in a black man's land, where the Gendarme chief and I are the law. I'm confident you know all about last night's display of gold in the bar and, unless you give me the facts immediately, I'll have you thrown into the local cells until you do."

"Throw me in the cells. I'm telling you nothing," was his obdurate reply.

He'd made himself clear enough, so my two giant assistants threw him into the back of the Landrover and bumped him over the bush, as far as the Sadiola Hilton. As I showed him into his accommodation, he muttered something in Afrikaans, which I presumed to be extremely rude.

It was a very chastened subcontractor who emerged from the fetid cell next morning. On the understanding he would not be required to spend any more time in the Hilton, he promised to come to my office to spill the beans, once he'd had a much needed shower. He came as agreed and proceeded to tell me the most improbable, albeit wonderfully precise story about the three 'coloureds' involved in the gold theft. I allowed him to return to work, while I set about proving his testimony to be a blatant fabrication. There were only three coloured South Africans employed by SEMOS at this time; one was miles away at the Yatela mine, another was on leave and the third was a decent man who wouldn't say 'boo' to a goose. I sped down to the sleimsdam, bundled the lying toe-rag into a vehicle and took him to the administration offices. With the connivance of the Mine Manager, I contacted this featherbrain's boss back in Johannesburg and explained the whole incident to him. As his company did a lot of business with AngloGold, he knew Van der Kerkof's intransigence could have severe repercussions on his balance sheet. He asked to speak to his man. The sound of Afrikaner snivelling was hurtful to the British ear, so I repaired to my office and awaited the arrival of Van der Kerkhof. He apologised for his deviousness and promptly grassed on the culprits.

Armed with the low-down, next morning I crept into the Engineering department in the very early hours and broke open the locker of the main suspect. The water filled container in which the gold had been displayed was still there, as my informant had suggested. The metal, though, had been removed. No matter, I knew whose locker it was and he was the first guest to grace my office that morning. He was followed by no less than twenty others, all of whom were interviewed in regard to the gold theft over the next few days. The circumstances surrounding just how the gold came to be stolen were as follows:

Huge volumes of mud slurry, containing minute amounts of gold, were pumped around the plant through a maze of pipes that twisted and turned in every direction. Because the mixture was abrasive, it slowly wore away the insides of the metal pipes, especially where they went around bends. To prevent any gold bearing solids spilling out should the pipe fracture at these vulnerable points, a device known as a 'dead box' was fitted to catch any residue. Gold, being particularly heavy, tended to gather at the bottom of any faults in the pipe, of course. As soon as a pipe did break, an alarm sounded in the Control Room and the flow was stopped. Engineers then replaced the section of pipe, cleaned out the dead box and put the solids back into the system. The dead box could then be refitted and production started up again. It was a Standing Operating Procedure for members of the Security Department to be present to watch over the whole procedure, not least the return of any gold to the milling system.

When a pipe had fractured during the early hours of Sunday morning, a couple of streetwise South African subcontractors, in connivance with the control room staff, decided to omit the security department from the information loop. They would take their chances on stealing any gold present in the dead box. It amounted to a mere 22 grams and certainly wasn't worth the risk, but they took it anyway. Having kept the gold for a couple of days, even flaunting their booty in the bar, the pair set off for a goldsmith's shop in Kayes to sell it. They were accompanied by three other engineers, all of whom were aware that skulduggery was afoot. At a goldsmith's, the two main protagonists bought a gold chain, using the two small pieces they had stolen as part payment.

In a gold mine, theft of the product is tantamount to murder and connivance of the offence is viewed equally seriously. By the time I submitted my report, there were a lot of twitching bottoms around Sadiola. The normally taciturn General Manager transformed into the Malian version of Hanging Judge Jeffries and eleven vacancies suddenly needed filling at SEMOS.

Sadiola's open cast environment didn't expose us to the gold theft problems experienced by conventional mines down in South Africa. Unlike the deep mines, where gold came up in lumps, in Sadiola it was lying all around in the dust. The specks of gold were microscopic, almost impossible to see with the naked eye and equally impossible to recover without using modern mining methods. The locals panned for gold inside our concession area, but what they recovered was infinitesimal.

216

Despite some incredulous looks from the South African security bosses on their inspection trips to SEMOS, we simply let the local gold panners get on with what they'd done for centuries, as a goodwill gesture really. In the plant, mining was a new concept to the Malian workers and, as experienced and innovative gold thieves, they lagged far behind their South African brothers.

When the price of gold had been high, asset protection in the mines, whilst stringent, wasn't taken quite as seriously as it was now. Security was high of course, but plenty of gold still found its way out illegally thanks to increasingly inventive methods adopted by miners with a criminal bent. In these days of unparalleled low gold prices, especially as it was getting increasingly more difficult to get the stuff out of the ground, there were many mines where the difference between a mine continuing to operate and closing down could well depend upon stopping theft. Suddenly, asset protection assumed an importance never before considered and thefts were treated very seriously indeed.

During the mining of oxide based ore, as in Sadiola at this time, the only place where gold was to be found in amounts worth stealing was in the smelt house. This place became my second home and I spent an inordinate amount of time in there during the working day. Unfortunately, I spent a fair proportion of my non-working hours in the wretched building too. The smelthouse alarm system had been installed before my time, by a person possessed of a compulsion to ensure nothing was ever stolen from within its thick concrete walls. Not only did this warning system activate when the doors were opened to allow workers access, as it should have done, but it could scream into life for a multitude of other reasons, often in the middle of the night. Whenever it activated at night, then the smelthouse foreman, me and the duty mine manager needed to drive down from the village to the site to investigate. There was never a single incident to cause concern. During my time in Sadiola, however, the alarm was activated by thunder, lightning, excessive noise and an eclipse of the sun; not to mention frogs, spiders, praying mantises, lizards and a host of minor technical problems I really didn't understand. Was the system a mite too sensitive? I certainly think so.

I saw all sorts of magic security equipment on my fact-finding trip to South Africa and was much taken by the 'electric chair'. Immediately upon my return, I put in a bid for funds to buy this intimidating machine and, much to my surprise, was instructed to order one. The piece of furniture bore a remarkable similarity to the chair in which Jimmy Cagney went to his doom in the old black and white film, 'Angels with Dirty Faces'. Perhaps the locals had seen the film on TV Mali because, to a man, they were terrified of the device. It worked on a simple magnetic circuit system and erupted mightily whenever the circuit was broken by any metal object. Before leaving the smelthouse, everyone was required to strip down to a pair of underpants and sit on the chair. Any metal object on the body, particularly in the anus or rectum, would set it off.

The word was put around amongst the superstitious Malians that, should they attempt to conceal gold and the chair detected it, then a charge of electricity would shoot up their bottoms and kill them instantly. The rumour spread like wildfire. Not surprisingly, reluctance to sit on the machine was considerable, even among the expatriates. The matter went to the Trade Union, to whom I gave a safety briefing and demonstration, whereupon the workers were instructed to accede to parking their bums momentarily on the chair. Unfortunately, or perhaps fortunately, the thing didn't function properly in the severe heat generated within the smelthouse during a Malian summer and *la chaise électrique* gave way to more traditional methods of searching.

Chapter 10

Part 6

Social life

THE WIVES in Sadiola had precisely nothing to do and all day to do it. Life must have been particularly tedious for them. They had little Afrikaner clubs and societies of course, but my wife, being a Filipina, was classed as 'coloured' and therefore unwelcome. The colour barrier prevented two other ladies from joining in with this occupational therapy: the chief accountant's Rwandan wife and a Russian girl, who was married to a Malian and therefore *persona non grata*. No matter, the three of them made up their own social club and met regularly at our house. Nothing remarkable about that you say, but it taught me something most elucidating—women don't listen to a word anyone else says! My wife spoke English and several Filipino dialects, the Tutsi lady spoke French and Kinyarwanda and the Russian girl, only her mother tongue. Nevertheless, they met a couple of times each week and had wonderful conversations. Presumably it's something only a woman would understand!

The Moslem religion predominates in Mali, with more than 95% of the population adhering to the faith. In Sadiola however, Christians formed 20% of the skilled workforce of locals. This apparent disparity was a result of schooling provided by the 'White Brothers and Sisters', Roman Catholic monks and nuns dedicated to furnishing academic and theological education in Africa. Our Christians held a fortnightly service and we went along to make up the numbers, although listening to a mass said in Bambara didn't do much for me. To fill the Protestant gap, the Afrikaners started to hold a service at the home of an engineer and, when I heard of this, I volunteered my support. My assistance was declined; they preferred their meetings to be kept racially pure and only white South Africans were welcome! Forgive the generalisation, but this just about summed up this race of people for me.

The list of those believing themselves gifted enough to show their paces at the forthcoming 'Grand Talent Evening' included a magician, assorted singers and dancers, a whistler, an alleged comedian and an animal act. With the exception of a parrot of unknown antecedents, the cast consisted entirely of South Africans. David, our Cornish general manager, was of the firm conviction there really ought to be a British element to the evening's fare, to add some star quality.

David was a born leader of men, a fine general manager and a gentleman out of the top drawer. Whilst an enthusiastic vocalist, not by any stretch of the imagination could he ever be accused of being a good singer. He thought otherwise and was convinced his voice was indistinguishable from that of Andrea Boccelli. He sounded nothing like the talented Spic but, to this very day, I can't hear Boccelli without thinking of David. Our small English contingent included Graham Harris, another man who, like David, suffered from delusions of vocal grandeur. That left me, a person blessed with the ability to shout musically, to provide the minimal talent of Sadiola's 'Three Tenors'. Despite hours of practice, we still sounded awful. David was sharp and Graham flat, which left me hovering somewhere in the middle. For operational reasons, the Grand Talent Evening was cancelled and the members of the Angel Choir were, mercifully, never required to expose themselves to ridicule.

You couldn't grumble about the leave cycle. We worked for a hundred days and then had twenty-one days leave, which might seem very generous, but three months was about the limit of anyone's stamina in this location. The problem with being domiciled in the Philippines meant it took us two days to travel in each direction and, from my perspective at least, it took me a week to recover from the jetlag once I'd got back to Cavite. We would set out from the mine airstrip by single-engine Cessna in the morning and fly to the Malian capital, Bamako. After a day spent lounging around in the company's guest house, it was off to the airport for an evening flight on Air France to Paris, oft times via Nouakchott in Mauritania. As an odd aside, in Mauritania a crowd of Chinese fisherman, or at least they smelt like fisherman, would always embark on their way back to China. The plane arrived at Paris Charles de Gaulle at 0500 hrs, whereupon we needed to stay in the airport until the evening flight to Manila. How irritating to know there was a decent hotel only a couple of hundred yards distant, but we couldn't use it because my wife only held a Philippine passport and wasn't permitted to leave the airport. Then there was the small matter of a 15- hour flight to Manila to contend with; no wonder I was buggered at the end of the journey home.

There was another Englishman married to a Filipina at Sadiola and they had recently purchased a condominium in Makati City, part of Metro Manila. They had still to see the place and, as I was going to the Philippines on leave before them, they offered me use of the flat in return for a report on the fixtures, fittings and utilities. I decided to spend the first weekend of my leave there and let my wife get on with seeing her family. The condo was located on an upper floor of a hotel in the 'P. Burgos' area, a locality where one was more likely to run into a lady of the night than a Mormon missionary.

Waking on Saturday morning, I discovered the place ankle deep in water and needed to call management to arrange for a plumber. It took him no time at all to discover the problem; all the waste pipes were blocked, a remarkably common occurrence in the Philippines. It took him rather longer to extricate several pounds of concrete from the pipes however.

In the evening, I elected to walk down to the Prince of Wales and sip on a few gin and tonics. My co-tester was a lonely Canadian I encountered at the bar, a man whose capacity for G&T was far greater than mine. It was after midnight when I bade the friendly Albertan a fond farewell and wandered back to my quarters on the twenty-third floor. Having fallen asleep on the sofa whilst watching TV, I finally readied myself for slumber at 0200hrs. After a half-hearted fight with the dials, I gave best to the complicated air-conditioning system and lay atop the bed instead. The moment my head hit the pillow, I became aware of a shuddering sensation, sat up and roundly cursed Gordon's Distillery. The shaking wasn't alcohol induced though and it soon gave way to lurching, as the room tipped wildly to the left. I was convinced the apartment was about to tumble down hundreds of feet to the ground and that my end was nigh. Just as quickly, everything returned to the upright once again. Screams coming from elsewhere in the building made me realize the phenomenon wasn't peculiar to Graham's condo. We were having a severe earthquake!

Grabbing a pair of trousers and a shirt, I burst out of the room and made for the emergency staircase. Unbelievably, a group of Filipinos, admittedly somewhat aged, were actually waiting for the lift! I descended those 408 emergency stairs barefoot, three at a time, minus my trousers and at a speed that, to this day, has only been bettered by a swooping peregrine falcon. The emergency lighting kept going off, but this didn't stop my speedy descent in any way, not until I hit something hard on the third floor. A female scream indicated a collision with a slower runner and I'd knocked her to the ground. Bending down to help this lady to her feet in the dark and dust, I discovered I'd taken hold of her by the bosom. She didn't complain and as this might have been the last chance either of us would have to dabble, we decided to enjoy the moment. What a relief to reach ground level just the same. I sat in the middle of the road with the other evacuees waiting for the aftershock until around 0400 hrs, when a group of bargirls going home after the late shift gathered around me. Whether they were plying for hire or not I never ascertained, but they took compassion on the bleary-eyed, shoeless Brit and one of them rushed off to buy me a pair of flip-flops. How very kind of her.

I tarried a while longer, still waiting for the aftershock, but it never did come. At the same time, I was trying to summon up sufficient courage to ascend the 408 steps to recover my things, for there was no way the 23rd floor would see me for a moment longer than necessary. The lift was working again by the time I found the stoutness of heart to make an assault on the staircase, but I was disinclined to use it. Once back up in the gods, I packed my stuff and was on my way down again in record time. A taxi took me back to Pacita Complex, to what should have been the bosom of my family. Unfortunately, our household was battened down against the elements and not a creature was stirring, not even a mouse. Lobbing rocks onto our metal roof had the effect of waking the majority of our slumbering neighbours, but hadn't the slightest effect on my lot. Tiring of the noise of a presumed artillery attack, a neighbour preparing for the first mass of the morning offered me sanctuary and a lie down on her settee until reveille was sounded at No. 17.

One of my leave periods fell over Christmas and, rather than suffer another Filipino Yuletide and New Year, I took a flight to Europe. A connecting flight to Johannesburg took me all the way back over Africa and thereafter, a shuttle flew me down to Cape Town. In Cape Town I stayed at the Holiday Inn in Newlands, very convenient for both the rugby and cricket grounds. It was a fine place to stay and, by British standards, exceedingly good value for money. It was the only hotel I've ever stayed in where the wine in my room's mini bar seemed cheap. Most days I took a ride down to the city centre, by using the suburban train that stopped only a few hundred yards from the hotel. After travelling on this train for several days, quite oblivious to potential problems, one of the hotel receptionists made me aware of the dangers associated with this method of transportation. Apparently, there were incidents of robberies and assaults on a daily basis. Ignorance is bliss!

I found a travel company catering to the discerning voyager and, during one excursion, visited the small town of Franschhoek (French Corner). Apart from being a delightful spot, it was the original home of the persecuted French Huguenots who escaped to South Africa and therefore of interest to me. Above the town stood the magnificent Groot Drakenstein mountains, which were simply begging to be climbed. I checked at the Tourist Information Office and discovered that, for the princely sum of 10 rand, climbers were at liberty to ascend the mountains by using defined paths. A couple of days later I returned to Franschhoek in my hire car to enjoy a day's hill walking. For my 10 rand, the lady at the Tourist Office presented me with a Photostat map sheet, a card giving me permission to be in the area and some really, really duff information. According to her, from the start point it would take me an hour and a half to reach the summit of the biggest peak and a further hour to come back down again. She'd clearly never been anywhere near the mountain and her information was badly flawed. After three and a half hours, I was still ascending and nowhere near the summit. As you get older, experience and good sense sometimes override your determination to get to the top at all costs. I gave best to the mountain and stumbled down to the empty car park and my faithful car. I never saw another person during the whole day and was left, once again, to contemplate the folly of tackling scatterbrained adventures alone.

Other trips with the friendly travel company saw me getting very merry on a tour of the wine producing farms in the Stellenbosch region, as well as visiting the Cape of Good Hope. Two of my fellow travellers to the Cape were British; a doctor and his accountant chum, both of whom were 'lovely' boys! Having been a good customer to the travel company, the husband and wife team invited me round for Christmas dinner, where I rather spoilt the splendid celebrations by finding all the old British sixpenny pieces in my wodge of Christmas pudding.

Walking around Cape Town, I happened upon the Central Methodist Church. Its doors were open and so I wandered in. Two kindly old ladies were dispensing refreshments to the passing public and their offer of a cup of coffee and a biscuit were gratefully accepted. Before leaving, they invited me to their next Sunday service. The church was full ten minutes before the service began, which gave several fellow worshippers time to come over and greet the stranger. It wasn't difficult to notice the common thread running through the host of friendly faces welcoming me. The same thread ran through the faces of every single person in the chapel that morning— they were all black or coloured. The minister was a middle-aged man, sporting an outrageous Hawaiian shirt and a pony tail. His gaudy attire wouldn't have gone down too well at Methodist Central Hall, but he turned out to be an inspirational preacher. As a result of talking to him after the service, I was roped in to help with the street-dwellers' Christmas Day party and, on Boxing Day, he took me with him to visit the Crossroads Squatter Camp, where I dispensed toys to the little children. Both events were eye-opening experiences.

On my penultimate day in Cape Town, I finally found time to climb Table Mountain; no 'girl's blouse' cable car for an intrepid mountaineer of my pedigree. My South African acquaintances back in Mali had assured me Table Mountain constituted little more than an easy stroll, which only went to show how few of them had ever climbed it. I started out from the Kirstenbosch Botanical Gardens and, even as an experienced walker, found it a stern test. This wasn't altogether surprising, since the mountain stands 1087 meters above sea level. I certainly never expected to encounter sections where pitons had been hammered into the rock face to attach climbing ropes, not that I had any ropes with me, or even sufficient water for that matter. I was ill-prepared for such a long climb, but made it to the summit nevertheless. On the way down, I became very thirsty indeed but, by a stroke of good fortune, a group of Americans were making their way up and, without needing to ask, one of them offered me a bottle of water. There are a series of cross paths as one descends back towards the botanical gardens and, as I stumbled out onto one of them, I badly startled a hippie who was sitting on a bench contemplating his navel. As well as contemplating, he was drinking cans of Stella Artois and I felt duty bound to relieve him of a can, to sustain me on the remainder of my downward trek. Be warned; unless you travel by cable car and walk the last few yards, then Table Mountain is not a place for casual walkers dressed in trainers and shorts.

Some of the Afrikaners formed a microlight aircraft club, although membership was restricted; English speakers, coloured and blacks not being eligible to apply. I hadn't the remotest interest in joining, but made a mental note of the racial slur for use at a later date. They purchased three aircraft in South Africa and had them sent up to Sadiola, without making either the GM or the security department aware of the project. The first I knew of their activities was when they called my guardroom, demanding that the gates of the airstrip be opened to allow them to exit with their machines. Without a word to anyone, they had landed their microlites on the company's airstrip, a piece of real estate for which I was responsible. It was typical of the irreverence with which they treated everyone's interests other than their own. Our flight schedule seldom exceeded more than a couple of incoming and departing aircraft per day but, since they had no knowledge whatsoever of this schedule, they had committed a serious breach of security. What sublime indifference to the safety and even the lives of those arriving by plane! I forbade them permission to use the runway ever again and made more enemies. They still flew over the mine and surrounding area, but never used the airstrip again. Imagine a worst case scenario, where a microlight crashed into the cyanide tower, the office complex or, even worse, onto our beautifully manicured football pitch? I was able to scupper their whole enterprise some time later, by reporting them to a high ranking member of the Civil Aviation Authority. There were no regulations in Mali pertaining to microlight craft; nobody had even heard the term microlight and so, for a small financial consideration, my contact wrote to SEMOS banning all flights by this type of aircraft until regulations had been formulated. They may still be waiting.

We played a lot of cricket in Mali; on a pitch with rather less than a true bounce. Nevertheless, some intense and hard fought matches took place in the middle of what was, in reality, the football pitch. Initially, matches were billed as 'South

Africa v The Rest', until the Brits grew tired of losing every time. After that, just like at school, the two skippers alternately picked a man apiece until they were down to the duffers.

It was after one of these third class contests in Sadiola that I finally threw in the towel as a cricketer. For some time I'd realized my bowling no longer resembled the immaculate 'Payne line and length' of yesteryear. To be candid, only the unpredictable bounce at the Sadiola Oval prevented the better batsmen from making mincemeat of me. So bad was the bounce, I once saw a Canadian lady bowl her first ever delivery in cricket so wide, it had more chance of hitting the fielder at square-leg than the stumps. The batsman, a most able performer with the willow, shouldered arms with disdain. He then stared with incredulity as the ball pitched, hit a rock and turned through 90 degrees to clean bowl him. The following entry was duly recorded in the score book:

Pretorius b. Arnott 0

It was when the General Manager, a man not noted for his big hitting, hooked me for two consecutive sixes over square leg that I accepted my best cricketing days were behind me. A couple of overs later I was able to extract a modicum of revenge, by catching him in the deep. In taking this magnificent catch however, I fell backwards and hit my head on something very hard in the rock-strewn outfield. Enough was enough I declared; my career had come to an end.

My cricketing career might best be described as modest. It was marked by a solitary century in goodness knows how many hundreds of innings, only a handful of fifties, but some tidy bowling figures provided the opposition wasn't too hot. Alas, it will be as a result of one infamous incident that I'll assuredly be best remembered by the MCC. Wisden have always been reticent to confirm or deny the facts, but it's probable I'm the only person in cricketing history to have been sent off the pitch for violent conduct during a Leicester Churches' League match.

John Hunt and I were at the crease for St Augustine's in a match against Hinckley Road Methodists, when I skied a ball into the clouds. We had actually run one and were crossing back, when I saw a fielder still waiting to catch the ball as it descended from the heavens. This appeared to be an opportune moment to give him a tiny little nudge on the way past and so I did. As a result, he failed to pouch the catch and, in the ensuing uproar, I trotted to safety. In the meantime, John Hunt was run out at the other end and walked. As the first offender, I ought to have been given out for obstructing the field of course, but since John had gone and the laws prescribe that two players can't be dismissed from the same ball, I stayed put. This wasn't good enough for the guy who'd been bumped though and, for a small man, he became very aggressive. He was advised, in language probably unbecoming of the Churches' League, to get on with the game, lest he be smitten down. This had the effect of making him even angrier and I found it necessary to push him back to his position at silly mid-off, using the minimum amount of force necessary naturally. Just after I returned to the crease, there was an apparent eclipse of the sun. It had suddenly grown much darker and an appeal against the light might have been in order. The phenomenon had nothing to do with the heavenly body, however; it was caused by the shadow cast by their exceedingly large wicket keeper, who had advanced upon my person intent on continuing the battle.

"You threaten my brother again and I'll give you a good hiding," said the unsporting stumper.

"Oh yes, do you think you're big enough?"

What a foolish comment that was! It was patently obvious he was, but the words had already left my lips.

"Yes, I'm big enough," he replied.

"Well, you take one step in my direction and I'll wrap this bat around your ears," he was advised.

"Oh yeh!" he declared, as he took what was to prove his only stride in my direction.

My bat connected smartly with his left ear and he went down to stay. The umpire promptly dismissed me from Pitch No.8 and I decided upon an immediate strategic withdrawal from Western Park.

In theory, this should have marked the end of my cricketing career for a considerable period, as the League Committee suspended me for two years. In fact, I played scores of times during my suspension, by attending Melbourne Hall Church and calling myself Richard Dyson.

The topography around Sadiola lent itself perfectly to hiking; the sweltering heat didn't. Nevertheless, once acclimatised a little, I set off at first light on the first of my Sunday morning walks around the area. The first feature to catch my eye was a wonderfully weathered escarpment that was simply begging to be climbed and, by 0500 hrs, I was two-thirds of the way up its scree-covered slope. Suddenly, I happened upon a flattened out area that smelled appallingly and, at the same time, was struck with the sense of being watched. This was because I *was* being watched, by seventy or eighty red-arsed baboons into whose nest I'd inadvertently stumbled. The smaller animals and females made a run for it, but the dominant male and his lieutenants seemed intent on holding their ground. It took a roaring rendition of the Payne war cry, an utterance reserved for occasions when I'm scared shitless, to send them packing and leave me to ascend the increasingly steep slope without further ado.

This being a hard and rugged place to eke out a living, the majority of the wild animals in the area had been killed and eaten by the locals. Despite walking every Sunday and always unaccompanied in the early days, I saw precious little in the way of wildlife. My Malian guards were convinced a lion would eat me one fine day, but I never encountered *panthera leo*, or anything else with sharp claws. There were plenty of wild boar mind you. Some of them were bloody big things too, but if you gave them a wide berth they would patter away without a sideways glance. I once came across a large family of boar, whilst safely cocooned in my Landrover admittedly, and gave chase. The big fellow stood his ground until his family had reached a safe hideaway, before giving me a disdainful look and trotting after his charges. Wild pigs prospered of course, as the predominantly Moslem population wouldn't touch them. Lizards abounded, as did the hyraxes *(procaviidae)*, but little else. For the uninitiated, rock hyraxes, or 'dassies' to the Afrikaners, are small, furry creatures that scurry around between the rocks. They have a distinct rodent-like appearance although, according to my reference book, they are actually related to the elephant. That takes a bit of swallowing!

Snakes would have constituted my biggest danger, although I never saw one face to face until on my very last walk in Mali. On this occasion I was with my replacement, Bones Ketteringham, to whom I wished to reveal the joys of walking in this barren landscape. He had just enquired whether there were any snakes to worry about and, as words of emphatic denial left my mouth, we rounded a turn in the track to come face to face with a cobra. It was standing erect, hood spread and clearly in ill humour. We formed the opinion it was up to no good and beat a hasty retreat. I'm told this walk proved to be not only the first Bones made in Mali, but also his last.

My walking jaunts were made public, although it was a very long time before anyone elected to accompany me. The starting time was at first light, which may have been enough to put most people off, but it was essential if a challenging hike was to be undertaken before the heat made walking physically dangerous. One Sunday though, there was a taker—the very last person I would have expected to see. Although I barely knew the company's Belgian accountant, it was common knowledge he was a man not greatly beloved by the personnel working for him, or by those with whom he came into contact in the restaurant and bar. He had decided to get fit for the first time in decades and considered a Sunday morning stroll to be a sensible method of achieving his aim. When walking with me, he was soon to discover the word 'stroll' to be a misnomer. My walks were designed to allow me to stride as far as possible in the four or five hours available before it became painfully hot. There was no room in my walking band for those intent on taking a Sunday morning constitutional, nor for 'casuals'— plimsole wearing types, without rucksacks, water or vitals.

The Belgian proved to be my Tonto and was ever present, right up to the day I left the country. We were joined by others: our fairly regulars, the 'occasionals' and, the most common species of all, the 'never agains'. Despite having an Army map-reading qualification tucked away somewhere, under my directional guidance the name 'Sadiola Strollers' became synonymous with being hopelessly lost. I will confess to having made the odd error, but humbly suggest not all the blame could be laid at my size 11 feet. The only map sheet available covered the immediate area of the mine, whereas our hikes often took us onto the next sheet—except there wasn't a next sheet. Then the tracks never corresponded with the map and, if there was a magnetic variation, it wasn't noted on the map either. Come to think, it's a wonder our bones aren't still out there being bleached by the scorching sun.

The National Geographic Channel sometimes shows programmes about adventurers getting horribly lost in deserts, tundra and jungles. If our motley crew had been in possession of a video camera, then we could easily have added the Sahel to the list of places in which to go missing. Despite having to wade swollen streams up to our necks in the rainy season, having a Landrover stuck in the mud for a week, needing to stop a motorcyclist and steal his machine in order to search for our Landrover parked some miles away (the result of a small map reading error), suffering falls down scree slopes that ripped the backside out of many a pair of shorts and walking around in ever decreasing circles in the searing heat, we all lived to fight another day.

In the days when my only walking companions were the mosquitoes, I once set out for the village of Wala. The sole reason for selecting this minute settlement as my destination was that, in Tagalog, *wala* means 'nothing'. The tiny village was aptly named and, after introducing myself to the village chief, I paraded the half dozen village kids playing among the scrawny chickens. They were duly presented with the only gift I could offer; a single Polo mint apiece. It was a puny offering for sure, but the kids seemed delighted. Having climbed an escarpment behind the village, I returned an hour later prior to heading back to the mining village. The kids all came out to greet me and I could hardly disguise my mirth, as each of them had the Polo mint dangling around their necks on a piece of string.

My supreme act of trekking lunacy was to arrange a night walk from Diamou to Sadiola, a distance of more than thirty tough miles. A wiser man might have consulted a witch doctor before selecting a date for the walk, but how was I to know this would be the only moonless night of the year? Seven of us set out on the gruelling march, only three finished. To my eternal shame and massive loss of face, I limped into the back-up vehicle after twenty miles, with a pulled muscle. My plucky attempts to continue were futile; my body was trying to tell me something. Next day, I used my 'reoccurrence of an old war wound, but I don't like to talk about it' ploy as an excuse for my failure. It may have convinced the gullible.

There was a period when our regular group consisted of me, Tonto the Belgian and a French medical assistant from Paris. We would use two vehicles, with mine invariably parked at the end of our route. When we finally strode into the rendezvous, I would demand a chorus of 'God Save the Queen' from those of Gallic descent before they were permitted to get into my British-made Landrover. This met with some dissent initially, although when the alternative was explained, they saw it made good sense to comply and burst into song.

A group of seven well-dressed Malian strangers entered my office and slipped a sealed envelope over my desk. The alarm bells sounded. Was I being offered a bung to look the other way when we dispatched the gold? Then I realised their mission must have been kosher, or halal, seeing as they had passed muster at the main gate. Otherwise, the guards would have had them trussed up and boiling nicely in a pot by now. I opened the envelope and discovered it did contain a bribe, of sorts; tickets for a forthcoming football match.

My visitors turned out to be the President and committee members of Kaysienne FC, the Malian second division team from the regional capital. Their invitations offered grandstand seats to 'Mr Waly Pagne and wife' and 'Mr Gramme Horris and wife' at the big match taking place ten days hence, when Kaysienne FC would be entertaining neighbours FC Kita in the play-off for a place in the Malian First Division. I assured them Messrs. Wally Payne and Graham Harris and their respective spouses would be delighted to accept their kind offer. You get nothing for nothing in Africa though and, over coffee, the real reason for the deputation became apparent. It ran rather deeper than a simple invitation to watch the fixture. What they really wanted was to sign four of my players, to augment their team for the big match against Kita. They wanted my goalie Marka Dembele, the team's star Traore Siriki, playmaker Richard Gueye and defender Cisse Mohammed. It always struck me as incongruous that two of the toughest soccer players I ever encountered should be called Cisse and Gueye, pronounced 'sissy' and 'gay'. The lads were delighted to have been approached by a club with the reputation of Kayes, especially as they would undoubtedly have their palms crossed with silver to sign on the dotted line.

The stadium was in a deplorable state of repair, with a ramshackle stand running along one side and barbed wire fencing along the other three sides of the stone-strewn mud pitch. Only fifteen minutes before kick-off, the gallant groundsman was still vainly trying to mark out the pitch, with a malfunctioning line-marker. In the end, he resorted to taking a bag full of lime in his hands and sprinkling it as best he could. For our comfort, a dozen splendid armchairs had been placed in the stand and the English contingent was cordially invited to join the worthies of Kayes and Kita in these VIP seats. We were even plied with drink, non-alcoholic naturally.

Resplendent in their all blue strip, Kaysienne FC took to the field first and the partisan crowd of several thousand showed its wholehearted approval. The players from FC Kita were still kicking balls around outside the changing rooms, when Graham made an observation.

"Have you seen what colour Kita are playing in?"

"Royal blue, by the look of it."

"And have you seen what colour Kayes are in?"

"Royal blue, by the look of it."

When the referee called the team captains together, the fact both teams were attired identically appeared to pass him by. Put your glasses on ref! Perhaps he considered the narrow white band on the Kaysienne stockings sufficient to differentiate between the sides. He was wrong and I was soon sorry for allowing my players to get involved in this match, for it turned out to be an absolute fiasco. It was impossible to tell the players apart and the referee lost control within thirty seconds of the start. He was totally inept and a megalomaniac to boot. The match finished with only fourteen players on the pitch, four from each side having been dismissed and, with the exception of the two goalkeepers, everyone else had been shown the yellow card. As if all that wasn't bad enough, Kaysienne FC took a 5-0 thumping. It will surely go down in history as one of the most bizarre matches ever played.

Soccer is an all-consuming passion in Mali and our department already boasted a very decent side when I arrived. This couldn't have been attributable to Conroy, my predecessor, as he didn't know a football from foot-and-mouth disease. His insistence on recruiting physically fit individuals was to be lauded just the same, as our team were an intimidating looking bunch. The players must have been happy when they discovered their new boss possessed rather more than a passing interest in the beautiful game; even if he was determined to wean them off Manchester United, Arsenal and Liverpool, in favour of the mighty Leicester City. The team was to improve considerably under my encouragement and stewardship.

Our centre-half, skipper, coach, trainer, selector and backside-kicker of slackers was former Malian International Ambroise Camara, a man who was to become a close friend over the years. Our team's four-season unbeaten run was largely attributable to his ability and guidance on the field of play, as well as him having his finger on the pulse of everything to do with soccer in his country. Before news of an imminent increase in the security department establishment was common knowledge, I could be assured of a visit from Ambroise. He would produce a list of very decent players who would kill for the chance to join the Semos Security Department. Even top players in Mali were paid absolute peanuts and to have a well-paid job, as well as the opportunity to play soccer to a decent standard, would be the pinnacle of these guys' aspirations.

We won the Semos League and Cup double at a canter during the first two years and were well on the way to emulating the feat for a third season, when we became victims of some blatant cheating. It was child's play to 'buy' a referee, although if I'd ever been asked for money from an arbiter, I would have had no compunction in reporting him to the authorities. We were well able to win our matches without resorting to any form of chicanery. Some of the refereeing to which we were subjected during the third season however, went way beyond the pale. Nothing short of a compound fracture of both legs would induce a referee to give a penalty in our favour. Furthermore, our players were subjected to outrageous conduct from opponents, all of whom were secure in the knowledge that their amoral actions would remain unpunished.

Matters came to a head towards the end of the match against arch rivals, *Les Tricheurs de l'Administration*—The Administration Cheats. We were leading by a goal to nil and the opposition hadn't even been in our half for fifteen minutes, when my watch indicated the ninety minutes were up. The referee, however, despite being constantly advised to blow for full-time, had clearly been bought. He allowed the match to continue for a further 20 minutes, during which time the opposition had still failed to launch a single foray into our half. Then, with an outrageous sixty-five minutes having been played in the second half, an Administration player punted the ball forward into our goal area. With not a single opponent in our half, Traore Siriki booted the ball back downfield, whereupon the referee trilled on his whistle. To the stupefaction of all assembled at the Sadiola Stadium, with the exception of the opposition players and officials naturally, he awarded a penalty for handball. Immediately the penalty was converted, he blew for full time.

That evening, a deputation from our team came to my home and the decision to pull out of the league, thereby rendering the competition worthless, was unanimously carried. This caused consternation within SEMOS sporting circles for, as we continued to play against Malian first and second division sides, attracting huge attendances into the bargain, the league petered out into mediocrity. There was even a movement, led by *Les Tricheurs* naturally, to prevent us from playing on the turf at the stadium. Despite his total lack of interest in football, the General Manager showed uncharacteristic firmness, by insisting the football fiasco be drawn to an end. He believed morale within the mine was being adversely affected by the fact football wasn't what it used to be in the Mine League. I was required to assure him we would enter next year's competitions, which we did and, to no one's surprise, took the league and cup double once again.

With a solitary exception, I watched every single game played at Sadiola, whether Security were involved or not. Camara Ambroise called to see me a couple of hours prior the final game of my last season in Sadiola, suggesting I give the match a miss. The sly dog had arranged to throw the match against the team in third place; thereby allowing them to take the league runners-up spot at the expense of the universally disliked Moolman's side. We went down by a goal to nil, but I've never included the contrived result in our statistics.

In a side containing some top quality players, I must make mention of Traore Siriki. Football aficionados will undoubtedly recall the name of Paul Ince, the Manchester United midfielder with skill, drive and a will to win bordering on the manic. My man Traore Siriki not only looked like Ince, but was more skilful, equalled Ince's drive and was twice as hard as the overpaid *prima donna*. The tragedy was that Siriki could only aspire to playing in the Semos Mine League, when dozens of players with only a fraction of his passion and ability where earning millions in Europe's premier leagues. I went as far as making an appointment with Martin O'Neil, when he was manager at Leicester City, to enquire whether he would give Siriki a trial at my expense. Unfortunately for Siriki, my efforts fell on stony ground. FA regulations required foreign players to have international pedigree and to hail from a country ranked no lower than 70th in the FIFA order of merit. My star man failed on both counts—what a waste.

A year after leaving Mali, I was sitting in a cyber café in the Philippines when I opened an e-mail from Bones Ketteringham. It was to tell me Camara Ambroise had died suddenly, at the age of only thirty-nine. I wept unashamedly.

Quite where all the spectators came from to watch the matches at the Sadiola Stadium was a mystery. The entire male populations of Sadiola and the surrounding villages must have shown up for the big matches! Loving football as they did, especially the British Premiership, a good proportion of them took pride in wearing a cheap copy of an English team's strip. Manchester United proliferated, with Liverpool, Chelsea and Arsenal also well represented. On a clear day, one might spot the jersey of another side but, despite having scoured the touchlines at every single match, there was never a Leicester City shirt in evidence. Then, at the Engineers v Geology match during my fourth season, who should be crossing the pitch prior to the game, but a magnificent fellow sporting the royal blue of my favourite team! He knew me and, when he saw me approaching, immediately made for the touchline. I cut off the man who was convinced he was about to be nicked for something.

"Where did you get that shirt?" I demanded.

"I didn't steal it Monsieur Wally, I bought it in Kayes," he stuttered.

"Do you know which team it is?"

"No Monsieur. I only bought it because it was on special offer."

"How much did you pay for it?"

"Five hundred CFA."

I went to Kayes a couple of days later, to try and find the bloke selling Leicester City jerseys for fifty pence a throw, but he'd sold out and moved on.

The inaugural and only Sadiola Darts Championships, organised by a pair of dim-witted Boers who would have had difficulties with the proverbial 'piss up in a brewery', were held in the club. Starting in the early evening, the matches stretched on indeterminably. None of the inept competitors could hit a double to save their lives and the 'best of nine' games was a farcical format. Even with my very average ability, I actually reached the quarter finals, but scratched when the little hand reached two and the big hand twelve. I had a busy day to face on the morrow and needed some shut-eye. Apparently it was daylight when Billy Jacobs triumphantly raised the winner's trophy to the sky, by which time there was only him, the runner-up and the barman left to witness the occasion. As the editor of the *Sahel Baro*, the mine's tongue-in-cheek newsletter, I interviewed Billy in an attempt to ascertain his emotions upon lifting Sadiola's supreme sporting trophy. His reply may have lost a little in the translation from Afrikaans to the Queen's English, because he declared himself, "As 'appy as a pig in Palestine."

Chapter 10

Part 7

Farewell to Mali

I'VE ALWAYS been a vile tempered individual; the sort of person who doesn't bear fools gladly and who isn't slow to let folks know when they're annoying me. From the outset at Sadiola, I found the South Africans to be a truly aggravating race. Thanks to my British phlegm and the fact my salary was huge, I had been able to bear their ill manners for almost four years. Recently though, things I'd normally have shrugged off began to bother me. The first manifestation of my problem occurred when, for no discernable reason other than the fact he was a Yarpie, I bawled out a bloke who came into my office to have an ID photograph taken. Next day, whilst discussing the England cricket side's magnificent victory over South Africa with the H&S man, I suddenly could only make out half of his face. What was even worse than only seeing half of him, was the absolute conviction that my end was nigh. It was time to consult the doctor. The good physician gave me a thorough examination and declared me to be as fit as a flea. Notwithstanding the worthy doctor's assurance, it was clear to me things just weren't as they should be with me.

Walking towards the manager's office some days later, my back suddenly seized. Prior to this happening to me, people with bad backs were always fair game for my barbed wit. Let's face it; after the piles, a boil on the bottom, flat feet or an in-growing toenail, what could be funnier than a bad back? Following several days of constant agony however, during which time I couldn't stand, sit, kneel, or lie without suffering the severest pain, anyone so indisposed now has my heartfelt sympathy and compassion. The doctor insisted I see an orthopaedic surgeon at the earliest opportunity. He also hit me with a body blow, by arranging for me to see a psychiatrist at the same time. Now, I'll admit to having done some pretty daft things in my time and my impetuosity is well documented, but not for a moment did I ever consider myself certifiable. We were all covered by BUPA as part of our contracts and I had a choice of seeing specialists either in Senegal, or in the UK. As there is a BUPA hospital in Leicester, the choice for me was made easy. Leicester it was.

An orthopaedic surgeon saw me first. He diagnosed a fairly pronounced lumbar lordosis, narrowed disc spaces in my lumbar spine and degenerate facet joints. Lordosis is curvature of the spine and the diagnosis worried me for a bit, until I realised I'd always been a bit round-shouldered. The narrowed discs didn't concern me unduly, but to have my facet joints described as degenerate was a bit thick! He had me kneaded, somewhat painfully, by the Leicester Tigers rugby team physiotherapist, who declared me fit to soldier on. Since that day, I've never had a recurrence of a back problem.

Next came my appointment with the Trick Cyclist! Doctor Khoosal's surgery was tucked away around the back of the hospital. You can't have proper patients mixing with the mentally disordered now, can you? Despite the initial disappointment of sitting on an upright chair, rather than lounging on a leather couch, I consider the hour spent with Khoosal to have been life changing. He opened with twenty minutes of questions, which went along the following lines:

"Is there anything that irritates you particularly?"

"Yes, there is."

"What would that be?"

"My wife."

"That's simply a fact of life my friend, get used to it. Anything else?"

"Yes, bloody South Africans. They are the most arrogant, ignorant, self-opinionated, racist braggarts I've ever come across."

"I'm sorry to hear that. I'm a native of Durban you know?"

Then, without further ado, he told me exactly how I was feeling. His diagnosis was spot on. Mine, he opined, was a classic case of depression, brought about by a series of events only I could rectify. In a nutshell, it was time for me to take a long break from Africa. He taught me a couple of simple and yet brilliantly effective breathing techniques; gave me a relaxation tape and a book to read, before sending me on my way rejoicing. Doctor Khoosal's expertise didn't come cheaply; AngloGold paid plenty for this session and another hour long period a week later, although the psychiatrist and I agreed the second hour was quite unnecessary. Sound both of back and mind, I returned to Mali a few days later. Heeding the psychiatrist's sound counsel, I took the precaution of informing the GM that I was giving serious thought to tendering my resignation. At the thought of losing his table-tennis partner and the probability of needing to find a replacement editor for the mine magazine, he tried hard to talk me out of the idea.

Considerable reserves of gold had been discovered at Yatela, a village only twenty-seven km down the road from Sadiola. What a pity it hadn't been found a hundred and twenty-seven km away, whereupon a separate mine would have been established and life in Sadiola would have continued in its pleasing fashion. The avaricious directors at AngloGold, however, realised high returns could be obtained for minimal outlay by combining the Yatela and SEMOS operations. With no consideration whatsoever for the departmental heads, most of whom gave their all for the Sadiola operation, everyone was required to don a second hat. They offered not a penny piece extra by way of remuneration; an unscrupulous move by a company devoid of morals.

Unlike departments in the mine whose effectiveness could be ascertained from how much gold hit the refinery in Johannesburg, the effectiveness, or otherwise, of the security department couldn't be measured. Did the low crime figures stem from our not inconsiderable efforts, or were we just lucky? Whatever the answer to the conundrum, I gave every minute of my waking hours and burnt much midnight oil to uphold a high quality security service. There was simply no way I could take on Yatela and give a performance of the same excellence. There were many other department heads who expressed the same reservations about the extra burden, but when push came to shove, they all obediently toed the line. I told management they would either need to find me a second-in-command, or they could shove the job up their bums. The matter was shunted off to Johannesburg for a command decision. They offered me a deputy for a three month period, so I recruited my chum Bones Ketteringham and promptly gave them three months' notice.

There's only so much you can take of mud huts and bare-breasted women. This fact, combined with the company's decision to burden the SEMOS heads of department with Yatela, meant it was definitely time for me to go. The job of running the construction phase at Yatela had fallen to our previous quartermaster and, despite him being a good chum since my arrival, we were to fall out badly over the security of the new mine. For a start, they expected my men to live in mud huts, which wasn't acceptable and I made my feelings known. In an attempt to appease me, my lads were moved to a bigger mud hut. As if such a puny carrot would be likely to influence me! Graham had a huge task on his hands and it's conceivable

I did little to make his load lighter. In my view though, he developed something of a superiority complex as a result of having been elevated to the upper echelon. Our giant bust-up occurred in the club, on an evening set aside to welcome the top brass from Johannesburg. With rather too much drink taken and with inhibitions cast to the wind, Graham drunkenly declared he'd hatched a plan to catch out my security guards. I assured him he would do no such thing and a row ensued, during which his table was pushed over and he was threatened with violence. Being a Liverpudlian and, as such, inured to raucous behaviour, or perhaps because he was rather pissed, he didn't bat an eyelid. Since I'd given my notice, pursuing a career with AngloGold was the furthest thing from my mind, which was just as well, as my over-reaction had been witnessed by everyone who mattered. Early next morning, the GM came into my office and I braced myself for the worst.

"How's your head Wally?"

"Dreadful. How do you feel yourself?"

"Wretched. Quite a night though?"

"Yes indeed. I presume you've come to sack me after last night's escapade?"

"No, of course not! We're all rough, tough gold miners, remember. This sort of thing is bound to happen on occasions. No, I've come to see if you fancy playing table tennis tonight?"

I'd survived another bout of impetuosity.

Technically a Malian enterprise, SEMOS was required to adhere to the labour laws pertaining to the country. Whenever a worker over the age of fifty-five left their employ, they were required to pay him a sum of money calculated by some convoluted mathematical equation specified by Malian Labour Laws. The rationale behind this pay-out was simple; it provided the worker with sufficient funds to build himself a mud hut. It was certainly never designed to give the grossly overpaid expatriates another lump of money when they returned to their homelands. Nevertheless, as employees of a Malian company, we were legally entitled to this payment, no matter how immoral it may have appeared. The chief accountant called me to his office one day, to point out certain sections of the labour regulations. As far as I could tell from reading the French text, a sum approaching US$20,000 would be payable to me upon leaving the company's service. Now, Tonto was particularly well versed in civil labour matters and he assured me that, should I care to apply, then my application couldn't fail. Well, I did care to apply and, despite the best the dishonourable South African company's lawyers could do, they coughed up, albeit with extreme reluctance. Strange how they stuck to Malian regulations when it suited them, but not when the reverse applied. To prevent another Wally Payne screwing them though, all SEMOS expatriate contracts were rewritten to exclude them from benefiting from section 53 of the Labour Laws. Their remedial action was probably illegal, but unless an employee agreed to sign away his birthright, he didn't get a job in the first place.

As usual during the afternoons, the Mining Village was largely deserted as people hid away from the searing heat. As one of the South African wives was walking past the bungalow occupied by a Canadian engineer and his wife though, she heard sounds she later described as, "Someone screaming as if fighting for his life." After a couple of minutes, during which time she didn't dare venture inside the dwelling, the door burst open and two black locals emerged. Mrs Knud recognised them both. The houseboy Traore emerged first, hotly pursued by Diallo, the village tailor. Traore was bleeding profusely from wounds to the head and back and Diallo was doing his best to kill him, by slashing at him with a large knife. When they reached the driveway, the pair fell to the ground and continued to fight viciously. At this point, one of our pilots appeared. In his statement, the reserve South African police sergeant stated, "I was walking past the 'ouse when I saw two bleks fighting on the ground, so I gave them both a good kicking to make them stop." It wasn't the British way of doing things, but remarkably effective by all accounts. His action actually had the desired effect and undoubtedly saved Traore's life.

Two of my security guards arrived on the scene and one of them assisted the badly injured houseboy to the clinic. The other guard entered the bungalow, where he discovered Antoinette, the lady of the house, in a very poor way. He carried her down to the clinic and, unbeknown to him at the time, most certainly saved her life. Diallo the Tailor meanwhile, had disappeared.

It took me six minutes to speed up from the mine to the village, by which time both Diallo and Antoinette were being attended at the clinic. I went directly to the house to view the scene and could scarcely believe my eyes. It was like something out of a police training film, or even Cluedo! On the floor was a length of cord which, it transpired, had been used to throttle Antoinette from behind. Then there was a machete, a kitchen knife, a broken pick helve, a stout wooden stick and, the star item, a 9mm pistol with a round up the spout. The Gendarmes had primary jurisdiction over any police matters in Sadiola and, as this investigation would undoubtedly be of a serious nature, I called the Adjutant Chef and asked him to get up to the Mining Village with all haste. That gave me time to visit the two injured parties. Traore's wounds needed stitching, but weren't life threatening. The poor lady wasn't at all well though and the doctor's examination was hindered by the fact he didn't speak any French, whereas she spoke nothing but French-Canadian. I translated for him. As she explained where she was hurting the worst, I tried to ascertain exactly what had gone on in the house. She was aware she'd been throttled from behind, but didn't know which of the two men had tried to kill her. Before I could continue, the doctor insisted on giving her a sedative and asked me to leave my questioning until later. I never had the chance to speak to her again, for she never spoke to anyone else ever again! Having succumbed to some post incident stress disorder, she was struck dumb and finished up in a mental hospital back in Canada. Meanwhile, my lads collared Diallo and brought him to the clinic for treatment. Whether his injuries were inflicted by the houseboy during their fight to the death, or by my lads whilst affecting his arrest isn't clear and in any case, I wasn't inclined to probe any further.

Having finished his coffee and eaten his fill, after an hour or so the Adjutant Chef condescended to make an appearance at the scene. He appeared mightily disinterested in proceedings, apart from waving the loaded pistol around in an alarming fashion. I had everything photographed, gave him a detailed briefing, gathered all the evidence and promised him statements of the witnesses, before having him confirm that he would accept responsibility for all further investigations. Thereafter, he didn't hang around. I accompanied him to the clinic, where he arrested both Diallo and Traore and had them shipped off to jail in Kayes. He never bothered to collect the statements I'd had translated into French for him, nor the photographs; he never interviewed any of our witnesses, nor did he ever visit the scene of the crime again. This was a classic example of an in-depth Malian police investigation.

I was leaving Mali for good a couple of weeks later and enquired on a daily basis exactly how his investigation was progressing. His response never varied:

"We have the man who tried to commit murder in custody. My investigation is therefore closed and we are merely awaiting a date for the trial."

"You also have an innocent man in custody," I countered.

"Irrelevant Monsieur Wally, as we also have the guilty party. One day, the guilty man will confess and the innocent man will walk free."

Rumour Control within the village had, without any evidence whatsoever, condemned Diallo the Tailor. I began to tire of the deputations of do-gooder women coming to my house, all demanding something be done to secure the houseboy's release. Even if I'd had the inclination to fight his corner, jurisdiction was in the hands of the Gendarmerie.

My private summation suggested the following:

Departing for Canada on leave within a couple of weeks, Antoinette had invited the tailor to her house some days previously, to measure her up for some new clothes. He had required a deposit in order to buy material and had watched as she opened her wallet to peel off a couple of large denomination banknotes. The wallet contained all her holiday money, a sum equivalent to more than the humble tailor could hope to earn for many years' hard toil. On his next visit, in addition to items of clothing, he also had a ligature in his possession. When her back was turned, he throttled her almost to death, before running into the bedroom to rifle through her things in an attempt to locate her wallet. He failed. By this time, the houseboy had seen his mistress lying on the floor and came into the house armed with various weapons, ready to confront her attacker. The pair of them had then commenced their bloody battle. The loaded pistol however, remains a mystery, although I'm certain it lived in the engineer's house.

When I left Mali, both contestants were still in jail and still accusing each other of being the assailant of poor, innocent Antoinette. At the trial, they were both sentenced to long periods of imprisonment, which was more than a little hard on the innocent party. A year later, the guilty man felt compelled to confess and let the innocent man walk free. Diallo is probably the prison tailor by now.

On a leisurely afternoon ride out, I'd once driven ten miles or so along the poorly paved road running through Diamou in the direction of the capital Bamako, but no further. It was said bandits patrolled the route and attempting to drive a Landrover to Bamako would be a foolhardy undertaking. Just the same, I really wanted to see what such an adventure had in store. I found a volunteer driver, Mady of course, and submitted an application to make the road journey to Bamako airport for my final journey out of Sadiola. The GM refused the road option out of hand, but agreed to let me to take the train.

The train to Bamako left Kayes before sunrise, so Mady and I set out from Sadiola in the middle of the night. It would take two hours to reach the station. To my considerable surprise, there was a fellow security man aboard the train; the good Captain Sanogo had detailed Marka Dembele to accompany me to the capital, just in case of trouble. Marka was our goalkeeper and a veritable man mountain; who better to have alongside you as a bodyguard!

Having taken my leave of Mady with considerable sadness; I boarded the first-class carriage and promptly fell asleep. The first stop was Diamou, where I was awoken by a knocking on the carriage window. I looked out with bleary eyes, to see the police chief of Diamou and his men assembled on the platform to bid me farewell. It was quite a moving experience. Malian railways operate on narrow gauge lines and we never topped 30mph throughout the journey. After four hours, although we hadn't covered an immense distance, I detected the need for a visit to the toilets. What ought to have been a simple undertaking proved quite impossible. The aisles were crammed with people and, when I finally bundled them aside and reached the lavatory, discovered a family inside cooking their lunch. Marka told me the train would stop inside an hour, so I held on gallantly.

In the middle of nowhere, the train stopped at a station thronging with vendors. Marka informed me this was a regular stop and we would tarry here for a thirty minute lunch break. There must have been five hundred people on the train and, as soon as it halted, two hundred and fifty men sprinted towards a goat enclosure to relieve themselves. The women did something similar on the other side of the carriages presumably. I wrote to the Guinness Book of Records, to register the record for 'the most people voiding urine simultaneously', but they didn't take me seriously. Bladders emptied and stomachs filled, the train continued its sedate journey to Bamako, where we arrived almost on time. Just for the record, it was a trip I'm glad to have made, but would be reluctant to do again.

Next day, my family flew down to Bamako and I met them at the airport. The morning after, we returned to the airport and caught the plane for Paris.

The last four years had been very good to me.

Chapter 11

China

A YEAR PREVIOUSLY, I'd met up with an old RMP chum at Hong Kong's Happy Valley racecourse. He'd just taken up an appointment in the former colony with the security company 'Combination Eight', but had soon discovered Hong Kong wasn't the place for him. Not only did he find the place and people irritating, but he disliked his job with a passion. The abrasive and demanding nature of his Singapore-based boss was the last straw, but having signed a year's contract, he felt obliged to see the twelve months out. Knowing I would kill for a position in Hong Kong, Mark said he would arrange for me to replace him just as soon as his contract expired the following March. He was as good as his word.

Thanks to Mark's recommendation, the Regional Vice President (RVP) of Combination Eight (C8) contacted me just after the turn of the year. He suggested I travel down from the Philippines to his office in Singapore, so he could take a look at me in the flesh. My reputation had undoubtedly gone before me and his decision about my suitability, I fancy, already made. All we did for two days was drink beer and I'd landed a job with a famous company in ludicrously simple circumstances. My first impressions of both the company and its RVP though, weren't good. Despite having done nothing except prove myself a man not averse to a glass of beer during my jaunt to Singapore, the company's next move was to invite me to attend their Regional Annual Conference, to be held in Thailand a week later. Four nights all found, in a decent hotel on Koh Samui Island wasn't something I was about to thumb my nose at.

Everyone gathered at the Koh Samui hotel during the course of the day—to drink a few beers, chew the cud and steel themselves for the rigours of the forthcoming conclave. Making a carefully stage-managed entrance, the last person to show was the Regional Vice President, known to his area managers as 'Rottweiler Robin'. Most of his subordinates were scared to death of him.

The term 'annual conference' was something of a misnomer, I was to discover. Rather than being a forum at which planning and ideas might be discussed, the sole purpose of the gathering was to allow the RVP to hold fort. Throughout the three days of the conference, he indulged in the most painful self-glorification, gave full vent to his megalomania and belittled his weaker delegates most cruelly. Up to this point I hadn't signed a contract and, had he included me in his character assassinations, there never would have been a contract. The wisdom of working for this man was already giving me food for thought. His self-aggrandisement and loutish behaviour continued into the final day, when he was rash enough to hurl a weighty calculator at the manager of the Indonesian office. He really ought to have been able to make the simple computation he was asked to provide in his head, but the poor chap hardly deserved a large adding machine around the ear for his failings.

The Rottweiler took me out for a beer on the final evening and asked me how I felt about signing a year's contract as Deputy Manager of the Hong Kong office. In reality, I'd have done anything to get a job in Hong Kong and so agreed to sign the document; once he'd accepted that, should a calculator ever be hurled in my direction, it would be returned with interest. He would never be permitted to bully me.

The Hong Kong company offices were located at Sha Tin, up in the New Territories and had been occupied for many years by a firm recently acquired by C8. My official title was Deputy Manager, although the responsibility for the HK operation was mine. Part of the take-over agreement with the previous company had been to retain their long-serving Chinese manager. Despite his obvious limitations and piddle-poor English, it would have been unacceptable for him lose face by being demoted. Loss of face is a peculiarly Asian thing and hugely important, especially to the Chinese. There were barely a dozen of us in the office and, if balance sheets for last few years were any yardstick, the operation hadn't made money for a very long time. Unless I could turn this trend around, then my career here would be a short one. Rottweiler Robin needed a quick profit from the Hong Kong office, or his take-over decision would be seen as a serious error of judgement.

C8 was a fully paid up member of the Hong Kong Security Association and, as the Association's AGM took place a couple of days after I took up my post, I elected to attend and show my face. Hong Kong expatriates suffer horribly from delusions of self-importance, with security professionals being some of the most arrogant of the lot and the swell-heads were well represented on this particular Thursday evening. The meeting was chaired by an immensely tall lady possessed of an exceedingly authoritarian air; her four acolytes on the top table appeared full of themselves too. I listened to proceedings with supreme disinterest, until the chairwoman announced the results of voting for those required to serve on next year's committee. Horror of horrors, our company had been selected to provide a delegate to sit in 'top field' and that someone would have to be me. Having been press-ganged into sitting on a multitude of committees and gatherings whilst serving Her Majesty, I had solemnly vowed never to grace such an assemblage ever again, not under any circumstances. Before there was time for anyone to table a vote on the proposition, I arose to face the foe.

"Madam Chairwoman," I declared, "As honoured as our company is to have been proposed as a committee member for the forthcoming year, regretfully I must decline your kind offer. I have been in Hong Kong a mere forty-eight hours and know nothing about the association, or even the workings of my company. By accepting, it would be doing the association, my company and myself no service whatsoever. At next year's AGM, we would be happy to be considered for a post."

This brought about a scathing response from the chairwoman; a sleight that was hard to bear in front of such an audience. Summoning up my reserves of dignity, I waited for my moment and, as she was leaving the dais at the end of the meeting, I collared her. She was left under no illusion; if she ever dared to talk to me in such a manner again, especially in front of an audience, then I wouldn't think twice about slapping her in the kisser. She apologised unreservedly, but I never went near the Hong Kong Security Association ever again.

There's a strange postscript to this tale. The following evening I went to the American Club, to dine with my old boss Joe Champagne. During the course of the evening, I related the story of the previous night's clash with the tall chairwoman. Joe was desperate to know what she was wearing and appeared intrigued when I gave details of her flowery Laura Ashley dress, sensible shoes and handbag. My description of her flowing blond tresses however, left him agog.

"That's really most interesting, Wally. How I wish I'd been there," said the man from Connecticut, "You see, until very recently, SHE was a man. I knew him well in fact."

Actually, the 'lady' went up considerably in my estimation following this disclosure. I don't pretend to understand this type of person, but it must have taken some guts to turn up and face her associates of decades past dressed in a printed cotton frock, rather than a lounge suit.

It didn't take me long to realise that C8 wasn't my kind of security outfit; I was used to pipelines, deserts, ports, goldmines, people attacking installations and the like. My job here was to sell security guards and I'm not and don't ever aspire to be a salesman of any description. Thanks to some local contacts in Hong Kong though, I managed to pull a few strings and get some of our guys employed at sites around the old Colony. Nepotism counts for a lot in the security world, especially in Hong Kong, where there are hundreds of guarding companies vying for too few contracts. One valuable sale of manpower, which came about as the result of a complete fluke, convinced Rottweiler he'd employed the right man. Someone called up to speak to my predecessor, to tip him off that a large hotel in Causeway Bay was looking to change its security server. Armed with this intelligence and with the able assistance of a speedy taxi driver, I managed to convince this hotel's management to hire several dozen of our men before anyone else got wind of the opportunity.

Included in the host of Rottweiler's failings was the erroneous belief he could recognise a good salesman from a thousand miles distant. Well, he made a grave error in marking me down as a rising star. Mind you, it wouldn't have taken much to shine in this organisation, if the quality of the people I'd encountered in Koh Samui were anything to go by. In truth, the majority of my time with C8 in Hong Kong was spent playing with my computer, or wandering around visiting old chums. What real work there was to do was still being undertaken by the Chinese employees, with very little input from me. Someone was drawing his money under false pretences.

I had taken over Mark's flat, on the thirteenth floor of a decent building in Sha Tin. It was conveniently located for the office and, more importantly for me, was only a stone's throw from Sha Tin racecourse. Along with some pots, pans and cutlery of inferior quality, Mark had bequeathed me his TV set and its accompanying magic box. This wonder-working device enabled the selection of both local Hong Kong channels and cable TV too. I've never been any good at anything remotely technical and this TV and box were way beyond my modest capabilities. The matter came to a head when I wanted to watch an important soccer match and simply couldn't switch over to cable. Despite being almost certain of the sequence of buttons needing to be pushed, try as I might, the TV was stuck on a programme showing Cantonese opera. I resorted to Plan 'B' and gave the set a severe look, flicked the power on and off several times and was about to assault it violently, when my exertions were interrupted by the ringing of the telephone.

"Wally Payne, technical incompetent," I declared.

"Sir, I think you are trying to turn your TV set to cable?" said a distinctly Filipina voice.

"Yes I am, but how on earth would you know that? Who are you anyway?"

"I am the Filipina maid in the block next to yours, but on the fifteenth floor," she explained. "I do not have a TV and Mark used to leave his curtains open and turn the set a little bit towards the window, so I could watch at the same time as him. If you want to see cable, you need to press number eleven—you have been pressing number fifteen."

It wasn't Big Brother who was watching me, but his sibling Big Sister and, by golly, she was right. I watched the match as planned and, ever thereafter, viewed with the curtains open and the television set conveniently angled towards the fifteenth floor of the adjacent block.

Not only did this lady know how to adjust Mark's TV set from afar, but she knew his portable telephone number too. She took to calling me on a regular basis and we chatted about a good many things. Like so many hundreds of thousands of her kinswomen scattered around the world, she was the sole breadwinner for an idle family living a life of leisure back in the Philippines. Lackeying for an obnoxious and unappreciative Chinese family and receiving the minimum wage for being treated as a chattel was this poor girl's lot. She deserved better. Her calls to me were her way of escaping from the drudgery of ironing, cleaning, cooking and babysitting for eighteen hours a day.

As often happens when boy meets girl, our calls developed a somewhat suggestive undertone and it became apparent this was one very frustrated young lady. We continued in this telephonic vein for a while, until I demanded to see her in the flesh. She declined, on the grounds of being unable to escape from the gaze of her employers. Without having the slightest idea who she might be, it appears I was already known to her. Seemingly I'd walked close to her several times in the courtyard and had even passed the time of day. Since I spoke to almost everyone whilst crossing the precinct, the field wasn't narrowed much by this admission. During her next call, the brazen hussy chose to tease me about the fact I'd never seen her; whereas she knew the man available to her as a fantasy figure. She was presented with an ultimatum. Either she came to my flat before 0800 hrs next morning, or I'd never answer her calls again. A trifle harsh perhaps, but being kept at a disadvantage by a mere woman wasn't acceptable.

I was dressed and about to set off for work next morning, when the doorbell rang. On opening the door, I discovered a most attractive young lady standing shyly outside. Once indoors, she became overwhelmed with embarrassment, averted her eyes and seemed incapable of talking. She was invited to take a seat but, after just three strides, fell to her knees and performed an unexpected, albeit perfectly acceptable act. She wasn't in the same league as the great Gisela Strangemann, the gourmet gorger of Gelsenkirchen you understand, but then again, very few women are. Actually, I'm something of a traditionalist when it comes to introductions, a handshake and offer of a cup of tea being my standard operating procedure. This unorthodox opening gambit met with my approval just the same and served to break the ice in a most acceptable fashion.

She served her purpose for several weeks, until I tired a little of her harsh handling techniques. Perhaps she noticed my ardour cooling because, on her next visit to my bawdy billet, she was accompanied by a friend. Our *ménages à trois* were memorable and it was with some regret that circumstances forced me to bid farewell to these two cool operators.

Like most entrepreneurs, the RVP considered China the place to be involved in business and, to this end, C8 had set up an office in Shanghai. The chap in charge of operations up there was a retired British Army infantry officer. He was only a year my senior, but looked considerable older; something which had not escaped Rottweiler's observation. Furthermore, the former major had done very little in the way of business since the office opened its portals six months previously. This lack of success had irritated the ill-tempered Rottweiler considerably and, not being a man to bear failure gladly, he saw me as a readymade replacement for Borthwick. The old major wasn't nearly as inept as the RVP perceived him to be and he had certainly tried his utmost to get the show on the road. Sadly, his lack of presence and personality were indisputable; both flaws were considered unforgivable failings in the eyes of the Rottweiler. In reality, the biggest impediment to doing business in Shanghai was something way beyond

Borthwick's control; C8 didn't have a valid licence to operate in China!

Something even more irritating to Rottweiler Rob, more irritating than the company's failure to strike gold up in China, had nothing whatsoever to do with business. Despite his age and lack of personality, Borthwick had managed to bed the particularly attractive Chinese company accountant. The RVP had designated this lady to be a high priority sexual target and, unusually for him, he had drawn a blank. In line with his distorted view of life, this was another reason for the warped personality to dispose of Borthwick's services. The loyal Shanghai staff had gathered around the old guy and so, with the exception of the accountant who still caused the RVP's loins to stir, Rottweiler promptly sacked the lot of them.

He and I made a preliminary trip up to Shanghai, in the first-class compartment on DragonAir. Rottweiler's avowed intention on the first morning was to give his sexual opponent notice and announce my appointment. To really rub it in, he also promoted me to the rank of Managing Director China and gave me a sizeable pay rise. Having delivered the *coup de grace* to Borthwick, the RVP was insensitive enough to plan an afternoon round of golf for the three of us. Unsurprisingly, the old major declined the invitation to play and who could blame him? Rottweiler and I played regardless, on a links course many miles away from Shanghai. Despite leading by 3 shots at the turn, I managed to run out of steam and lost by a shot or two, much to the delight of my opponent. He did waft at a couple without counting them and then took severe umbrage when I pointed out his arithmetical failings but, as a big pay rise was in the offing; I took my defeat like a wimp.

A couple of days later it was back to Hong Kong again, this time to make preparations for a trip to Copenhagen, where C8's International AGM and bonding exercises were to be held. Despite imminent changes in the batting order, Borthwick and the Hong Kong Chinaman ought to have represented China, but both men proffered puny excuses for their inability to attend. It fell to me to grace the event with my presence, in the capacity of 'Managing Director China'. The reluctant couple's absence wouldn't have gone unnoticed; he who had to be obeyed would undoubtedly extract some unsubtle revenge at an opportune moment. Quite how much money the company spent on bringing its delegates from every corner of the globe, for what amounted to nothing more than a massive piss-up in a castle, defies the imagination. Nevertheless, I had a wonderful time at their considerable cost.

At C8's expense, my travels during a very short space of time had taken me from the Philippines to Singapore, back to the Philippines, then to Hong Kong, Thailand, Hong Kong, Shanghai, Hong Kong, Denmark and now back to Hong Kong again. All I had to do now was mess around in the office for a few days, awaiting the directive to travel to Shanghai and take up my new post. Most inconveniently, the call came on Friday evening, just as I was preparing to have a night out with my chum Lin. In fact, I was actually aboard a Kowloon bus heading for the Tsim Sha Tsui bars. My orders from the Rottweiler were explicit: travel to Shanghai with all haste and boot Borthwick out of the company offices and the apartment. Despite his insistence that the journey north be made immediately, I travelled up on Sunday evening instead. What was the point in going any earlier, only to hang around all weekend? The eviction notice could wait until Monday.

In a city with a population of goodness knows how many millions, what would be the odds on me spotting Borthwick doing his shopping whilst on my way by taxi to the company's apartment on Sunday evening? I arrived at the splendid flat to discover the keys waiting for me in the foyer and the place already vacated. Thus, any nastiness between the sacked man and me was rendered a none event. He was certain to think there was complicity afoot in this seamy affair, whereas I was totally innocent of any ill intent. We did meet subsequently and I attempted to convince him of my honesty, but he wouldn't buy it at the time. Later he did.

The entire C8 (Shanghai) team paraded at the office on Monday morning. Numbering precisely two; me and the sexy accountant, I considered our complement somewhat lightweight. With the rest of the staff having already been sacked, it seemed improbable that things could deteriorate any further. I was wrong. My first phone call of the day came from the Rottweiler.

"Where's that bitch of an accountant?" he screamed.

"She's in the next office, preparing some notes for me."

"She's been in touch with my boss back in the UK and told him a pack of lies. That's disloyalty in my view and I don't accept disloyalty. Sack her!" he said.

"If I sack her, I'll be left here all on my lonesome. Knowing nothing about the place or the job, I'd prefer to keep her for the time being."

"Sack her!"

"I'm the Managing Director here. In my view, we need to keep her, at least for the time being."

He could hardly contain himself.

"I'm the Vice President. Sack her!"

So, I offered the poor girl my profound apologies and sent her on her way. Unfortunately, with her went the computer passwords, safe combinations, keys, details of where we banked and where our records were kept. Now I was all alone and clueless in an office located somewhere in the Pudong area of Shanghai. I hadn't even discovered where the nearest toilets were, or McDonalds; hell, I didn't even know the way home. None of that mattered to Rottweiler; he had sacked the woman who had refused his advances and exposed his indiscretions to the C8 hierarchy. As far as he was concerned, all was well with the world.

By mid-afternoon, I'd had enough of the unequal battle. It was time to shut up shop, find a posh hotel and drink several beers at the company's expense. Before taking her leave, the accountant had kindly given me a pile of index cards, on which the names of locations were written in English and Chinese. Without the card bearing the address of my flat, I might still have been in the hotel bar to this day.

I'd only been in the office for five minutes on day two, when the phone rang.

"What are you doing in the office?" he demanded.

"I'm trying to piece together the chaos you've caused."

"You should be on the streets, wearing out your shoe leather and drumming up business!" he said, and then put the phone down on me.

What a twat!

When I called him back later, the Lord High Executioner gave me permission to recruit a lady who had worked for the company previously. Miss Zhang had been sacked by Borthwick for an alleged misdemeanour, so she was deemed acceptable to the RVP. The whole Shanghai situation was unfathomable but, with the able assistance of Miss Zhang and another new female recruit, I managed to blunder through and get a vague idea of what went on in the office. By having our business licence translated into English, however, a dark and very worrying secret was revealed. The company didn't have permission to sell guards in China! Our licence to trade permitted us to carry out security training and teaching, nothing else. I called Singapore to enquire whether Rottweiler was aware of this fact. Of course he was; he just didn't want me to know how badly hobbled we were when it came to doing security business.

"Don't worry about it, just do the business anyway," he said, from the sanctuary of his office 2,358 miles away.

"Listen chum; let's get something clear. I have no intention whatsoever of learning Mandarin from the inside of a Chinese prison cell. We must have a meeting up here as soon as practicable, to hammer out a strategy for this place. Failing that, I think you might want to get in touch with Superman, because he's the guy you need to run this place under present conditions."

He accepted my proposal and promised to spend a week with me in Shanghai, to put things on a firm footing. Despite the excellent salary this post attracted, my top class accommodation and an honest desire to stay in China, I sensed this whole affair was going to end in tears.

I went to the airport on Monday morning to meet him off his plane from Singapore and was stunned to discover he had a woman in tow. Even more bizarre was the fact that I knew her! She'd been at the AGM in Copenhagen, in her capacity as manager of business in Sweden. They booked into a plush hotel near the office and Rottweiler went to work—on the Scandinavian blonde. This bounder was supposed to be giving me the benefit of his experience and helping me to formulate a feasible China strategy. As it was, he never came near the office until Thursday morning.

He must have had a bad night with Pernille, because he immediately set about me in no uncertain terms. Now the way I'd sacked the accountant didn't meet with his approval apparently. She had wasted no time in reporting the seamy story surrounding her dismissal to the UK office and had included the fact that I'd expressed regret at losing her, which was the absolute truth. Following a sound bollocking from his bosses, Rottweiler needed to vent his spleen on someone and I was nearest. He accused me of disloyalty, something which was anathema to him, before booting me out of my office while he made some phone calls. Later in the day, from an enormous pile of CVs, he and I selected a group of people to be interviewed next morning for vacant posts within the office.

The morning interviews proved to be an ordeal, as Rottweiler belittled both the interviewees and me. Despite his undoubted ability when it came to selling security guards, he knew nothing about dealing with Asians and even less about getting the cooperation of Wally Payne. Following yet another sleight, I let him have a verbal volley. He sat in my chair, sulked and sent some e-mails. He paid me not the slightest heed as I went around the office, gathering my things together. Instead of eating lunch, I took a taxi to the flat, packed my bags and hired another cab to transport me to the airport.

The 7th June marked the end of my probationary period with the company and it wasn't by accident I'd chosen this day to make my escape. I called the Gauleiter from the airport, told him he had failed to impress me as a boss during my time with the company and that I had no desire to continue in his employ. For once in his life, he was stumped. Putting the phone down on him, I took the plane back down to Hong Kong and went directly to the office.

The Chinese manager was waiting for me in Sha Tin, with a cheque for considerably more than I was due. Methinks Rottweiler was well used to blokes walking out on him. He probably found it advisable to offer them a financial sweetener, in the hope they might think twice before spilling the beans about his conduct. Another of his frailties was the compulsion to lay the blame elsewhere than on his own doorstep. To explain the rationale behind Wally Payne's rapid departure from Shanghai, he circulated an improbable story around security circles in quick time. News of my nervous breakdown came as something of a surprise, both to my doctor and to me. In his view, this work of fiction adequately deflected any blame for the loss of his Managing Director China away from him. Well, thank you, Rottweiler Robin—archetypal coward and total shit. Just to cover my own arse, the whole sordid Shanghai story was passed onto the chief administrator of C8 in the UK. My story would certainly have served to corroborate the testimonies given by both Borthwick and the accountant.

I stayed in Hong Kong to consider my options and did some walking in the hills on Lantau Island. Whether my state of mind was still affected by the Shanghai shenanigans or not, I'll never be sure, but I did something totally out of character on one of these walks. With no fear of contradiction, I claim to be a very experienced and most safety conscious hill-walker. It wouldn't cross my mind to set out without carrying all the aids an experienced walker would pack as a matter of course. Since my plan this day was to walk only a short distance and in an area well known to me, the golden rule was broken and I went off ill-equipped.

My target was a clearly visible track only half a mile away, albeit on the other side of a steep, tree covered ravine. Descending the precipitous gradient, I soon realised how very hot and humid it was and soon needed to tuck into some water. My downward route was obstructed by thick vines, which made progress painfully slow and retracing my steps impossible. I continued down through the thickets at a snail's pace and then, disaster of disasters, falling backwards, my remaining bottle of water was broken. After an hour or so of extreme physical effort, it was clear I was getting nowhere fast and was in trouble. No water, no portable telephone and no coverage in the area anyway, no compass, no map and no likelihood whatsoever of any other walkers coming this way. At the bottom of the slope was a serpentine, dry stream bed, which I followed for what seemed liked hours. It was necessary to lie down every few minutes in an attempt to cool my body temperature, but flies and mosquitoes soon made moving on a necessity. Heat exhaustion was setting in; the associated symptoms of shivering and vomiting made this obvious. My rate of progress was pathetic, but the heat and lack of water rendered me incapable of moving any quicker. The fact I might not make it out of this mess occurred to me and panic was about to set in, when I happened across a slow moving stream of unknown provenance. Taking on what might be fetid water is of secondary consideration in such circumstances; better to have the shits than be dead is my philosophy, so I drank deeply. My vomiting was spectacular and I felt appalling, but at least my survival had been secured. Finally, having negotiated a waterlogged field with great difficulty, there, on the other side, lay a footpath, albeit not the path I was originally aiming for. Crossing this paddy really took its toll and it was an exhausted and sorry looking individual who lay on the path recovering for a considerable period of time. The walk back to my hotel was child's play after the rigours of the afternoon.

Next morning, I wandered along a track above the ravine that had proved so testing the day before. To my astonishment, the trees and thickets extended no more than thirty yards either side of the dried stream bed. A left or right turn at any time would have led me to open ground within five minutes!

Whilst still waiting to see what might transpire on the work front, a company in Indonesia contacted me with the offer of a short term contract. Mark, who had handed me the C8 position on a plate, was at work on my behalf once again. He did take the precaution of telling me he'd worked for this company before and wouldn't touch them again with a barge pole. The boss of this outfit was an Austrian, with an English accent adversely affected by spending rather too many years in the French Foreign Legion. His proposition was for me to travel to

Jakarta and take up a month's contract, writing Standing Operating Procedures at an industrial site.

"It's only for a month, but the contract may be extended," he explained.

"What are the hours of work?" I enquired.

"Office hours, 0900 – 1800 hrs, but I'd like you to be there at 0600 hrs."

"What's the reason for that?"

"Well, the site is a toxic waste dump located in a residential area. The locals start rioting at first light and you need to be there before it starts, just in case you have to control an emergency evacuation."

"What's the pay?"

"US$5,000 a month."

"In the circumstances, I'd need US$15,000 to take the job on."

"That's beyond my means."

"Thanks for calling. Goodbye."

Werner wasn't to be put off by my rejection of his first offer. Within a fortnight he was on the blower again, with another interesting proposition. He was looking for someone to manage a security team engaged in anti-illegal logging activities on the island of Sumatra. This sounded more down my street.

"What's the situation? What does the job entail?"

"It's reasonably quiet and the job involves arresting illegal loggers and handing them over to the police."

"Who's in charge at the moment?"

"Nobody, the position is vacant."

"Who ran the job before?"

"There were two joint managers, one a Swiss and the other an Aussie."

"Why did they resign?"

"They didn't resign, they left the site."

"They simply walked off the site?"

"I'll be honest with you. Their bodies were last seen floating down a river."

"Thanks for calling. Goodbye."

Ah well! Back to the situations vacant pages!

Chapter 12

Ferrar House

I'M PRONE to bouts of piety and during one of these periods, I resorted to looking in the *Church Times* for a post suitable for a man of my ability. To be perfectly honest, the realization that positions in the security industry might be difficult to find at my age may also have tempered the decision to cast my net wider than hitherto. Lo and behold, there in the situations vacant section and heaven sent perhaps, was just the job for me. Ferrar House, a religious retreat centre located in the tiny hamlet of Little Gidding in rural Cambridgeshire, was looking for someone to take over the running of the place. In response to my e-mail expressing interest, they sent me a rather odd job specification. Initially, it led me to believe they were looking for a navvy rather than a chap like me; a man of varied talents, although not, admittedly, in the religious retreat line. Having to get my hands dirty was never a hindrance to me undertaking a task, which was just as well, since cleaning the toilets, carrying dustbins and sorting out years of clutter were all part of the job description. It seems as though the bogs may have been a long-running problem at the house, since '**keeping the loos sparkling clean**' had been elevated to a chapter all of its own, in bold print.

In addition to the warden's obligations on the water closet front, keeping the house clean and tidy, making beds, doing the laundry, cleaning the kitchen floors and mowing the lawn were all considered tasks of some importance. Welcoming visitors, making coffee, taking bookings, handling daily cash income and keeping a check on shop stocks were the technical tasks.

The job description was obviously not penned by a person with military antecedents, since it went on to say: 'any ideas for the development of Ferrar House will be welcome' and 'there will be opportunity to help with maintenance of the property, if interested'. No self-respecting military man, of course, would ever dream of volunteering for anything.

A series of e-mails winged their way to and fro between the Philippines and Ferrar House until, at my suggestion, I offered to present myself to the directors of the house. I wanted to let them have a look at the aspirant toilet cleaner and 'general factotum' in the flesh. They seemed suitably impressed, although one of them, a man of the cloth no less, later confessed to having harboured suspicions about me. In his view, anyone inclined to travel from the Philippines to Cambridgeshire in order to serve coffee and perform the rest of the menial tasks, must have had an ulterior and perhaps even a criminal motive. His misgivings weren't totally unwarranted, given the numerous valuable documents and artefacts housed in the building and adjacent church. Just the same, they appointed me on the spot and at a salary which, although by no means a king's ransom, was higher than the amount I'd expected. I agreed to start work a couple of days later.

Little Gidding is one of three villages known collectively as 'The Giddings'. Little Gidding is undeniably little, Steeple Gidding has a redundant church with a steeple and Great Gidding, whilst boasting the largest population, was named by someone with delusions of grandeur. An example of the exciting lifestyle enjoyed by the residents of the area might be judged from the list of highlights advertised in the *Village Clarion*: candle making, papier-mâché moulding and the weekly visit of the mobile library. The monthly issue of dog clean-up bags, it transpired, was the most eagerly anticipated social event!

Little Gidding actually has an interesting history, although none of it was known to me as I reported for my toil. Back in the early days of the 17th century, a spiritually motivated individual by the name Nicolas Ferrar brought his family to the area, a place devoid of people and consisting of nothing more than a dilapidated Manor House and a church being used as a hay barn. The Great Plague had decimated the village in 1348 and, apart from a few houses reportedly existing in the village in 1566, it had been abandoned since 1594. Although Nicholas Ferrar died in 1637, the religious community he set up on the site in 1625 continued their work and worship, until what remained of the Ferrar family left the area in the 18th century. King Charles the First visited Little Gidding in 1642, just before the outbreak of the Civil War and spent a day as a guest of the Ferrar household. Unfortunately, Oliver Cromwell's troops also paid a visit some time later, sacking the place and scattering the members of the community in the erroneous belief they were Roman Catholics.

In the middle of the nineteenth century, a man called William Hopkinson acquired the property and set about restoring St John's church and the estate. He demolished the old Manor House, which had fallen into disrepair once again and constructed Manor Farm, the current day Ferrar House. The place gained prominence in more recent times when, in 1936, the American-born writer and renowned poet and essayist TS Eliot visited the church. The visit proved to be the inspiration behind him writing the last of the poems in his sombre 'Four Quartets', which is actually called 'Little Gidding'. By the mid-1900s the farmhouse and buildings became redundant once again, until they were purchased by Tony Hodgson. During the 1970s and into the 1990s, a considerable amount of work was carried out on the various buildings and the farmhouse became home for the members of the Little Gidding Community; subsequently renamed the

Community of Christ the Sower. This community dispersed at the end of the 1990s and its demise is still the subject of acrimony and much heated local debate. Since the departure of the zealots, Ferrar House had functioned as a place of retreat for those desirous of some peaceful and contemplative time in the Huntingdon Wolds.

Having settled into my humble lodgings on the first floor, I spent the first couple of days making an appreciation of the task ahead. The place was in a mess and there was plenty for the new warden to be getting on with. Nothing seemed to be organized and I made some suggestions to the directors, based on tried and tested military administrative methods. As it stood, nobody knew what was going on. A common goal needed to be specified and a plan formulated to achieve our aims. My ideas were well enough received, especially the weekly meeting I instituted to monitor progress and swap ideas. Simple minutes of proceedings were produced by me and most of the matters marked 'action to be taken' seemed to fall on the same person's shoulders. The weekly meeting felt like a good step forward, but it appears I was mistaken. On the day following the third of these weekly meetings, I discovered a dissenter in the ranks. One of the female directors came into the house during the course of the morning and, as a gentleman is prone to do, I rose from my chair and greeted her cheerfully. She ignored my cordial approach and strode past me into the kitchen without even deeming to acknowledge my presence. Clutching a cup of weak tea and breathing fire, she returned almost immediately to confront the Keeper of the Sparkling Latrines.

"Have I done something to incur your wrath?" I enquired in all innocence.

"Yes, you most certainly have," she snapped.

"Would you care to make me privy to whatever has angered you so?"

"You slung a paper at me during yesterday's meeting. That was both rude and disrespectful and I won't have it."

During the course of the previous afternoon's meeting, I had gone into an adjacent room to pick up a pile of papers that needed distributing. These papers, I then pushed across the polished table to each of the members. Under no circumstances could my action have been construed as 'slinging' and I told her so in a firm manner.

"Don't you dare talk to me in that tone of voice," she declared, "or you will be out of a job very quickly. I am a director of this house and you will afford me the respect my position demands."

My hackles rose.

"Madam," I replied, "you have no need to threaten me with the sack. You can stick your fucking job right up your scrawny arse! And furthermore, since I'm not bound by the strictures of the social strata you inhabit, let me tell you something else. If you ever talk to me like that again, I will have no compunction in giving you a slap right across your arrogant face."

With that, I donned my Barbour jacket and marched off along the lane leading to the Great Gidding road. I'd had my first dose of the snobby attitude prevalent among country-dwelling folk with loads of money; the sort who can't bring themselves to live in a house with a street number. They prefer living in Old Vicarages, Old Rectories and converted water mills, with nothing better to do than involve themselves in running charities and boasting of their patrician origins.

It was bloody cold out there, so I only walked as far as the top of the lane and put a letter into what was a definite contender for the nation's most isolated post box. Although still seething with anger, I was unwilling to subject myself to hypothermia for the sake of this haughty bitch and returned to the House, intent on packing my bags and looking up the flight schedules from Birmingham to Manila. She was waiting for me. This time butter wouldn't melt in her mouth. She offered an unreserved apology for her climacterically induced outburst and gave me a hug a Grizzly might have been proud of. Had I made a sexual advance at that juncture, I'm convinced she'd have let me take her over the seventeenth century font, there and then. For her though, it was too late. She was already, and irrevocably, on my shit list!

The minister responsible for the spiritual welfare of Ferrar House was a retired man of the cloth, a former canon at Ely Cathedral no less. He also held a non-stipendiary post as vicar of the Anglican Church at Hamerton, a village some three miles from Little Gidding. Although a Methodist by denomination, I considered it my duty to attend Sunday Morning Prayers at Hamerton and, by becoming a regular worshipper at this church; I effectively increased the congregation by twelve and a half percent. For whatever long-forgotten reasons, the church had been constructed out of all proportion to the size of the tiny village it served and could have housed several hundred worshippers comfortably. One would be forgiven for thinking a congregation of eight or nine souls might have been lost in such a huge building, but nothing could have been further from the truth. The regulars included an organist who, in her own words, could screech magnificently, as well as several members of the Huntington Philharmonic Choir. The sonorous sound of the songsters, combined with the voices of the rest of us shouting musically, served to produce a joyous sound. Like so many Anglican communities however, the tiny Hamerton flock seemed to do little to encourage new blood into the pews. In fairness to them however, perhaps they had already exhausted every avenue before I arrived?

The overall managerial set-up at Little Gidding consisted of five trustees, all of them toffs and each an alleged expert in some business or academic field. They formed 'The Little Gidding Trust' and looked after the small estate of six dwellings adjacent to the House, dispensing the resultant income to charitable causes. Ferrar House Ltd. was an independent entity, although one member of the Little Gidding Trust also sat as a director of Ferrar House Limited, along with another pair of worthies. They were responsible for the paltry amount of business transacted by the house. Now, even a lad with Durham mining village roots and a Leicester housing estate upbringing could see there was a mathematical anomaly associated with the set up. The 'chiefs' numbered seven, which left one solitary 'Indian' to do the work. This problem notwithstanding, I threw myself wholeheartedly into the task of sorting out the myriad of problems.

Trustees are a funny bunch and one could be forgiven for wondering why they take on such responsibilities. It's certainly not for financial gain for, not only are they unpaid for their labours, but can be held legally liable should financial discrepancies come to light. No, it's all undertaken for the perceived honour of being a trustee; something that's simply 'done' in the upper echelons. There might be some truly well-meaning souls out there I suppose, but from my experience, they would certainly be in the minority. Were it not for the fact trustees are the sort of people born into money and position, precious few of them would earn a crust in the real world. There I go again; letting my working class background emerge to haunt me, but I truly do despise snobs with a passion.

Since I was employed by Ferrar House Ltd, I neither knew nor cared about the Little Gidding Trustees, with one notable exception—Mary. She served on both committees and was a most decent, dedicated and hard-working soul. She was a good looking bint to boot. The remainder of the crew comprised a

276

supercilious lawyer from nearby Hamerton, a horsy lady from Newmarket and two others, who lived a good distance from the Giddings and never graced the place with a visit. Excluding Mary, the remainder were too old, too ill or too disinterested to continue and had reached the end of their useful lives as trustees. A few weeks after my arrival, the Annual General Meeting of the Little Gidding Trust was held at the horsy lady's stables down in Suffolk. Mary dutifully attended the afternoon meeting, arriving back at Ferrar House late in the evening. She asked me to help her unload some documents from the back of her car, a task that might easily have tested a gang of labourers. Once all the crap was inside, she burst into tears. The other four trustees had thrown in the towel, handed her documentation going back for many years and left her to get on with it. She didn't know which way to turn. I felt inclined to give her a shoulder to cry on, but managed to control the urge.

Now, if there's one thing at which you become particularly adept as an Army administrator, it's sorting out years of crap left behind by incompetents. Getting the better part of this mountain of paper sorted out was easy enough therefore; it was when it came to making sense of the accounts that I hit a brick wall. Nothing had been recorded for many months and apart from piles of documents and invoices, there was nothing to go on. Moreover, as the trustees had all thrown in the towel, there was nobody around to ask. Normally a devotee of the 'draw a red line under it and start again' school of military accounting, it was clear these books needed to be tackled rather more attentively. At some time they would be audited by the Charity Commissioners, whose methods were totally unknown to me. A pal with a hidden cache of Army swag provided me with all the necessary military accounting stationery and I transferred the whole mess of potage into workable accounts, albeit in a military fashion. After several weeks of hard labour I made a tentative trial balance and, to my astonishment, all looked well. What was even more remarkable was that the cash column balanced to within a few pence and the bank figures were spot on. The remaining trustee and directors of the House breathed a huge sigh of relief. Thereafter, both the House and Trust accounts became my responsibility, although my job description was never amended to record the fact. I was content enough to assume the role, especially since my pay appeared to have been increased by 25% when I received my end of month salary. I was in for a rude awakening at the end of the following month; the additional sum had merely been an ex-gratia payment. Walter was more than a little miffed by this revelation.

There were a host of things needing attention because, in its current run-down state, the house wasn't the kind of place I wanted to be associated with. There were two large rooms at the back of the building, each filled to the ceiling with a decade's worth of detritus. It took me a week to empty them out and then I needed to tip the dustmen generously, just to have them haul the mounds of rubbish away. Sorting out the kitchen took a couple of days, likewise cleaning a myriad of mucky windows that weren't opaque, as everyone thought. Then, with the connivance of an equally inquisitive director, I dug up several square feet of hollow-sounding floorboards, in an effort to find out what was causing the buzzing noise keeping me awake at nights. We found nothing and the buzzing conundrum was never satisfactorily explained; perhaps I was suffering from tinnitus after all, as one of the directors suggested? Blinds needed fitting to the bathroom windows, to prevent solicitors' letters citing indecent exposure dropping through the letter box. As it was, folk wandering abroad on the Wolds were currently afforded unrestricted views of those performing their ablutions. I erected a bird table on the spacious lawns and attracted a veritable profusion of wild birds, arranged for exterior security lighting to be fitted and had signs made, directing would-be punters to the house. In addition, I honed my skills as a top-notch coffee maker, washer-up (admittedly with the aid of a splendid dishwashing machine), Dyson vacuum cleaner minder, dustman, bed-maker, laundryman, hewer of wood and drawer of water, beast of burden, supermarket shopper, weed puller, grass cutter, carpenter, locksmith, painter and decorator, plumber and gardener. From being a guy without a single practical molecule in his body, I was rapidly being transformed into a genuinely efficient handyman. What's more, I was thoroughly enjoying it.

My introduction to plumbing came about when the industrial washing machine, located in a back room, began to flood the place out each time it discharged water. A former member of the Christ the Sower mob, the former laundress no less, assured me the water flowed out of the laundry room and into a cesspit located under the lawn. I had resolved to dig up the lawn, until a little research revealed an old plan showing that the water, implausibly it must be said, seemed to flow uphill to a sewer located on the other side of the building. Armed with an array of bamboo poles, scrapers and shovels, an inquisitive director and I set about the ancient pipes. Apart from nearly being sick as a decaying rat was pulled out of a pipe and getting the rods stuck every five minutes, the job of clearing the waste water outlet was accomplished inside a couple of hours. The canon, conspicuous by a pair of clean hands, proffered advice from the touchline, but was largely ignored.

My arrival had coincided with the annual migration of the Cambridgeshire Chapter of Cluster Flies from their summer habitat to their winter quarters at Ferrar House. Somehow they entered the roof space of the rambling old building and then set out to infest the upper floor in their tens of thousands. When they were up to establishment and paraded in regimental formation, it was quite impossible to see through the dormer windows on the top floor. The village's 'Controller of Nuisances' claimed to know a thing or two about cluster flies, probably through having been called up to the house each year since time immemorial. He fumigated the roof space every couple of days for a fortnight and killed flies weighing several pounds. It was all to no avail, as there were always thousands more in reserve. I assumed the role of Flycatcher General and found sucking them up in the vacuum cleaner to be an effective method of keeping the numbers down. Nevertheless, it was impossible to let these rooms to guests in the circumstances. We had every space twixt roof and rooms sealed by Arthur the handyman, hired the controller of nuisances to fumigate once again and I waded in with my Baygon in the mornings and the Dyson each evening, but nothing worked.

In the Fox and Hounds at Great Gidding, I discussed the subject of our infestation with an old rustic, a man who knew both his onions and his cluster flies. He maintained there was no way to control them once they had 'clustered' for the winter. The only thing to do, he advised, was to prevent them from getting into the building in the first place. I left a copy of the old man's instructions in the diary at Ferrar House when I left. It read: "Spray the south walls of the buildings with a diluted disinfectant solution once a week, from the beginning of September until the end of October." Following my acrimonious departure, it's doubtful whether those snobs would have taken the least bit of notice of advice left behind by a mere plebeian, no matter how relevant. I'll warrant the cluster flies still hone in on the house each winter.

The brick wall running down the far side of the Ferrar House lawn stood only ten yards from St John the Evangelist Church. Between the church and the wall though, ran a parish boundary and the care of St John's actually lay with those responsible for the Anglican church in Great Gidding, a couple of miles away over the fields. People who came to visit the church invariably came into the house for a coffee and slice of cake and, conversely, those visiting the house would always make a pilgrimage to the church. A situation to benefit both entities, you would imagine? Not a bit of it! A bitter feud existed between those responsible for Ferrar House and those devoted to the upkeep of the church. The reasons behind the animosity were shrouded in the mists of time, but were perpetuated by those in positions of responsibility nevertheless. These days, the main gripe concerned money. The St John's crowd felt, perfectly reasonably, that the house made money because the church drew in visitors. They wanted their cut of the cash. What they didn't take into consideration was that the money made from dispensing cups of tea and Jamaica ginger cake is minimal, especially when the number of people visiting hardly registered on the Richter scale. The truth was, the house lost money hand over fist, especially since I'd been appointed as resident warden and needed paying. There was no money to give and only the generosity of the Little Gidding Trust kept the house afloat.

It was me who took the first step towards pouring oil on troubled waters. Having seen four members of the church committee visiting St John's one morning, I scurried over and invited them to the house for coffee. Despite holding positions at St John's for decades, two of them admitted they'd never been inside Ferrar House before. During this chance meeting, I tentatively tried to start a little bridge building between the warring factions. The church was open from dawn to dusk, seven days a week and, can you believe it, people actually travelled from as far away as Cambridge to perform the task of locking and unlocking the door? My first step towards establishing some entente cordiale was to volunteer my services as 'Door Opener Extraordinary'. It took me a full minute to march from the house to the church, even when walking into the teeth of a howling Huntingdon headwind. They accepted my offer with apparent gratitude, although I'll warrant my unexpected show of charity provoked discussion. Actually, being the first person to enter the unheated church at dawn was a great joy. There is definitely something 'special' about this place, as generations of visitors will gladly testify.

When the house was occupied by the religious community, it was designated a dwelling house and, consequently, not subject to any Health and Safety rules or Fire Regulations. The place was now managed by a warden and used by paying guests, thus rendering it accountable under a profusion of government legislation. This fact was either unknown to the directors, or, if they were aware, they chose to ignore the fact. I brought them into the real world at one of the weekly meetings, having first prepared some unpalatable facts. The financial implications came as a huge shock. The burglar alarm system needed overhauling, Health and Safety implications would need to be considered and acted upon and, the crowning glory, fire regulations needed addressing. I arranged for a fire adviser to visit and give an opinion.

One glaring anomaly in the house's fire evacuation system caused the Fire Adviser to collapse with mirth. Those clambering down from the upper floor would need to stop at the first floor corridor and, as the flames licked around them, climb out of the window and onto a metal ladder running down the outside wall to the ground. This method of escape was particularly recommended for the aged and infirm! His assessment revealed the crippling cost of implementing even the basic work necessary to conform to Government regulations. It would be necessary to approach the Little Gidding Trust with a very large begging bowl.

With its religious history, Ferrar's connection to Clare College Cambridge and Little Gidding's association with TS Eliot, the majority of visitors to the house tended to be intellectuals. I knew bugger all about Nicholas Ferrar, whose tomb lay outside the door of St John's and less than bugger all about TS Eliot. Rather than have the guests consider the warden academically inferior, I swatted up on both subjects and was soon able to talk about either of the great men without making a complete fool of myself. In addition, as the dining room wallpaper was William Morris and always attracted comment, I quickly acquired a working knowledge of the Arts and Crafts Movement as well. Guests tended to be learned folk; some so wrapped up in their narrow fields of expertise as to be oblivious of what was going on around them. Others, whilst supremely gifted, possessed the ability to bore at an international level. Just the same, many had worthy tales to impart. The canon was a great help in every regard. Not only was he a brilliantly intelligent man, but he would dispense his knowledge willingly, albeit a tad too expansively on occasions.

Not every visitor to St John's Church intended to visit the house too, but I was an uncompromising custodian. Anyone darkening the church entrance, my doorstep, or even having the temerity to look in my direction was unceremoniously bullied into the house for coffee and a sticky bun. They were never charged a penny piece for their refreshment either; I simply pointed out the location of the donations box and left it to their consciences. This method, I discovered, had the effect of doubling our income from comestibles.

Ferrar House attracted its fair share of odd sorts:

In his desire for solitude prior to taking an important theological examination, a would-be vicar locked himself away in the Upchurch Room for three days. He was not only odd, but clearly impervious to cluster flies. I used to leave his food outside his door, rather like a prisoner on Devil's Island, and pick up his plates afterwards. When he emerged from his self-imposed isolation, he declared himself refreshed, happy and more than ready to tackle his exams.

Susan Farrar claimed to be a direct descendant of Nicholas Ferrar, despite the subtle change of the first vowel. That's as may be, but she inherited little of the fellow's brilliance. She claimed to be a violinist of note, but if the tripe she played on the CD I was foolhardy enough to purchase from her was anything to go by, then she most certainly wasn't.

I spent an entire afternoon chatting to a plain young lady, who was making a reconnaissance of the house with a view to spending some time there with her partner. No matter if they weren't married I mused, provided they were willing to stump up coin of the realm for the pleasure of staying at the Anglican Church's version of Fawlty Towers. Her partner was a priest it appeared; a minister studying at Clare College in Cambridge of all places. In these enlightened days, perhaps it didn't matter if they were having a bit on the side prior to tying the knot? What really stunned me though, was the revelation that her partner was a female minister! Perhaps it was the look on my face, but they decided to do what homosexuals do away from the House and my gaze.

An Australian vicar arrived with his wife and young children. He had the vision of setting up a religious community back in Australia and had come to Ferrar House to pick up a few pointers, in the false assumption the community was still in residence. His reference books must have been very much out of date, as the Christ the Sower mob had departed years previously. Several Sowers still called in from time to time it's true; to gaze longingly at the kitchen where they'd baked bread, or the storeroom where their printing presses had churned out religious books nobody bought. The folks from the

Antipodes stayed a week just the same and appeared to enjoy themselves immensely. The good reverend listened intently as I explained the situation at Ferrar House and he said something I considered particularly wise: "No matter how important a place or a vision, when it has served its purpose, there comes a time to let it die."

A couple happened by on a tandem, intent on some refreshment before cycling all the way back to Peterborough. He was a retired pathologist and his wife a practicing GP. They were about to sell up and move to Nepal, on behalf of Leprosy Mission International. I felt like putting my bike-clips on and going with them!

There are a surprising number of people in the country with the surname Gidding or Giddings, many of whom were driven to make a pilgrimage to the villages. There exists an improbable, but true, story about one such visitor. A lone motor-cyclist from the south of England, by the name of Giddings, found great inspiration in the place. Something affected him so profoundly that, when he returned home, he confided in his father. The teenager impressed upon his father that, in the event of a premature death, he wished to be buried in the graveyard at St Andrew's church in Steeple Gidding. A couple of years afterwards, he was killed in a traffic accident and, perhaps as he foresaw, his remains lie in Steeple Gidding churchyard.

There were some valuable objects in the house; ancient books, a unique font and valuable paintings. They were all alarmed, but the house was so far from the nearest police station, any would-be felons could have screwed the place, incapacitated the warden and been halfway up the A1 towards Doncaster before there was any response. The church housed some precious objects too; notably a rare brass lectern, which would have fetched a pretty penny in the USA. Those responsible for the church insisted on the building being open to the public during daylight hours. This was tantamount to begging to have the lectern stolen, as they seldom had anyone around to keep a watchful eye out for thieves. Whenever I was at the house, any visitors would be pounced upon immediately, if only for me to force feed them; but I wasn't always there. A couple of years after giving up the retreat house game, I chanced to call into Little Gidding for old times' sake. I found not only the church open as usual, but the house insecure, unoccupied and with the alarm system disabled.

My job description required me to be nothing more than a cleaner and bottle washer; any additional tasks were undertaken with good grace, but were by no means my responsibility. Taking minutes of a meeting was something I'd done often enough in the military and, since there was nobody nominated to perform the task at the first meeting of the new trustees of The Little Gidding Trust, I sharpened my pencil and honed up on my speed writing.

The meeting turned out to be little more than a stage for the dominant male to mark out his territory. The new trustee responsible for finance and buildings used the gathering to wield the sceptre and subjugate the rest. To this end, he was highly successful. The only minute directly affecting me was proposed by this self-appointed supremo; he wanted the accounts be audited by someone specialising in Charity Commission matters and I was in full accord. The resultant six-page draft of the minutes was, in my view, a pretty fair representation of proceedings, especially since those proceedings had been largely double-dutch to me. I distributed draft copies to the six members of the brains trust and awaited their response. Five of them thanked me for my efforts and a couple suggested cosmetic alterations to the record. The sixth, the financial wizard, not only tore my minutes apart in red ink, but pissed me off severely by sending copies of my massacred effort to the other members. He didn't need to do that. By the time the next gathering of the trustees came around, I refused absolutely to involve myself.

The next time this man seriously angered me was when he wrote to a lady accountant who specialised in matters charitable, inviting her to meet me at the house to discuss the way I'd cooked the books. In his narrative to her and copied to me, he wrote, "Wally is something of a dinosaur. You'll find him more 'quill and parchment' than computer." Perhaps he thought he was being witty; I thought he was being bloody rude and wrote back to him at once. He was made aware of his gross error of judgement in using me as the butt of his perceived humour. I was angry enough to 'bat his lugs' and told him if he considered himself tough enough to ridicule me, then he ought to come to Ferrar House at the earliest opportunity. I'd have showed the contemptuous braggart just how unfunny his ill-considered comments were. I ignored his attempts to contact me by phone for a whole week, before finally permitting him to offer his apologies. This dimwit's arrogance was to be the catalyst behind me leaving a place where I was most content.

At the time of my residence at Ferrar House, I don't suppose the three Giddings had a population of more than five-hundred between them, with Great Gidding being easily the largest—big enough to boast a pub in fact. Being in the heart of foxhunting country, perhaps it was obligatory for the hostelry to be named the Fox and Hounds. I paid a couple of visits a week and seemed to get on well enough with the locals, most of whom seemed strangely suspicious of the goings-on at Ferrar House. This reservation undoubtedly stemmed from the time when the house was run as a community. Happily, I seemed to be exempt from the whispering and was readily accepted at the pub, at Patel's corner shop and in the travelling library. To prevent me from feeling too comfortable with my status in the village however, I was informed by an old fellow that a newcomer couldn't expect to be fully accepted in the community until he'd been there for twenty years or more. My 'stranger in our midst' status was no impediment to them offering me the position of Parish Administrator just the same. Alas, circumstances dictated that I would leave this part of the world before the post became vacant.

Living alone at Ferrar House wouldn't suit a person of a nervous disposition. Some said it was advisable to put your watch back 200-years before you drove down the narrow road, with grass growing through the middle, to the house. The building stood on a ridge above the valley that sloped down towards the Alconbury Brook. It attracted the wind like a magnet and creaked and groaned alarmingly on occasions. The corridors were lined with old paintings of Ferrar and his family and, especially when you were in the place alone, the eyes seemed to follow you as you wandered along. Added to this was the odd buzzing noise, only apparent once I was tucked up in bed. I lost count of the hours spent creeping around the building like a spectre in the night, vainly searching for the cause of the droning. Fortunately for me, I'd spent eighteen months as the sole occupant of a really spooky place, the Officers' Mess in Edinburgh Castle, and was thus inured to living in haunted houses.

Despite the rural nature of Little Gidding, I really felt Ferrar House might be the ideal spot for me to take root. My wife and daughter came over from the Philippines to spend a couple of weeks and see how they fancied the place. Their arrival coincided with a deep depression over Huntingdonshire and it began to snow, blow and freeze. The little one was delighted to see snow for the first time, but enduring a fortnight of the worst our British weather could produce did little to endear the Huntingdon Wolds to them. Perhaps I ought to have brought them over in June, rather than January? At the end of their fortnight, they packed their bags and departed without a backward glance. To support my family in the Philippines whilst labouring for a barely adequate salary didn't make economic sense, so I reluctantly considered giving my notice. I was still in two minds about calling it a day, despite the excesses of the warped accountant trustee, until an almost irrelevant incident occurred to convince me.

One afternoon, I discovered a 'Post-It' note left on my office table, making me aware of the deficiency of a toilet roll in one of the ladies' toilets. It would have taken the author far longer to locate a 'Post-It' and write the note, than it would ever have taken her to walk into the conveniently located storeroom, pick up the bum fodder and put it into the lavatory—surely! That though, would have been beneath the dignity of a person born with a silver spoon in her mouth.

I was required to give a mere 7-days' notice and, as there were Bank Holidays on both Friday and Monday, I delivered my letter of resignation to the Ferrar House directors on Thursday evening. I then went to Leicester and didn't return until Tuesday morning. My letter wasn't well received and, from being good old Wally, I suddenly became *persona non grata.* Barely a soul spoke to me and I departed with my handover notes still in my pocket. The canon wrote me a farewell note and some of the astute priest's words probably summed me up perfectly:

"You are, I think, somewhat of a wanderer on the face of the earth—not necessarily a bad thing provided you remember the celestial city as your destination and that there are others with you on your pilgrimage."

Chapter 13

Arzew

HAVING THROWN IN THE TOWEL at Ferrar House, I flew back to the Philippines to contemplate my next move. Almost immediately however, a glance at my e-mails revealed a tip-off about an opening in Algeria. I contacted my former employers PCL and without doing more than chat briefly with the boss and forward a copy of my CV, I was on my way again; this time to Arzew, a small port on the north-west coast of Algeria. The exhilarating world of water desalination and electricity generation was beckoning.

Despite working on an array of different projects over the years, my knowledge of desalination plants was non-existent. This deficiency of understanding was of little consequence in the early days, since the site was nothing more than an open space and, in any case, it soon became apparent that our Japanese masters, Ishikawa-Hirabayashi Industrial (IHI), knew precious little about the subject either. An eminently respected company in the world of heavy industry, it's doubtful whether the Japanese economic miracle owed anything to IHI's performance as constructors of power production and desalination plants. To be fair to them, tunnels and bridges were more in their line and this was, I understand, their first bash at the water purification business.

The project had been running for several months before I arrived and boasted an expatriate security team of four: two men working in Algeria for 8-weeks, with the other pair on leave. The system is known as 'back to back' in the security game. Every two months, the arrival of a refreshed pairing was followed, only a few hours later, by the departure of the knackered, outgoing team. This left precious little time for a meaningful handover, especially as so many changes occurred during the two months away from site; each successive tour was, in effect, like starting anew.

The quiet, self-effacing, steely-eyed, considerate, charming, courageous Gordon ran the security operation[1] and I was his back to back. A former Lancashire policeman was Gordon's night man, with a giant called Miguel da Silva my partner in crime. I'd been called upon to replace a former French Foreign Legionnaire, who had considered one 8-week tour of duty sufficient to sate him of the Japanese work ethic, despite the considerable financial rewards the job offered. Ought I to have smelt a rat?

Da Silva and I saw very little of each other, which was just as well since the Portuguese/ Brazilian mongrel's swaggering, pompous, vainglorious manner irked me considerably. That the narcissistic young man possessed a remarkably well-developed frame was undeniable, but his prancing around in a pair of tiny underpants at every opportunity and compulsion to kiss his seriously bulging biceps whenever anyone was around to observe the perversion, I found somewhat worrying. When Gordon returned to site following my first two-month stint with the muscle man, I told him he would need to choose which of us he wanted to return. There was no way I could work in harmony with this character. Fortunately, da Silva chose to resign, thereby relieving Gordon of an awkward decision. Preferring the appearance of the arrogant Adonis to that of an ageing superstar would have been an easy error for our Japanese bosses, who knew the square root of nothing about the security game, to make.

---

[1] *Gordon insisted upon this selection of adjectives!*

Any self-respecting security man would have been astonished to see the glaring anomalies at the Arzew site; the most obvious being the exterior fence, which only extended along three sides of the enclosure! Then, the number of guards employed on the worksite numbered precisely zero! This glaring irregularity came about because the number of men required for policing the area had been calculated at the very start of the project, when only management and administrative staff were present in their office complex. Since then, construction had started on the site and the number of workers increased every day. Our guards, meanwhile, still only managed access control and their numbers had actually been decreased at a recent manning conference. When I first started the job, Gordon had asked me to phone him after a couple of days, to give my considered opinion on the current situation. During my call, I expressed serious reservations about several matters and discovered that we were in absolute accord. He was only too well aware of the problems and had tried, numerous times, to address our mutual concerns. The stumbling block had always been the IHI General Manager, Kendo Nakabayashi. Seemingly, the Samurai had been badly screwed over manpower by a British expatriate security team on a previous project and was determined never to have his fingers burnt again. Gordon suggested it might be worthwhile me approaching Nakabayashi, to see if a new face might convince him to give our department the necessary tools to work with. Gordon also asked me to broach the subject of the Project Evacuation Plan, a document of crucial importance, especially in a volatile country like Algeria. He had written the plan months previously, but it had been gathering dust on the GM's desk ever since.

I waited a week before arranging an audience with Nakabayashi, by which time I had a better idea of the problems affecting our department. In addition to the minor

292

consideration of the missing quarter mile of security fence and the paucity of guards, the site was as porous as a colander. Access was available to all and sundry, the site was in darkness at night, the few guards we did have were both inept and in collusion with the baddies; the electronic card access system didn't work and standing operating procedures weren't followed. In addition, the Japanese flatly refused to be subjected to the security regulations imposed on all other races, thus reducing the whole policing effort to a farce. There is a simple security adage, which, had it been implemented in Arzew, would have gone a long way towards solving the fiasco. That is, "Fence it, Light it and Guard it."

The GM spoke no French and only a smattering of English, but he flatly refused to use an interpreter when speaking to me. My first question was perfectly simple and a reasonable enough enquiry in my view:

"When might we expect the site to be fully enclosed?" I asked.

"No, no, no, no, no. You don't understand," he replied, answering precisely nothing.

"I understand all too clearly Nakabayashi san. Unless we enclose the site, there will be thefts on a daily basis. Mark my word!"

"No, no, no, no, no. You don't understand."

"What is it that you consider to be above my comprehension?"

"Fence very expensive. Not cost effective."

"OK. I will talk to you again on this subject when the value of stolen equipment exceeds the cost of installing a fence."

"Humph!" he replied.

"Since we seem to have resolved this issue, could I ask you about the Evacuation Plan? Is there any progress on its acceptance by Tokyo?" I enquired.

"No need for Evacuation Plan."

"What if we need to evacuate the site in the event of terrorist action?"

"Everybody got return plane ticket."

"And if the route to the airport should be blocked?"

"No, no, no, no, no. You don't understand."

This, I was to discover, was his standard response to any question he was incapable of answering, or didn't want to answer. Like Gordon before me, I left his office confused, frustrated and more than a little annoyed.

Our remit in Algeria was to offer security advice, with both Gordon and me well qualified to proffer counselling about living in and, more importantly, surviving in shitholes like Algeria. We each had experience in Algeria itself, as well as knowing our way around many of the world's less hospitable countries. Our Japanese masters, though, were disinclined to listen to our sagacious suggestions.

Everyone's contract specified bachelor status as a strict condition of employment. Why then, did sub-contractor Mr Coulls arrive with his memsahib and live in marital bliss throughout his contract? Another rider to contracts dictated that travel to and from Oran must be made by scheduled flights on Air Algérie. One member of the supervising engineers blithely used the Oran-Alicante ferry whenever he travelled and continued to do so, until he was sacked for an unrelated reason. Many sub-contractors booked their consultants into 5-star hotels adjacent to the airport, rather than have them suffer the rigours of the residential camps and then allowed them to travel up to site by taxi, or hire car. My written reports about these dangerous diversions from security regulations were blatantly ignored by Japanese management. A truly bad example was being set by people in positions of responsibility, the very people who should have known better. The Japs would have done well to adopt the Royal Military Police motto to get them on the right track. *Exemplo Ducemus*—by example we lead. As time went by Gordon and I agreed that, as long as we gave pertinent advice and documented the fact, then if they chose to ignore it, we couldn't really give a damn.

Just the same, the question of the fence demanded a resolution and I arranged for the subject to be raised at a meeting of Heads of Departments. I tried to explain just how much stuff was being stolen simply because the site wasn't secure and how easy it was to enter the area, even in a lorry. With more and more valuable items arriving on site each day, I suggested that the prognosis for the future was bleak. What an abject waste of time!

Nakabayashi deemed to respond to my futile efforts to make them see sense.

"Anyway Payne san, fence no good. You say so yourself."

"I said no such thing!"

"You say Ari Baba can easiry cut fence with wire cutter."

"Not if you put 20,000 volts through it!"

He thought about this for a moment before adding, "You try be humorous?"

"Given the scintillating sense of humour displayed by you and your fellow kinsmen, I fear any attempt to add a jocular air to this conversation would be a forlorn undertaking. To put it in the British military vernacular Nakabayshi san, 'If wit was shit, you lot would be severely constipated'."

"No understand."

"Yes, I am trying to be humorous and, by all accounts, failing miserably."

"Ah so! No try be humorous prease, this serious matter."

"You could have fooled me."

Any perspicacious person could see what was wrong with the security in Arzew, but not the Japanese seemingly. I'd had enough of this meeting and so, amid much Nippon mumbling, took my leave of those assembled.

A few days later, I decided to make one last effort to get the GM to talk some sense about the Evacuation Plan. There were several important points that simply had to be resolved; otherwise the draft would never become a viable plan. My first question was:

"Who is responsible for purchasing boat or aeroplane tickets in the event of an evacuation?"

"No, no, no, no, no. You don't understand. All people got return ticket from Oran to Paris."

"You and your Japanese compatriots may have return airline tickets from Oran to Paris. The Turks, Indians, Malays, Chinese and Wally Payne don't."

"Subcontractor must buy own ticket."

"Have they been made aware of this? I don't think so."

"Tell subcontractor must buy ticket. You write letter."

"Nakabayashi san. In the event of trouble here, do you really imagine the fifteen hundred expatriate workers will simply be able to drive down to Oran and board a plane?"

"No, no, no, no, no. You don't understand."

"Thank you for your invaluable assistance sir, you've made everything crystal clear."

The Evacuation Plan was consigned to an office drawer, where it stayed until our contract finished.

We were billeted in Camp 10, alongside the regimented Japs and other expatriates of diverse provenance. The camp also housed a squadron of Algerian Gendarmes, whose task was to escort our convoys and provide small arms cover. Left to the elements, this miserable piece of real estate would have reverted to desert within a year. The buildings might have been good by Algerian standards when they were constructed as temporary accommodation by the Yanks 25-years previously, but now they were insanitary hovels. The quarters, extravagantly referred to as villas, still needed fumigating regularly to control insects and assorted nasty things that wandered abroad, while a resident pride of feral cats were tolerated to keep the vermin at bay. The uphill battle of keeping the billets habitable was down to Jacques, the Mauritian camp manager, who must have had the worries of the world on his narrow shoulders. I'd actually come across Jacques previously, when he was our supermarket manager down in Mali. The expatriate world is exceedingly small on occasions.

With its double row of savage barbed wire fences, watchtowers, security lighting and CCTV cameras, Camp 10 might have given a visitor the illusion of sanctuary. Financial restraints imposed by the cheese-paring Japanese meant the place was anything but secure, however. There were insufficient guards to man the watchtowers, no means of communication existed, light bulbs were seldom replaced, the CCTV system was forever malfunctioning and the generators only provided electricity intermittently. Furthermore, the guards were paid a pittance and, consequently, were poorly motivated, ill-equipped, often hungry and either freezing or suffering from savage heat, depending on the season. It broke my heart to see these men scrabbling around in dustbins looking for scraps to eat, when so much was thrown away by the camp kitchen staff. The niggardly Japanese, though, preferred to sell the excess food as animal fodder, rather than give it away to deserving causes. That, after all, might have exposed them to accusations of benevolence, which simply wouldn't do. We did our best to provide sustenance for the guards and, in the time-honoured British Army tradition, we 'found' equipment, food and clothing that hadn't yet been lost. Just the same, our men remained a shambles and I was grateful for the presence of the armed gendarmes. As shabby and inefficient as they were, at least each man was equipped with a Kalashnikov.

The majority of the Japanese seemed perfectly content to work, eat and sleep their four-month tours of duty away. Consequently, there was nothing in the way of amusement in Camp 10, although Gordon had installed cable TV in our villa and this helped keep us informed and sane. It even took the management a full year to decide upon opening a bar. Even then, you needed to purchase beer chits from the administration office beforehand, or you went thirsty. Without the Europeans and a small, stalwart band of young Japanese, the place need not have been there at all. The fortnightly whisky and beer issue showed the Japs in a different light however. The undisciplined charge to the store room, where brave volunteers dispensed the bottles, indicated considerable clandestine in-house alcohol consumption.

The restaurant, wherein noodles, boiled rice and raw fish ruled supreme, was the domain of a machete-wielding Japanese chef. His assistant was an Algerian, a man much beloved, both for his pleasant demeanour and excellence with a wok. He won the trust of the head chef and, on the occasions when his boss was having a snooze or getting his leg over with a chalet maid, he was entrusted with the store keys. Quite how much swag he stole before he was finally caught by the camp manager is debatable, but he left without a whimper when dismissed. He also coughed to the theft of several dozen bottles of whisky, but since an investigation would have exposed some lax administrative accounting, I was instructed not to pursue the matter.

I'd never met any Japanese before, but had heard about their voracious appetite for work. Setting out for the site each day at 0630 hrs and not returning to camp until 1830 hrs would represent a good day's work for most men you'd imagine. Not a bit of it; many of the engineers stayed on site until 2200 hrs and I've known them to work around the clock. To me they showed their true colours as workaholics, or first-class suckers-up, when a Gendarme-escorted trip to a nearby beach was organised one Friday. Since Nakabayashi elected to work that day, with the exception of a paltry dozen men, they all elected to go to the site as well. The expatriates and Filipinos weren't bothered about what their bosses might think and we trooped off en masse to enjoy a well-deserved break.

Work only occupied IHI employees for 99.9% of their waking hours; the other 0.01% was taken up by the Annual Christmas Bingo Game. Abe the administrator came into my office a day before the auspicious occasion:

"Payne san, you speak very good Engrish. You prease be Bingo crawrer."

"OK Abe, old bean. Give me the place, date and time."

"Me no understand."

"What time you want me be Bingo crawrer?"

"Ah so. Tomollow in lestaulant at 2000 hours."

Sometimes I wonder if I ought to have been a performer, because give me an audience and I'm in my element. OK, so calling out bingo numbers isn't Royal Command Performance stuff, but the Japs lapped up the spectacle. It went something like this:

"OK, listen in for the first number," I announced.

"Rissen in for first number," they echoed in unison.

"Legs eleven, one and one, number eleven," I articulated.

"Regs erevan, one and one, number erevan," they all repeated, followed by a mass rendition of, "Continue Warry san, continue."

"Next number is Kelly's eye, number one."

"Kerry's eye, number one. Continue, continue."

"Next number is two fat ladies; eight and eight, eighty-eight."

"Two fat radies, eighty-eight. Continue, continue."

"Next number is six and six; clickerty click, sixty-six."

"Crickerty crick, sixty-six," they enthused, "Continue, continue."

And so it went on to the great excitement of the IHI personnel, until all the prizes were allocated. They had never enjoyed an evening so much for years. For my stalwart efforts, they presented me with a memento of the evening: a paperweight, with a scorpion entombed inside the glass. It was something I'd always wanted.

The expatriate workers on the site—downtrodden Chinese, Indians, Malays and Turks—lived in the direst conditions at Camp 3, a place with accommodation facilities comparable to those on the Burma Railway. These men went to work for twelve hours or more each day and were confined to camp each evening. In fairness to IHI, this wasn't a regulation put in place by them, but by the Algerian Government and pertained to all projects employing expatriates in the industrial zone. Arzew was vitally important to the Algerian economy and the last thing they wanted was the murder of a guest worker. IHI never gave a second thought to the welfare of our underlings and, not surprisingly, there was trouble. My award for 'Most Blood Spilled during a Punch-up' went jointly to the Chinese and the Chinese-speaking Malays, for their spirited joust following a card game.

Whereas the Chinese, Malays and Indians stood out like sore thumbs in Algeria, the Turks didn't and with them, discipline became a major problem. If there was a chance to buck the system, the Turks would grasp it with both hands. They bribed our guards to let them out of camp and back in again; with the connivance of the drivers they jumped off the buses bringing them back to camp after work and went to Arzew town; fences were climbed and holes dug to escape; whores were brought in, drink too and they committed a plethora of other 'soldier-like' misdemeanours. Every offence was made the subject of a concise report but, despite threatening draconian punishment, Nakabayashi did nothing at all about the situation. The bottom line was purely financial; replacing a miscreant with a replacement from Turkey was an expensive business, whereas keeping an already trained guy on site didn't cost a yen.

Each morning, bus-loads of men descended upon the desalination plant and, in the evening, they took the reverse route. They were guarded, in a fashion, by disinterested Algerian gendarmes and a security man without a gun—me! What sitting ducks we would have made if the terrorists had been inclined to make their point. The reality was though, even at the height of the troubles in Algeria in the early 90s, there was never much of a problem in Arzew, or in the nearby port city of Oran. Nevertheless, we published a blood-soaked weekly situation report, designed to emphasize the dangers of working in a terrorist infested country like Algeria. By perpetuating the myth of danger and impending doom, we were able to keep hold of our well-paid jobs.

Despite having his ear bent by both Gordon and me on a regular basis, Nakabayashi remained resolute in his assertion that we didn't require guards on the building site. He remained equally adamant about the building of a fence along the eastern side and it was never to rise! Meanwhile, huge amounts of equipment and materiel continued to arrive in readiness for the main construction phase. It was stored in flimsy containers, secured by even flimsier padlocks, on a site which was unlit, unguarded and wide open. It came as no surprise to me when the incidence of thefts began to increase dramatically.

There was one magnificently brazen theft from the site, when a team entered in a lorry during the night, helped themselves to hundreds of brand new tools and simply drove out through the side without a fence. There would undoubtedly have been some brisk business on Oran's black market next morning. When the news reached the GM's ears, he summoned me to his office.

"Big ploglam with Ari Baba!" he announced.

"Big ploglam with Ari Baba indeed," I confirmed.

"What you do catch Ari Baba?"

"I have informed the Gendarmes and they will carry out an investigation."

"How they take away many things?"

"They drove a lorry onto site from the east, where there's no fence; they broke off the cheap Chinese locks that I've told your department heads to replace a hundred times; loaded the booty into the lorry and drove out again via the east side which, you may be surprised to know, ISN'T FUCKING FENCED OFF!"

"No, no, no, no, no. Guards steal."

"There aren't any guards; you won't let us recruit any."

"No, no, no, no, no. You don't understand."

"Look Mr Nakabayashi. Until you construct a fence, illuminate the place and allow me to employ more guards, you'll never stop Ari Baba."

"No, no, no, no, no. You don't understand."

I suffered this sort of nonsense every time Ari Baba, or one of his forty thieves, sneaked off with a screwdriver, wrench or, the Algerian favourite, a sanding machine. Conversations between us would undoubtedly have been different had he accepted the obvious requirement of an interpreter, but his Asian compulsion to 'gain face' by speaking English meant he couldn't be seen to need assistance.

Given the retribution meted out to thieves in Arzew, firstly by the gendarmes and then by the courts, I wondered why locals attempted to steal from the site at all. Arabs, though, are driven by a 'if it's not nailed down then why not take it' attitude to life. I made the mistake of leaving my mobile phone lying on the desk of my unlocked office one afternoon and, returning from the urinals a mere sixty-seconds later, found myself the victim of a *klefti wallah*. I called my number immediately from the office phone and the cheeky thief had the brass neck to answer. He could only speak fractured French, but was perfectly happy to chat to me, even though he couldn't have been more than a couple of hundred yards away from my location. My assistants called the number regularly for a week afterwards and, although he conversed with them, he resolutely refused to fall into any trap to catch him. It was IHI's phone anyway, so he was welcome to it.

That evening, everyone and his dog was subjected to a search at the main exit. Although my phone wasn't found on the night of the 'big search', we did nab a bloke who had a couple of gas bottle regulators secreted in his bag. He would do! The gendarmes were summoned and the local brigade's top man arrived to investigate. He was a huge black man, with a distinctly rustic style of dealing with miscreants. He began by smiting the unfortunate fellow mightily in the face and, when he arose somewhat unsteadily to his feet, he smote him down a second time. When the baddie staggered to his feet again, he was instructed to get into the rear of the police van. He made the error of turning to pick up his bag first, whereupon he suffered a third trip to the canvas. This man spent a week in the gendarme brigade cells, before appearing before the local magistrates. A six-month jail sentence seemed a bit severe to me, but foreign investment sites were important to the Algerian economy and theft needed to be discouraged.

Despite the ridiculous nature of our horn-locking sessions, Nakabayashi was no fool. He knew the mounting cost of losses through theft was becoming a real issue, but remained adamant that IHI funds would not be made available to beef up security. Instead, the crafty fox had a cunning plan and called the sub-contractors to one of the most outrageously scheming conferences I've ever attended. The contracts manager, a permanently pissed Glaswegian with an almost unintelligible accent, held court. The language of communication at conferences was supposed to be English, although I didn't understand much as McSporran read through the parts of the legal documents dealing with responsibility for materiel on site. Nakabayashi, pretending to understand, but clearly as baffled as the rest of us, nodded enthusiastically the whole time. I wondered exactly what the Turkish, Malay and Algerian bosses made of the whole affair; very little I shouldn't wonder. Finally, the GM rose to announce his understanding of the contracts with regard to the financial responsibility for materiel on site and, at a stroke, diverted all the costs of stolen items to the sub-contractors. It's doubtful whether anyone understood exactly what had gone on but, in any case, there were seldom dissenters to a Nakabayashi proclamation.

The outcome of this conference proved catastrophic from our perspective, as each subcontractor hired his own security men, under the guise of Heath & Safety aides. The following story will indicate the kind of nonsense I was forced to endure:

Two Turks employed by the Istanbul based consortium of Alarko had assaulted an Algerian on the site. Quick, somebody call the security manager! I was in the process of pulling on my corn and bunion inducing steel toe-capped boots prior to entering the site, when an Algerian, not of my acquaintance, appeared outside my office.

"You are not needed," he declared in excellent English, "I am dealing with this incident."

"And exactly who might you be?" I enquired of the Arab.

"My name is Kadi Siddiqi, the Assistant Safety Manager of Alarko," he announced with considerable pride.

"Well Kadi Siddiqi, Assistant Safety Manager of Alarko, I just happen to be the Security Manager of this crappy organization. Now, let me assure you of something. Contrary to your erroneous assumption, it's me who will be dealing with this matter," I replied, without any pride whatsoever.

He wasn't to be convinced though and, like an annoying little dog, he followed me down to the site. I began an investigation into what appeared to be a simple matter, the likes of which had been bread and butter stuff for me a thousand times before. The previous day, a Turk called Gündoğdu had found a mobile telephone on the site. Unencumbered by any morals about trying to find its rightful owner and perhaps believing he had chanced upon a heaven sent opportunity of augmenting his pauper's salary, he'd handed the phone to an Algerian. This man agreed to buy a local SIM card for the telephone and return it to Gündoğdu next day. The Turk would then sell it to a gullible fellow countryman and split the profit with the Algerian. In this part of the world however, the law of the jungle prevails and, next day, the Algerian denied ever having seen the phone. He was promptly set upon by Gündoğdu and his chum.

By the time I'd ascertained these few facts, there were more Turks gathered around me than were involved in the Battle of Gallipoli. A strategic withdrawal, I considered, might be a wily ploy. A couple of minutes later, all the main players were gathered in my office: the two Turks, the assaulted Algerian, an Arab interpreter, the Turkish Safety Manager, me and—Kadi Siddiqi. Siddiqi, without considering the possibility of the dire repercussions of his foolhardy action, had actually parked his bottom on my chair.

"Tell me again who you are mister."

"I am the Assistant Safety Manager of Alarko."

"Well, since we have the Alarko Safety Manager here, I think we can dispense with your services. Cheerio."

"You must ask me more politely," the wretch had the temerity to say.

"Mr. Siddiqi," quoth I, "fuck off out of my office before you are thrown out. And never come back unless you are specifically invited."

He made an exit, his bottom lip all of a quiver. I continued with the convoluted investigation for precisely two minutes, whereupon the GM arrived with Siddiqi in tow. He demanded to know what was going on. My attempted explanation was cut short by the Nakabayashi classic:

"No, no, no, no, no. You don't understand."

"Oh, but I do understand Nakabayashi san."

"No, no, no, no, no. Why you insult this man?"

"This man is sticking his nose in where it's not required and I sent him out of my office."

"No, no, no, no, no. You no be rude to rocal people."

At this juncture he started berating me in his best Samurai Japanese, with just a hint of English thrown in to confuse matters. Although he was the only one who really understood what he was saying, it was clear enough to those assembled that the Security Manager was being soundly reprimanded by the General Manager.

The verbal lambasting of a departmental manager, I pointed out to him with commendable restraint, ought to be delivered in private and certainly not in front of an audience of subordinates. It didn't stop him, so I suffered in silence. Once his verbal assault on the Briton was completed, he strode purposefully out of my office, still muttering Japanese oaths. The Turks and Arabs made a strategic withdrawal from my office and I never did complete the investigation into this case. I felt duty bound to prepare a letter of redress at once, without giving a hoot about the impact it might have on my job prospects. The following memorandum, penned in simple Engrish, was on Nakabayashi's desk within twenty minutes.

As the Security Manager on an industrial site, one is occasionally required to make unpopular decisions. This is a simple fact of life, as is the supposition that everyone, regardless of nationality, rank or creed, knows more about security than the Security Manager does.

The incident on site on Monday 28th illustrates these assertions admirably. Mr Kadi Siddiqi , HSE Alarko, involved himself in investigating an occurrence that, in my view, ought to have been dealt with by my department. Kadi was intrusive in my investigation; was rude and arrogant. Consequently, I found it necessary to require him to leave my office. He did so with bad grace. It was then, as I was attempting to establish the facts surrounding this case, that you entered the outer office.

It immediately became apparent that Kadi had complained to you about his treatment at my hands. Refusing absolutely to listen to my point of view, you then delivered an attack on my actions. As GM you are perfectly entitled to criticise my performance, but to do so in front of three Turkish and three Algerian subordinates is bad management practice and, frankly, rude. Had you required me to visit your office, or spoken to me in private elsewhere, then your attack on my performance would have been marginally more acceptable.

By berating me in front of these people, you have made me lose the respect of those over whom I am expected to exercise control. Word soon gets around a work site. Furthermore, you have accepted Kadi's word and taken action, without ever listening to my defence. You have now opened the floodgates, allowing any subordinate who doesn't like the sound of my instructions to come into your office and complain, confident in the knowledge you will take action, in public, against the Security Manager. In short, you have made my position untenable!

I feel I showed remarkable restraint, by keeping my composure when you were demeaning me in front of six *workers. I hereby advise you that, should I be faced with such unprofessional conduct again, I might not be guaranteed to exercise such restraint.*

Should you be dissatisfied with my performance or demeanour, then you are at liberty to give me notice. I shall, in any case, be leaving the site on 23rd Apr.

He never deemed to reply to the letter; in all probability he didn't understand a word of it anyway. During the course of the afternoon however, the Administration Manager appeared in my office. This busy man, who had never spent longer than ten-seconds in my presence on previous visits, actually accepted my offer of a seat and cup of coffee. Adopting a most unusual and certainly un-Japanese approach, he conceded that the GM could be a difficult man on occasions. He then astonished me, by presenting me with a bottle of whisky, compliments of Nakabayashi. This was the nearest thing to an apology one was ever going to get from the General Manager, so I accepted the bottle. Never having touched a drop of the stuff since Hogmanay 1962, I presented the bottle of Dimple to a grateful McSporran.

One thing still bothered me about my role as Security Manager. During his command performance in my office, Nakabayashi declared it wasn't the responsibility of the security department to investigate thefts on site. If this was the case, then there was precious little point me being in Arzew at all. I decided to clear the air, by asking for clarification, and penned the following note:

During your verbal assault on the Security Manager in front of six subordinates on 28th Mar, you stated, quite categorically, it was <u>not</u> the responsibility of the Security Department to investigate thefts or assaults occurring on site. Would you kindly confirm or clarify this comment?

He never replied. Thereafter, I took details of thefts for the record, but never bothered investigating the circumstances. Apart from being in my office each day and keeping the lid on potential security disasters, I certainly never earned my money. A Welsh engineer on site had a job which, as far as I could ascertain, required him to do even less than me. He gave me some pertinent advice—"Grin and bank it boyo!"

The Welsh engineer was one of the four Britons engaged on the desalination contract; along with the drunken McSporran, Bartlett the circumferentially challenged Health & Safety manager and me. Jones and Bartlett were outstandingly boring, but I enjoyed their mid-morning visits to my office for coffee and cake for two reasons. Firstly, it afforded me the opportunity to speak English rather than French but, more importantly, they were good for my self-esteem. These guys were veritable giants in the weight department and made me, a man who tipped the scales at a mere 210 pounds, very much the weakling at our coffee morning assemblages.

A new gendarme captain arrived at Camp 10. To demonstrate his power and authority and to make it clear he was not a man to be trifled with, unless you bribed him first, he promptly withdrew all his gendarmes from the IHI operation. This seemed an odd decision to me, since the sole purpose of his men being in Camp 10 was to provide us with armed escorts and police support. My petitions fell on deaf ears, although he agreed to reconsider the position and give me a decision within a week. In the event, my irresistible offer of a package of goodies to be brought back from the UK when I next went on leave, succeeded in eliciting a promise to have the gendarmes returned to their posts next day. For the price of a new suit, a costume for his wife, a bottle of the Glenmorangie, a Liverpool football strip and some toys for his kids, I had bought the corrupt bastard. Unfortunately, the return of the

309

gendarmes next morning wasn't soon enough to avert a major incident.

It was the evening of the 20/20 cricket finals at Lords and the games were being shown live on Sky TV. Since Leicestershire had made it to the final, I decided to break my self-imposed alcohol prohibition and was tucking into my second bottle of a rather rude Algerian Mascara red wine, as the Foxes cruised their way to victory. My viewing was interrupted for a couple of minutes, when my night man called to tell me a freak wind had removed the roof from the main administration block on site. There were no injuries and nothing could be done by way of repairs until morning, since the area had no lighting. For sure, an incident of this nature didn't merit missing the final overs of the match. With only a dozen balls left however, there was some loud thumping on my villa door. Just my luck, the first time I'd taken a drink in six weeks and there at the door stood the three head Japanese honchos—Nakabayashi the Terrible, Takahashi the pernickety administrator and Takashima, a truly supercilious toad. Takashima's forbears would almost certainly have been Second World War POW Camp Commandants.

"Arrange vehicles and gendarmes. Go to site now," the GM ordered.

"Can't be done I'm afraid, we have no gendarme cover. You may recall I explained the situation to you this afternoon. In any case, the night security man assures me all is well and so there's nothing to be done until first light."

"No, no, no, no, no. You don't understand. Arrange now."

"It's you that doesn't understand Nakabayashi san. We have no gendarmes—we cannot go to the site without gendarmes."

"No, no, no, no, no. You don't understand. Roof blow off, we must inspect."

I attempted to explain to Takahashi the administrator; he spoke fine English, but was very wary when it came to countermanding the Samurai's instructions. Slimy Takashima, always ready to ingratiate himself with the General Manager, identified the perfect opportunity to score 'brownie' points.

"When the GM tells you to do something, you do it immediately. Do you understand?" he shouted for best effect, simultaneously poking me in the chest with his yellow forefinger.

It wasn't the wisest thing he'd ever done in his uneventful life, especially since I'd just supped a couple of bottles of rough red. Without stopping to consider the possibility of him being a 5th Dan karate exponent, I took him firmly by the throat and marched him backwards down the road for twenty yards.

"Listen to me, you slant-eyed bastard! If you ever try to belittle me in public again, I'll break you scrawny, yellow neck. Do you understand?"

After three slaps around the ear, he deemed to nod to the affirmative. Feeling I was onto a winner, another verbal dig at the slimy creep was surely in order.

"And if you should ever poke me in the chest again, I'll break all your fucking fingers. Do you understand?"

He understood.

"In fact, as long as I'm here in Arzew, don't ever talk to me again. If you want anything from my department, you will send me a memo."

I let Takashima loose and returned to face the music. My credence and most probably my job were saved by the timely intervention of the gendarme captain. He had been alerted by the cacophony and, undoubtedly realising the problem was actually of his making, immediately produced three gendarmes. With the exception of Takashima, who had retired to lick his wounds, we trooped off to the site. As I had prophesied, it was dark, nothing could be seen, nobody had been injured, bugger all could be done until first light and we had wasted our time. The incident was closed and, as was the case with Nakabayashi, by next morning he'd completely forgotten the whole event. There were two pleasing postscripts to the evening's entertainment. Takashima never uttered a single word to me for the next year and Leicestershire lifted the 20/20 trophy.

If the antics of the IHI administrators were any yardstick, it would be very difficult to find a more parsimonious bunch than the Nips. The IHI crew responsible for stores would have professed prudence and financial awareness, whereas in truth, they were as tight as Japanese Dabbling Ducks' arses. It's not unknown for people to dislike security personnel; they represent authority and nobody likes being told what they can and can't do. The Abe/Fuji quartermaster partnership within the Admin Department though, really went beyond the pale when it came to their dislike of this particular custodian of the law. No matter how short the duration of their stay, every single person coming onto the site was provided with IHI uniform. This pair though, was determined Payne san would never stand sartorially resplendent in the company's garb. A multitude of requests for being allowed to dress like everyone else invariably met with the same excuse for refusal—I was too big. I've always been a big lad and will concede to carrying a pound or two of overweight these days; nevertheless, to suggest I was anything other than a stocky, well-made individual would be grounds for a defamation prosecution. Within the walls of Fuji's well-guarded clothing container, there simply had to be a suit to fit me. Not all Japs are skinny, buck-toothed workaholics after all; and what if a retired sumo wrestler came to work in Arzew? Confirmation of a personal vendetta was proved beyond any reasonable doubt, when the company recruited my British coffee drinking companions.

Jones, from Haverfordwest, stood 6'4" and tipped the scales at something well in excess of twenty stones. His chum Bartlett, the amiable Grimsby Town supporter, might only have stood 5'7" in his platform heels, but his poundage couldn't be measured on my bathroom scales, not by a long shot. Neither of these men had ever bought anything off the peg in their lives and yet, thanks to a miracle of Japanese technology, they were both sporting IHI uniforms within a couple of days. Their garments weren't exactly Saville Row it's true and only fitted where they touched, but at least they had some work clothes.

With the exception of the allegedly misshapen Wally Payne, everyone on site proudly wore the company's IHI logo on his breast. This caused considerable mirth amongst the Filipinos and struck me as an apt testimony to this rotten organisation. You see, translated into English from Tagalog, 'ihi' means 'piss'!

Despite being unarmed, we were responsible for escorting personnel to and from the international airport at Oran, some forty miles distant. The two accompanying gendarmes did have weapons, but since they were either asleep, chatting, or chanting the Koran throughout the journeys, we would have been terribly vulnerable should any baddies choose to take exception to our presence. Escorts, it could be argued, were unnecessary anyway, since Oran saw very little in the way of terrorist activity. The requirement for escorts was laid down by Algerian legislation however and was not open for discussion. From my perspective, the trips to town and back were a welcome diversion from being stuck in the office all day, waiting for precisely nothing to happen.

Oran Airport was an absolute shambles. Planes never left or arrived on time, the facilities were poor, the toilets reeking and the airport devoid of air-conditioning. To make things worse, the Algerian Airport Police wouldn't issue me with an access permit to the arrivals and departure areas. Since the only reason for my presence at the airport was to facilitate the smooth arrivals and departures of expatriates, this could have rendered my journeys futile. Simply because I greeted the policemen and customs men cordially however, as well as giving them a cheap ballpoint pen or a handful of toffees whenever the mood took me, I was able to walk brazenly into the forbidden areas without causing a single inquisitive head to turn.

Unlike other airlines, Air Algérie didn't give out arrival documentation on the plane and there was an unholy scramble for forms once passengers reached the Arrivals Hall. The scrimmage in the hall was exacerbated by an inept team of baggage handlers, who often took an hour or more to unload the baggage from a single aircraft. Luggage conveyors breaking down on a regular basis; baggage from a flight being placed on two different carousels and, the ultimate; two or three flights arriving simultaneously, all served to make an afternoon in the arrivals hall sufficient to make a person go off his head.

The escort team included me, the sensible one; a movement's administrator with a mind of his own, two dozy gendarmes and a brace of manic drivers. A prerequisite for obtaining an Algerian driver's licence is lunacy and our chauffeurs were eminently well qualified. One of our drivers had a compulsion to drive at breakneck speed, especially when it was foggy. He was one of the few people I've ever sacked during a lifetime in management. Another of our drivers crashed spectacularly into the rear of a parked lorry, which was strange given it was bright daylight, the weather dry and the road devoid of traffic. He had braked sharply when a handcart, laden with fish, spilled its load onto the main thoroughfare. With each of his wheels improbably balanced on a large fish, he had skidded as if on ice. As the cause of an accident, it was certainly original and neither the investigating gendarme nor I had ever seen the likes before. It wasn't easy trying to organise these guys into an efficient team; they went off for a coffee at the most inappropriate times, their attacks of diarrhoea were synchronised to coincide with our departure and every driver felt compelled to move his vehicle around the car park to find a shadier spot on a regular basis—without telling me naturally.

A delegation of IHI top brass was arriving on the Air France flight from Paris Charles de Gaulle. It was important for me to ease their way through customs, move them slickly through the arrivals hall and out to the vehicles for the journey up to Camp 10. The drivers were instructed to reverse their vehicles into one of the less populated car parks and stay with them, then the Algerian gendarmes were briefed on exactly what to do—twice! It was with guarded confidence that I marched into the airport with the administrator. Everything went swimmingly, until I gestured for the big-wigs to cross the road to the car park. I looked up, only to discover there wasn't a single one of our vehicles to be seen! My fury was interrupted by cries of "Monsieur Wally" emanating from another parking area, located to the left of the exit. The bloody fools had decided to move all the trucks to get them nearer to the exit, without them taking me into their confidence naturally. I would still have got away with the last minute change of plan had we been able to depart immediately, but we couldn't. The emergence of the VIPs from the airport had coincided with the gendarmes' overwhelming desire for coffee and croissants. Alas, it's the sort of thing you have to get used to when working with people from this part of the world.

Another crowd of Japs arriving on an afternoon flight from Paris included the IHI Supremo. For once, the flight wasn't horribly late and the group of eight were successfully escorted over to the airport car park. We were all aboard and hot to trot, when one of the Japanese was suddenly smitten by an overwhelming desire to urinate. He simply had to go! The boss gave his nod of approval, so I took the enuresis sufferer by the hand and led him back to the main hall, showed him where to find the toilet and waited discretely outside for him to finish his call of nature. Several Algerians went in and out of the malodorous lavatory, but after ten minutes, there was still no sign of the newly arrived Nip. I went to investigate and found him surrounded by an angry crowd of locals. Unfamiliar with the layout of an Arab style toilet, the Asian had relieved himself in what he thought to be the communal urinal, but was in fact the trough where the faithful washed prior to prayer. It took several minutes of negotiation, with coffee and croissants all round for the religiously offended, before they agreed to let him progress with his head still attached to his shoulders.

Visible from the main road to Oran airport was a cemetery with, unusually for this part of the world, crosses on all the graves. The gendarmes and drivers with whom I travelled each day referred to the place as the American Cemetery, although not a single one of them was remotely interested in taking me there to investigate. After months of lobbying and plying him with bottles of whisky and wine, the gendarme sergeant was finally won over; he consented to return to Arzew one morning via the American Cemetery. The cross-covered hillside visible from the airport road was just a tiny part of the graveyard it transpired; on the other side of the slope and not visible from the main road lay a far larger burial ground. The gravedigger-in-chief appeared delighted to have a guest and the visitors' book he presented for my signature indicated why. I was the first person in four months to darken the doorstep of his immaculately maintained cemetery, which contained the remains of six-thousand servicemen killed during the Second World War.

The majority of the fallen were not Americans, as the Algerians erroneously believed, but Frenchmen. They were

316

predominantly matelots, killed during the Anglo-American attack on the French fleet off Oran in 1942. The French had capitulated by this stage of the war and the scuttling had been ordered by the Allies, to prevent the ships being commandeered by Rommel's Afrika Corps. A small enclosure containing barely a dozen graves marked the US losses during the campaign, unless they had taken the majority of their fallen home for burial. The French graves were marked with wooden crosses, all of which were grotesquely infested with dozens of snails. Tired with the unequal struggle of scraping inedible snails from the memorials year after year, the French Government had capitulated, as usual, and begun replacing the wooden crosses with some constructed of concrete.

I asked the custodian if there were any of our heroes lying in his graveyard. He led me to a small British War Graves Commission maintained cemetery called 'Le Petit Lac', where one hundred and sixty immaculately kept stones lay in four neat rows. Those lying under the sod were predominantly sailors and airmen, but the odd soldier's name was also to be found chiselled into a marble marker. There was one solitary Black Watch soldier's grave and, having an affinity for the Black Jocks following a tour of duty in an adjacent barracks in Germany, I contacted the unit's Regimental Headquarters. I wanted to report the grave well maintained and to enquire whether they would like our small British contingent to lay a poppy wreath on Remembrance Day. The Regimental Secretary wrote a charming letter in response to my offer and, as a postscript, asked whether I was the Wally Payne who played for the RMP soccer side in the 80s? "Because if you are, I've still got the scars you bastard!"

As construction progressed, workers began to require access to the seawater-intake area, down by the shore. This was located on the opposite side of our desalination plant site's north wall, in a zone controlled by the feisty Béthioua Port Police. Any IHI personnel entering the port area were required to be in possession of a distinctive brown-coloured pass, which needed to be shown at a guard post manned by one of our inept security guards and an even more inept port policeman. The sad fact was, anyone and his dog could enter the port, simply by greeting the occupants of the guard post and slipping them a couple of Mars bars. To make matters even more farcical, a twenty-metre section of the doughty fence separating our site from the port area had been cut away, to allow the work of installing seawater entry pipes to be carried out. As a result, rather than walk two hundred yards to the guard post and a further two hundred yards back up to their workplace, the majority of workers simply scrambled through the hole and saved on shoe leather. I told Nakabayashi we needed to post security guards at the breach. His reply was not exactly unexpected. "No, no, no, no, no. You don't understand."

Despite my sure and certain knowledge to the contrary, Nakabayashi remained convinced that IHI workers didn't need port access badges at all, claiming the Chief of Police had told him so at a recent conference. This was unmitigated bilge of course, brought about by yet another linguistic misunderstanding. Had an incident involving an IHI worker not in possession of a valid badge occurred in the port police controlled area of responsibility, then all hell would have broken loose for certain. The Samurai, meanwhile, blithely continued to believe what was patently wrong.

Soon the point was reached where more people were crawling through the hole in the fence than were being monitored at the guard post. So, early one morning, I secreted myself by the hole and prepared to do a little surveillance. Who was the first person to walk through the illegal entry point? None other than General Manager Nakabayashi! At this juncture, I lost interest in the port area too.

For reasons known only to their inscrutable selves, IHI refused to apply for Algerian work permits on behalf of our little security team of four. As a consequence, we needed to obtain a new business visa prior to each journey back to Oran. It was debatable which Algerian Consulate was nearest to my home in the Philippines: Tokyo, Kuala Lumpur or Beijing, but none of them was exactly on the doorstep. For this reason, I always opted to return to the UK a fortnight early and toss my passport in at the consulate located near the Albert Hall. The Algerian Consulate in London worked such short hours and at a pace so sedate, it took up to ten days to obtain the necessary stamp. Once the initial pilgrimage to London was completed, time was no longer my master and I'd join an organised bus trip. Five days in some boring seaside resort accompanied by a bus load of OAPs wasn't exactly my cup of tea, but it was cheap, cheerful and it killed the time. This way, I became well acquainted with the coastlines of both Cornwall and Norfolk and met a lady from Nottingham.

The hotel in Newquay was full of old ladies from our bus tour, all of them way beyond the age of wanting a bit on the side. At the next table in the dining room however, sat a reasonably attractive lady of some thirty summers. She was looking after her aged grandmother and was hopelessly out of place among the geriatrics. On the second night of the tour, the hotel bar closed at an obscenely early hour and everyone, with the exception of the young lady and me, repaired to their rooms in time for News at Ten. She retrieved a couple of bottles of red wine she had stashed in her boudoir and we sipped a few glasses in the foyer as we discussed the price of cheese. Even the management had gone to bed by the time we decided to take a walk outside, to look at an incoming thunderstorm. As the door clicked behind me, the realisation I'd left my hotel front door key on the foyer table hit me. We had a problem;

hers was in her handbag, which was also lying on the foyer table. The cold and rain soon dampened any enthusiasm for looking at nature and I rang the doorbell to summon the duty manager, or anyone else who might let us in. A period of increasing panic ensued; nobody would answer the door, nobody would answer the phone and there was absolutely no way of gaining access back into the rotten hotel.

Finally, I hailed a passing taxi and instructed the driver to take us to an alternative hotel. This was close season in Newquay though and, at this hour, every inn, hostelry and doss-house in the town was in darkness! We returned to our place and tried again to wake someone in the building, but to no avail. It bucketed down, the wind blew and tempers were beginning to fray, especially mine. The poor lady, scantily clad and without footwear, was becoming hypothermic. With some reluctance, I divested myself of my Barbour jacket and gave it to her, only to borrow you understand? An hour passed and we still hadn't seen hide nor hair of a fellow human being, let alone a vehicle when, as if heaven sent, a van finally came around the corner. The driver must have thought he was being hijacked when I stood in front of his vehicle, but he stopped just the same. When he wound down his window, I related our tale of woe in the hope of eliciting sympathy.

"You're a lucky bloke," he said, "My hotel's just around the corner. Jump in and I'll take you there."

What a decent fellow and what a stroke of luck. I was reluctant to book into a double room, but the moist lady from Nottingham convinced me she was scared and needed company, so I gallantly acceded to her request. At this late hour only slumber was on my itinerary, so I simply bade the lady goodnight and climbed into bed. Dozing off in my single bed, I was suddenly awoken by the not unfamiliar feel of soft, warm flesh. Unless I was very much mistaken, a woman was trying to share my pit. Turning over to confront the trespasser, her eyes met mine.

"I want to have your baby," was her corny opening gambit.

Just my luck to pull a broody female but, like any self-respecting former soldier would do in the circumstances, I gave it my best shot. To complete what turned out to be not such a bad night after all, next morning the hotel owner waived any charge for the room.

Weekly meetings, which all heads of department were required to attend, were held last thing each Thursday afternoon. To be frank, it would be difficult to imagine a more criminal waste of time than the unproductive hours spent around the conference room table. Each departmental head was required to give a weekly report, in English, with Nakabayashi the Samurai chairing the meeting. We each had a copy of all departmental reports in front of us, which was just as well, because apart from Takashima and the administration manager, the remainder spoke only rudimentary English. A fast talking, thickly-accented bloke from Grimsby, an unintelligible Scot and yours truly made up the remainder of the assembly. Battle commenced when Nakabayashi murmured, "Hai! Administration!" Abe san would then do his thing and, if all went well, he would be rewarded with a second, "Hai!" Thereafter, the engineers gave their reports in some incomprehensible dialect, which may or may not have contained the odd word of my mother tongue. The truth was, even if the content of their reports had been delivered in the Queen's English, it still wouldn't have made a scrap of difference to me; I'm an engineering illiterate and am content to remain so. In any case, whenever there was a serious matter to discuss, they burst into Japanese. Why didn't they do it all in Japanese and have an interpreter to translate the British fellows' efforts?

I was a tail-ender and went into bat ninth. Upon the words, "Hai! Security", I would bore everyone with security statistics, interspersed with terrifying tales of terrorist atrocities, complete with gory photographs. Each week, Nakabayashi would ask the same question, "Where you get all this information?" My response would always be the same, too: "Confidential sources Nakabayashi san." In fact, the vast majority of my intelligence simply came from reading the local newspapers.

From the general tone of our weekly management meetings, it appeared as if things weren't progressing on site as quickly as they ought. Nevertheless, buildings rose from the sand and miles of pipes, tubes and wires were connected up. The heart of the whole operation was the Turbine House, where three enormous gas turbines were built for the purpose of producing electricity for the Algerian National Grid. The generating process resulted in masses of heat being given off and this was used to boil seawater, the steam from which was then condensed to produce sweet water.

Dawn rose on an auspicious day at Arzew; the mighty turbines would be fired-up for their first test run. Although by no means an expert, I understand that specialist pieces of equipment known as 'injectors' allow a gas and air mixture into the big beasts and they turn rapidly to produce power. Within a couple of hours of starting the tests on the turbines, many of the injectors had melted! Heated words could be heard emanating from Nakabayashi's office and rumours abounded of swords being produced, to enable those responsible for the debacle to do the honourable thing. Each turbine needed fourteen injectors, costing US$20,000 apiece and, after testing all three turbines, IHI had managed to bugger up twenty-four of them. They were returned to Basildon in Essex, where a YOPS Scheme lad sorted them out within a fortnight and sent them back by GPO recorded delivery. Despite the setbacks, a month later the three turbines were running for hours at a stretch and producing much needed electricity for the Algerian grid.

To my great good fortune, I was at Es Senia airport on the morning of the disaster and was actually talking on the phone to the Grimsby giant. Suddenly he cried, "Oh my God, the turbine house is on fire. The flames are a hundred feet high." Thus, within five minutes, the project was set back many months. IHI were mortified, although many of us were perfectly delighted; we would be in employment much longer than anticipated. Investigations were carried out by the Japanese and, although accusing fingers were pointed in every direction, honest men were conspicuous by their absence. Culpability was never laid at anyone's door, despite there being grounds for sacking several department heads. The cause of the fire was risible, bordering on farce:

The American manufacturers of the turbines wanted some minor painting work done on a wall behind Turbine Number Two. IHI, however, had laid-off all their painters. They approached the two main sub-contractors but, guess what, they had laid-off all their painters too. Never mind, one of the Algerian drivers working for the Turks had a brother-in-law who was employed as a painter down in Arzew. He would be only too pleased to lend a hand and earn a few dinars on the side. What Nebi Chaa omitted to say was, his brother-in-law was a spray painter in a metal chair factory. Any port in a storm—he would do!

Enter, stage left, Kadi Smail; alleged painter of the Parish of Arzew.

Having been shown what to do, the best brains in IHI left Kadi Smail on his own in the turbine house, up on scaffolding, with his paint brush, blow-torch, scraper, pot of paint and two fire extinguishers, both of which were empty. Nobody told him about clearing away the rubbish on the floor and, when his blow torch sparks fluttered down...

A couple of months later, when everything was repaired and running as it ought, IHI decided it was time to dispense with the services of expatriate security managers. There were no tears shed on my part.

Chapter 14

Around and About

SCAREMONGERS told me it would be impossible to find a job once I'd reached the age of fifty and, had this popular misapprehension been the case, I'd never have worked after leaving the Army. As it is, I've laboured almost constantly. Nepotism has played a big part in me finding positions, but that's how life is in the big, bad outside world. Come to think, with scarcely an exception, every job I've had since leaving Her Majesty's employ has been obtained on the old boy network. After working for the Japanese in Arzew though, my search for gainful employment proved gloriously fruitless.

My pursuit of a job has invariably been in the security field, which isn't surprising, given that's all I know. The only other area to interest me is the church, which might surprise many who know me. Fertile areas in the hunt for positions with a religious bent are the *Church Times* and, until its demise in 2006, the *Christian Herald*. I'd landed the Ferrar House job through the pages of the *Church Times* in fact. I've applied for numerous jobs with the church, some rather beneath my station should the truth be known and have succeeded only in collecting more than my fair share of rejection slips. Perhaps these institutions were looking for someone rather younger than me? Had any Christian organisation cited my surfeit of summers as the reason for rejection, then I'd have had no hesitation in reporting them straight to God! He isn't ageist at all. Had He been, then neither Moses nor Abraham would have been called to serve and where would the world be then? Or, one final thought, perhaps they had read my first two books; in which case they certainly wouldn't want me anywhere near their choir girls or the communion wine.

The group that pissed me off most were the Trustees of Chichester Cathedral. They were looking for a gopher to work as deputy warden in their old peoples' hospital set-up, located within the cathedral grounds. I really fancied the job, knew Chichester well and, from a selfish standpoint, liked the idea of living in free accommodation. I ought to have realised my application was doomed from the outset, when acknowledgement of my submission was addressed to a 'Mr Wainwright'. Thereafter, there wasn't a squeak out of the Bishop or any of his acolytes, despite my regular requests for an update on the state of play. On the day of the interviews for the post, I took a sentimentalist's look at the job description of yet another failed application and discovered a caveat tucked away at the bottom. It read, "If you haven't heard from the trustees by the date of the interviews, you can consider your application unsuccessful." Good grief! This was a lowly position involving pandering to posh parishioners with private pension plans and calling up the undertaker when they snuffed it. Someone at Chichester Cathedral seemed to think they were dealing with applications for the post of CEO at ICI and I wrote to them to express my sentiments. The Church of England, I asserted, had a duty to behave more compassionately towards fallen job seekers. A lackey in the cathedral office was directed to write to me on behalf of the haughty, retired Naval Commodore, who masqueraded as Chairman of the Trustees. He declared through Mrs Sylvester-Bradley that, as a charity, St Mary's Hospital needed to exercise frugality in all matters financial and, to show what a clever ex-Jack Tar he really was, he explained how he'd saved a whole fiver on postage. What a pompous prick! With snobs like him in the Church of England, is it any wonder they can't fill the pews in the majority of their churches? I've not finished

326

with them yet though. The chances of any of my pound coins finding their way into a collection box the next time I go to Chichester Cathedral are precisely nil. What's more, they would do well to count their postcards once I've left! Methodists Rule OK?

There have been other ecclesiastical disappointments. St Mary le Boltons Church in South Kensington advertised a position as a caretaker and candle snuffer-outer and, by the cut-off date, I was the only applicant. A fair chance of landing the job you'd think? Nope! So unimpressed were they by my credentials, they re-advertised the post in the very next issue of the *Church Times*. Not partial to having a former soldier on the staff? *J'accuse!* At least they sent me an e-mail telling me to get stuffed, which is more than several other London churches did.

In Leicester, the Cathedral too deemed to send me a written rejection, thereby thwarting my aspirations to be an inter-faith community worker. Come to think, there couldn't have been anyone less suited to the position than me. The Wyggeston Hospital, on the other hand, ignored me completely when I applied to be a warden at their worthy establishment. Also in Leicester; after giving me enough encouragement to travel all the way from the Philippines to be interviewed, the Methodist Church in Glenfield decided they didn't want me after all.

It hasn't all been failure. After two interviews and numerous telephone calls, I was offered the post of warden at an almshouse set-up in York. When they told me the stipend however, I couldn't get out of the place fast enough. £250 a-month in 2006 seemed distinctly stingy to me. Exceedingly miserly salaries were also the reason I declined offers to work at St Anne's church in the town of St Anne's in Lancashire and also at St Martin-within-Ludgate, near St Paul's in London.

The Othona Trust was set to appoint me as manager of their retreat centre in Essex, but they were just too evangelical for my taste and I declined their offer. They promptly appointed a pair of homosexuals in my stead. I never followed up a position as an Army Bible Reader either; to me, they were a well-meaning outfit, but just a tad over-zealous for my taste.

The Sandes' Homes are a Northern Irish protestant charity doing good work in British Army barracks. They seemed set to appoint me to an assistant manager's post in Harrogate, until they discovered my wife was a Roman Catholic, whereupon I was offered the job on a single-man basis. They were told to stuff their job.

Whilst in Leicester, hoping in vain for the job at Glenfield Methodist Church to come to fruition, I unpacked my walking boots. It was a beautiful spring morning and a walk in the countryside was the order of the day. Nearing the village of Kirby Mallory, I stopped upon hearing the unmistakable call of a cuckoo. Spring had sprung! That evening, the *Leicester Mercury* carried a page about cuckoos and invited readers to phone in if they'd heard the call of a spring visitor. I dutifully phoned and asked to be put through to the 'Cuckoo Line'.

"Cuckoo line," said a disinterested Scots voice.

"Good evening, I heard a cuckoo this morning."

"That's pure, dead brilliant. Just a minute please."

He put his hand over the mouthpiece, but not well enough.

"Hey Charlie, take this bloody call will you?"

"What is it?"

"Another fucking cuckoo!"

Next day's paper carried a map of the county, almost obliterated by cuckoo sightings. I won't bother calling them again!

My unemployed status didn't curb my wanderlust and it was in Australia where an unusual incident befell me. Around the corner from my hotel in Sydney was a bar with a 24-hour

328

licence. What's more, it had a betting facility. What could be more acceptable to a 'gold-card' holder at William Hill's than a pint with his punt? Things went very well on the wagering front and, after the last race, I retired to the bar with my pockets full. The barman was an amiable Slovakian, with whom I conversed until he needed to cash up at the end of his shift. Just before he handed over, a homosexual entered the premises and sat down alongside me.

"G'day sport; do you mind if I sit here and chat to you?"

"Not at all."

"I'm a poofter. Will that make any difference?"

"Not unless you touch me."

"What do you do for a living cobber?"

"I'm a security man; and you?"

"I'm a barmaid."

I bought him a pint and told him to talk to someone else. At that juncture Johann bade me a fond adieu and a huge South-sea islander assumed responsibility for dispensing drinks. He looked at the queer and demanded to know what he was doing in the place, as he was barred. He also noticed the pint of beer in front of him.

"Who bought this poofter a beer?" he boomed.

"I did," I admitted.

"He's barred. He's not allowed to drink here"

"Unfortunately, I'm not clairvoyant old chap. As a stranger, how could I be expected to know that?"

"If you bought him a beer, then you're barred as well."

So, for the only time in my life, I was required to vacate licensed premises before closing time. The ignominy of it! The lure of a bet and a schooner of Victoria Bitter saw me back in the place the following evening just the same. Mercifully, the South-sea giant wasn't on duty.

Kuwait Airlines were offering great deals on business class tickets between Manila and London; not only were they the cheapest carriers at this time, but you also got to sit in the first-class section at the front of the plane. The only inconvenience on KA is an alcohol ban. No matter! The stewards turn a blind eye if you care to bring your own supply aboard and I drank a few brandies on the way back to the UK on this particular trip. After a few hours' sleep at Chateau Fisher, the abode of my chum Bob in Leicester, we reported to the home of 'Phil on the Hill' for Sunday lunch. As I was about to tuck into some pudding following a very decent lunch, I began to feel pains in my stomach. So severe was the pain that I needed to walk around the streets, wondering at the same time just why Phil on the Hill would want to poison me. I made my way back to Bob's house and, after vomiting blood several times, decided to call the doctor. Being a Sunday, my call was transferred to an Emergency Service where an anonymous recorded voice told me my call was in a queue. It must have been an awfully long queue because, by the time a real person spoke to me, I'd listened to Beethoven's Piano Concerto No 5 in E flat opus 73, Mendelssohn's Hebrides Overture and a selection from the Best of Shostakovich. The medical administrator was convinced I needed to see a doctor; perhaps my vivid description of vomiting blood clinched it for me? There was no ambulance available of course, so Bob drove me down to Leicester Royal Infirmary. So spectacular was my groaning, vomiting and diarrhoea by this time, Doctor Patel decided it prudent to admit me. There was a snag however; the hospital was so full of malingerers that there wasn't a bed available for a really sick person like me. The Indian doctor found me a place at Leicester City General Hospital, but again there was a snag. There were still no bloody ambulances available. Where were they all for goodness sake?

Rather than expire whilst waiting for the emergency services to put in an appearance, I took a taxi to the City General. The driver was the Sikh equivalent of a saint; he gave me reassurance and stopped regularly in secluded spots to allow me to be sick. At the City General, they admitted me to the emergency ward and a nurse stuck a couple of drips into my arms. I was in excruciating pain and my groaning, vomiting and voiding of the bowels were nothing short of spectacular. Despite my agony, the nurse couldn't give me any medication until a doctor had examined me. Doctors were particularly conspicuous by their absence on this day however and, after an inordinate length of time listening to my Oscar winning performance as a dying man, the nurse was compassionate enough to bend the rules a little and give me an injection to relieve the agony. I was in the City General for days and underwent a plethora of tests. Just the same, the physicians couldn't find the cause of my problem and, by the third morning, the pain had subsided completely. I could even eat without regurgitating. They arranged for an endoscope to be shoved down my gullet a week hence and, without coming to any conclusions whatsoever regarding my condition, they discharged me. I walked out of the hospital feeling perfectly well, although half a stone lighter. A few days later, the thought of having a tube rammed down my throat no longer appealed to me, so I cancelled my appointment. Anyway, my stomach was fine and there was never any reoccurrence of the problem, until a year to the day later.

I'd just eaten something innocuous for supper in the Philippines, when the very same symptoms manifested themselves. This time it was the doctors and staff of the Manila Adventist Sanatorium who were treated to my dramatic, award winning performance. My party piece was reserved for the Adventist choir, and a truly magnificent performance it was for sure. The very moment they came into my room to cheer me up by singing a hymn or two, the disgorgement began. My timing was immaculate and they made a rapid tactical withdrawal, even before the guitarist had time to play a single chord. Just as before, despite suffering terrible pain, by the third day I'd recovered completely. As a last resort, the doctor decided upon the ultrasound examination and this revealed my problem; my gall bladder was full of gall stones and needed to be removed without delay.

Had this been a British hospital, then I'd have been convinced the operation was going to be touch and go. Everyone, from the surgeon down to the lady who cleaned the lavatory, wanted to pray with me. It was a little disconcerting, wondering if they knew something I didn't, but praying with them was a great comfort. Even my own minister came to visit me and did something I'd only ever seen in films, but always fancied. He performed a 'laying-on of hands' and we took communion together in the ward.

It was a blessed relief when they came for me early next morning; this problem needed resolving once and for all and I wasn't the least bit apprehensive about getting the show on the road. The medical gown they required me to wear for my guest appearance in the operating theatre won no prizes for sartorial elegance though. I'm a big lad, whereas Filipinos are a small race and so, no matter how hard I tried to arrange myself, my working parts showed. This was embarrassing enough in front of the medics, but once they had me on the operating slab, who should march in to watch the show but a dozen trainee nurses! They all prayed for me of course, as did the anaesthetist and theatre staff until, finally, the surgeon deemed to stick in a shift. Once he'd prayed for me, they knocked me out and removed my gall bladder.

My whole body was shivering uncontrollably when the anaesthetic wore off and I was feeling 'proper poorly'. Everything was glowing white and there, at the bottom of the bed in the recovery area, stood my little girl. I was convinced I'd died and gone to Heaven, until I saw my wife by her side! My gall bladder had contained no less than 150 stones, which the surgeon collected and placed into a glass jar. Next day there was a small ceremony, during which he presented the stones to me, along with a set of equally unwanted Technicolor photographs of my offending organ. These gestures, however well meant, struck me as somewhat curious and the gallstones were consigned to the toilet bowl at the earliest opportunity.

My previously immaculate body contrived to go wrong again when I was back in the UK shortly afterwards. Helping to shift a deceased old lady's furniture down a flight of stairs, I managed to rupture myself. My hernia was described by the surgeon who sliced me open as 'substantial', as was his fee for repairing it. Initially, I'd sought help at the local NHS surgery, where the young lady doctor insisted on donning a pair of yellow Marigold washing-up gloves before deeming to grope my testes. She insisted on calling them testes, which I considered a load of bollocks! If I'd left the matter in the hands of the NHS, my hernia would have been repaired several years later, but I wanted the problem resolving rather more speedily and so called BUPA. So proficient are hospitals when you are paying through the nose for the privilege of being treated by them, they even asked me to name the day I wanted 'doing'. I subsequently phoned a surgeon, who offered me a slot a couple of days later, along with the offer of a discount of £200 if I'd accept the first appointment of the morning. First person on the conveyer belt it was then.

As soon as I came around in the recovery room, a male nurse came to enquire about my condition. The pain in my side was considerable, so I asked if he could oblige me with a few painkillers. Glancing at my medical notes, he took a pace back before remarking:

"It says here you're a former military policeman."

"Yes, but only for twenty-eight years," I explained.

"Well, I was in the RAMC and we hated the monkeys. Get your own bloody painkillers."

He strode away with a wry smile on his face, but returned with the necessary medication a couple of minutes later. By 1000 hrs I was back in my hospital bed. Two hours later, a nurse arrived with a tray of food she insisted I eat and, by 1400 hrs they had me walking up and down the ward. "It's good for recovery to be walking as soon as possible after the operation," explained the sister. I wasn't convinced. What she really meant was that they had another punter ready to occupy my bed space and so it proved. At 1500 hrs they booted me out. Modern day private hospital practices—in, out, no mucking about!

Just to prove I'm in terminal decline, my back started giving me gyp. Perhaps I oughtn't to have been surprised, since even as a teenager my bearing wasn't all it might have been. When I went into Burton's in Church Gate to be measured for my first ever new suit, the tailor scribbled some notes about my build on a buff-coloured chit. He attached the chit to my order form and off it all went to Burton's factory in Leeds. I bet this fellow will have been blithely unaware of just how badly his throwaway comments would affect my self-esteem in years to come. In fact, after so many decades, I wonder if there's any mileage to be gained from suing him for giving me a life-long inferiority complex. Knowing my luck, the statute of limitations governing such matters will have expired by now. Burton's allegedly made your suit to measure, although I'm convinced their warehouse in Leeds contained rows and rows of ready-made suits, to fit all but the most hideously deformed. I can still picture the 'custodian of suits' up in Yorkshire reading my buff chit, snipping an inch out of each shoulder and tacking an extra yard of pinstripe material into the backside, before putting my garment into the van and despatching it south. The buff coloured chit was still attached to my suit when I tried it on; it read, 'Slightly sloping shoulders, protruding rear.' How very hurtful. Just the same, my cheap suit looked the bee's knees and I couldn't wait to get down to the *Palais de Danse* to try out its bird-pulling potential.

I sometimes wonder if I exude a subliminal threat to other passengers on the bus, because the seat next to mine is always the last to be occupied. And so it was on the Number 16 and the spare place remained vacant right up to the moment the driver prepared to set off. Suddenly, a flustered lady laden with shopping boarded the vehicle at the very last moment and collapsed into the place next to me.

"Ah, to be sure, to be sure," she exclaimed, "Am I not the lucky one, to be sure, to be sure. Thank you Holy Mary Mother of God, to be sure."

"Good afternoon. You're Welsh aren't you? Your accent's a dead giveaway."

"Actually I'm Irish, from County Tipperary," she confessed.

She turned out to be an interesting, intelligent and articulate lady, but just a bit batty for all that. She was also a religious fanatic. By the time I got off the bus at Westcotes Drive, not only had she told me all about her family and her conversion, but had invited me for coffee at the Central Baptist Church the next Sunday afternoon. She was a member of a well-meaning band of Christians rejoicing under the name of *Agape*, which is Greek for 'love' apparently. On Sunday afternoons, Agape ran a retreat for the waifs and strays of Leicester, a place where the dross of the city could get a free meal and a drink of something non-alcoholic.

Ridiculously overdressed in comparison to the other punters thronging the Central Baptist Church Assembly Rooms, I stuck out like a sore thumb. A volunteer served me a coffee and made conversation—up to the point I confessed to having been a policeman in the city. "Don't let anyone hear you say that," he stuttered, fearing for my safety in present company. The lady from Tipperary never did appear, although I did talk to the handful of volunteers responsible for the care of seventy or eighty people who, in an opinion based on a lifetime of dealing with the dregs of the earth, appeared particularly unsavoury. There was only one male volunteer present and he would have been in real trouble had the throng of drunks and druggies turned nasty. These Agape folk were well-meaning people but, in my view, a tad out of touch with reality.

I tarried for just thirty minutes, but this was long enough to have my police experience put to the test. Firstly, by kicking open a lavatory door and pulling out an Indian who had overdosed and then, by disarming a West Indian, who was waving a knife around in a menacing fashion. To be honest, my gallantry in the face of the knife-wielding man from the Caribbean wasn't quite as meritorious as it might first have appeared, since the Jamaican's trousers fell down as he approached me and I grabbed his knife as he was pulling them back up again. I left with the firm conviction that there were better things to do with my Sunday afternoons than pissing against the wind trying to help people who didn't want helping.

It's not just on buses that my magnetism attracts oddballs, as I can get into bother on trains too. It was all the fault of Midland Mainline of course, for not putting enough carriages on the London stopping train. The truth is, I have a long-standing gripe against this company. Why do they always allow whining children, TB sufferers with hacking coughs, people with leaking Walkman headphones and mobile phone addicts into my carriage? It was never like this on the old LMS.

336

Age is no impediment to a person displaying ignorance, arrogance and a lack of consideration towards his fellow man I have discovered. Nor has age reduced my compulsion to redress such behaviour, even by using the minimum amount of force necessary if required. In fact, I seem to grow less and less tolerant of fools as the years go by. These sad facts were confirmed on the 0930 hrs train from Leicester to London one morning. It was clear the train was going to be full and, once the alighting passengers had emptied out onto Platform 3, we all pushed hard to get into the carriage. I was the second person through the door and confident of a seat, until the way into the seating area was blocked by a lady having trouble lifting her monster suitcase up onto the storage rack. I didn't feel inclined to strain myself on her behalf, but wish I had, because by the time she'd managed her weightlifting feat, the carriage was almost full. People had entered through the bottom door, the sneaky sods. I strode forward purposefully, only to find my way blocked yet again, by three older gentlemen standing in the aisle. They were attired identically, in cheap blazers with a trade union badge emblazoned on the breast pocket and ties with the same motif printed on them. They decided to sit on the left-hand side, then the right, with their backs against the direction of travel and then vice versa, until there was scarcely a seat left. I felt compelled to comment, before I finished up standing all the way to Kettering.

"Isn't there a seat in here to suit you old buggers?" I enquired, staring at each of them in turn.

"Shut your mouth," said the man nearest to me, "We've only been on the train two minutes."

"Exactly! And if everyone took two minutes to find a sodding seat, the train would be an hour late setting off," I declared.

He embarked on a go slow, so I pushed passed him.

"Get out of the way you old fart," I instructed.

"You swine! You're a bloody swine!" he spluttered.

I turned on the fat, grey-haired sloth and pushed him down into a seat. The possibility of him getting a punch on the nose was looming large, until I saw the look of fear in his eyes and decided to show mercy.

"Another squeak out of you fatso and I'll punch you in the mouth and break your top set," I said, wittily in my view, but with more than a hint of menace.

"You all heard that. You're all witnesses. He threatened to assault me," he said, addressing the other passengers once I'd set off for the other end of the carriage.

I rushed down the compartment and just managed to grab the last seat before a bloke with a Labrador and a white stick made his lunge. The noise of the fat bloke's continued bleating was easily discernable, even from ten yards distant.

Just before Market Harborough, the ticket collector made his rounds. He was accosted by Fatty and forced to listen to his tale of woe, before honing in on me.

"Are you the gentleman involved in the dispute," he enquired in a particularly effete voice.

"Yes, I am."

"Frankly sir, I didn't see what happened and don't really know what to do as I'm new on this job," he said honestly.

"Well, as a policeman of some thirty years standing, let me instruct you on the law pertaining to assault," I said.

Having convinced him it was Fatty who had started the problem, I then suggested he phone ahead to the Railway Police in Kettering. I was alighting there and the police could take up the investigation. He considered this course of action, but was still dithering.

"I still don't know what to do," he moaned.

"Shall I tell you what to do?"

"Yes please."

"Fuck off to the other end of the train and collect some tickets."

"I will. I will," he declared.

So, he sashayed off to the other end of the train to collect some tickets. A few minutes later, as the train slowed down for Kettering, I made my way to the seats occupied by fatty and his pals. I have an abnormal capacity for malice at times and this was such an occasion. I gave my opponent my severest glare.

"Right, arsehole! Get off the train with me here in Kettering and bring your pals with you. We'll all go and see the police and you can lay your complaint. On the way to the police station however, I'll give you a real reason to complain, by breaking your nose. Come on!"

He declined my invitation.

I wasn't back in the UK to become a contender for the veterans' heavyweight title though; my preoccupation with keeping a pay cheque coming in was a more pressing reason.

Chapter 15

Arzew again

I **WASN'T GETTING ANY YOUNGER** and my more pessimistic acquaintances in Leicester rated my chances of finding a decent job to be precisely nil. They even suggested that, even at fifty years of age, one would be hard pressed to be land a position of any description. Well, that shows you what 'they' know! I'd sallied forth for fair Albion just before Christmas, with the intention of making one final assault upon the job market before throwing in the towel altogether. Admittedly, I'd done a little job-hunting homework before heading back to England's green and pleasant land. Some months previously, a nepotistic contact had indicated the possibility of an opening with his company in Kent, although pinning him down to a starting date from afar had proved a difficult undertaking. Now I was back in the UK, this was certainly a lead worth pursuing. Several religious organizations advertising vacancies in the *Church Times* were also beneficiaries of a letter from yours truly, in which I expressed my interest in whatever they might have to offer, no matter how paltry to salary. As a result, I was in with the sniff of a chance at an almshouse in Leicestershire, where they were looking for a resident warden.

The first hint that things were perhaps beginning to move in the right direction came when I was invited down to discuss the post in Kent. Things went swimmingly it seemed, although the illusive starting date was never mentioned. A fortnight later, the trustees of the 'Hind Sisters' Homes for Widows of Church of England Ministers' gave me an interview date and then, on my way down to do penance by watching Leicester City at the Walker's Stadium on Saturday afternoon, my phone rang. It was an old SAS pal I'd previously worked with in Algeria. Right out of the blue, the Japanese company we had worked for in the Arzew Industrial Area, near Oran, had asked us to return on a new project. For contractual reasons he was unavailable, but he had put my name forward for the post. He suggested I call a person by the name of Moriki Hata in Arzew with all haste, since our former employers IHI were keen to appoint a security manager immediately, if not sooner. Not being a lad to look a gift horse in the mouth, I'd phoned Hata san even before the Posthorn Gallop had signalled the arrival of the Blues onto the field of play. He accepted my financial terms without demur and appointed me on the spot; his only question being, "How quickly can you get out here?" Talk about having a job handed to you on a plate!

As Sod's Law dictates, even before I'd obtained my Algerian visa, the company in Kent gave me a starting date. On the ecclesiastical front, I was short-listed for the job at the almshouse and, just for good measure, I was asked if I'd be interested in being the verger of a city centre church. Who says there are no jobs in the UK for oldies?

Not long afterwards there I sat, resplendent in my bilious-green, several sizes too small all-Nippon uniform, bluffing my way as the security manager of an LPG site in darkest Algeria. The journey from the airport at Oran to Arzew revealed that nothing in the area had changed a jot since my previous contract in the wretched place. The Industrial Zone, meanwhile, continued to spew out an array of noxious substances, most of them injurious to health. It would take a decree from the Emperor himself to alter the Japanese work ethic; so it was still all work and no play at IHI. Our accommodation was in Camp 10, a place I knew all too well.

Not so much as a lick of paint had been applied to embellish its dilapidated appearance and it still bore a worrying resemblance to Stalag Luft 17. To make living in the place even more trying than before, the muezzin of the nearby mosque had become hi-tech, by installing an amplifier in his minaret. His exceedingly irritating 'call to worship' voice was now enhanced by the loudest sound amplification device in the whole of Islam. His wake-up routine started at 0400 hrs, which was hardly conducive with a lie in, but enabled me to dispense with the need for setting my alarm clock.

Prior to being granted my own place of abode, I bunked with the construction manager, Moriki Hata. He was a man with a pleasing disposition and a well-developed sense of humour; he partook of a glass of beer or saké with relish and had an eye for the ladies. In fact, Hata san was an all-round good guy, but for his silly laugh, the habit of constantly cracking his knuckles and toes and a twenty-a-day smoking habit. A student of the Nakabayashi School of Engineering no less, he told me that Naka had personally recommended me for this job. Nakabayashi the Samurai had made my life particularly difficult during the desalination project and it seemed highly improbable he would have put my name forward, but I was assured he had.

Hata adopted a philosophy not normally seen on industrial building sites in these climes; he recruited female engineers and interpreters. His rationale being, should there be a bit of skirt around, then the guys were less likely to knock chunks out of each other. There were four Japanese ladies on the site and, at the construction manager's invitation, a selection visited our villa each evening for a noggin. As pleasant an interlude as this was, the ageing Englishman didn't stand a realistic chance with the slanty-eyed lassies but Hata, despite behaving impeccably in public, was certainly very close to at least one of them.

342

After a month of lodging with Hata san, I was granted sole occupancy of Villa 40—a weather-beaten, rudely appointed billet. Unlike Chateau Hata, Chez Payne badly lacked ambiance and was not exactly a hive of activity in the evenings. The most I found do within its confines after the day's labour was to watch a bit of TV, eat peanuts, drink diet coke and snooze on the well-worn settee. Thereafter, it was off to an equally well-worn scratcher for a read of 'Daily Bread' and a chapter of a book, before being quickly overcome by slumber. Not an exciting life, but I reconciled myself to the drudgery by calculating the not inconsiderable sum the Japanese were paying me for my toil.

Meals were prepared in an insanitary kitchen, by a less than wholesome Japanese chef and his Algerian assistants. Provided boiled rice, noodles, raw meat and seafood were to your liking, then this was definitely the place to eat. Actually, it was the only place to eat. The diet grated on me very quickly, as did the disgusting eating habits of the Japanese, who slurp everything capable of being slurped with great relish. After much complaining about the fare, the chef found a box of frozen chips from somewhere and I was treated to 'chips with everything' for a couple of weeks.

The work being undertaken in our section of Arzew real estate was officially described as: 'the construction of three gas separation trains'. A 'train' in this case referring to an enormously complex, almost Heath-Robinson like series of pipes and machinery stretching over hundreds of yards. The vast plant already had six trains in operation; the additional three would make it the biggest establishment of its kind in the world. It was all a complete mystery to me and, if the truth be known, a matter of total disinterest. My remit was simply to supervise access and egress to the site; the technical stuff could safely be left in the hands of the plethora of engineers. In simplistic terms, natural gas was pumped through pipelines from gas fields located in the south and east of Algeria. It entered our GP1Z plant and into the separation trains, where it was broken down into butane and propane. The residue was burnt off through lofty chimneys, while the valuable gasses went into storage tanks, to be processed and shipped off to various parts of the world. Don't quote me on any of that information; it may have lost a little in the translation from Hata's Japanese to Hata's English.

Quite why I should have been invited to attend the Tank Kick-off Meeting was a mystery, since the only tanks I knew anything about were British Army Chieftains and Conquerors. Even worse was that the printed agenda indicated some input by the Security Manager. This was only my second day on the site and I feared my total lack of technical knowledge might make it my last. Amid much talk of nitrogen purging and pre-stressed bottom insulation, I spoke on security—as if I knew anything about the subject! My opening comment was in the form of a cheery, "Good morning. I'm Wally Payne, your friendly and flexible security manager," and would have been happy to see the slightest sign of a smile of acceptance on someone's lips. To my astonishment however, the assembled multitude of Japs, Spics, Dutchmen and Frogs—with only the Health & Safety man and me representing Her Majesty's interests—burst into belly laughs and a round of applause rang out! Thereafter, a few words about boring old security were sufficient to convince the congregation I was a good guy. Years of bluff, honed to perfection in the RMP, had won the day once again.

The other British passport holder on the project establishment was Henry, the Health & Safety manager. This humdrum, soft-spoken ex-submariner was preoccupied with his subject, to the point of boring me to death. Once, upon returning to the office after a trip to the site, he rushed over to speak to me.

"You'll never guess what I've just seen and photographed."

"A flock of naked nuns?" I volunteered.

"No, it was something more exciting than that."

"Somebody smoking behind the bike sheds?"

"No, it was two guys sitting in the cab of a moving JCB; one with his back to the direction of travel!"

Well blow me down. What wicked people there are wandering the world!

Henry was an insular man and we seldom had a meaningful conversation; something exacerbated by his deafness and permanent sore throat. His inability to hear and talk affected his performance on site so badly that his position became untenable. He had made numerous visits to the resident doctor for tests and tablets, but nothing seemed to improve his condition. Finally, Hata asked me for an opinion about his suitability to stay on site. As loath as I was to see a bloke lose his livelihood, I told Hata he ought to find a replacement and send this guy back to the UK for some much needed treatment. That was the last anyone ever saw of dear old Henry. Some months later he wrote to tell me he was in Belfast's Royal Victoria Hospital, suffering from cancer of the throat and neck, with only a 50-50 chance of survival. We corresponded for a while, until his brave letters dried up. When I called the hospital some months later to enquire about his welfare, they told me he was no longer registered as a patient. Henry was dead.

Out of financial expediency, I'd accepted the company's harsh work cycle of 12-weeks on and two-weeks off. This rotation was perfectly acceptable to the industrious Japanese, but I was not blessed with their work ethic. Furthermore, I'd quite forgotten what a rotten place Arzew was, how arduous the work was and how miserable it was to live in Camp 10.

Guys were systematically being driven into the ground, especially the Indians, Filipinos, Chinese and Sri Lankans, whose contracts were even more severe than mine. On the bus to the site in the mornings, all but a handful of our IHI personnel were asleep within 30 seconds of the bus starting up. Those first three months in Algeria were some of the most difficult I've ever endured.

IHI had engaged a security company rejoicing under the name of Prosur to perform all the physical security on site and in the two residential camps. The same company had been similarly contracted on the desalination project, when their performance had varied between extremely poor and pathetic. Had I been in Arzew at the time they were awarding the security contract, then their selection would have been fought tooth and nail. I wasn't there however and, with parsimony being the IHI watchword, Prosur were chosen. Their men were pitifully paid and, as a result, unreliable, prone to taking a day off for a better paid casual job, inefficient and bone idle. I was to spend many months convincing IHI to amend their contract with Prosur, to ensure the men were reasonably paid. My firmly held opinion was that they were far less likely to steal and 'turn a blind eye' if they were paid a living wage. The guard's vastly improved salaries were set to commence on the very day of my departure from Arzew, so I can't confirm whether or not their 90% pay increment ever materialised.

The selection of Prosur didn't sit very well with our overlords Sonatrach, whose own '2SP' security outfit were traditionally used on all their projects. Since IHI were constructing the 'trains' on Sonatrach real estate, there were several senior security bosses in the area determined to make life problematic for Prosur and for their commander-in-chief, the friendly and flexible Wally Payne. Nepotism, corruption and high office go hand in hand in Algeria, particularly in the world of security and it was an accepted fact that a person seeking employment as a 2SP guard would first need to cross someone's sweaty palm with a 50,000 dinar sweetener. This equated to £400 Sterling at the time, a considerable sum in Algerian terms. With more than a hundred Prosur guards employed by IHI, several Sonatrach people of exalted rank were losing out on a nice little earner. My Prosur guards were obstructing the flow of graft and were prime targets for removal, by fair means or foul, at the earliest opportunity. Should the IHI security manager be encouraged to leave at the same time, thereby leaving the coast open for unrestricted duplicity, then so much the better!

The overall boss of Sonatrach security was an unapproachable man by the name of Lazreg, a devious megalomaniac. He worked at the main office down in Oran, never answered his phone to me and ventured over to Arzew only when there was something clandestine or immoral afoot. I would have hated to put my life in the hands of this despot. Had he been British and in the RMP, the corporals would have left something particularly nasty in his boots.

The principal anti-Prosur point of attack came through Lazreg's assistant, the despicable Ziane Chahi, security manager of the GP1Z complex. The only thing this wretched creature and I had in common was the same date of birth; along with the singer Madonna. Sonatrach, at the insistence of Lazreg, demanded that every expat request for movement in and out of the industrial zone be signed by Chahi, rather than me. Similarly, every request for a gendarme escort needed to be agreed by this devious creature. There was neither rhyme nor reason for any of this and to make matters worse, he would arbitrarily change his petty regulations on a whim. The fact was, I couldn't pass wind without obtaining prior permission from him, in writing. He, of course, never committed a single word to paper in all this time. I'll spare my readers the details of the farcical goings-on with which I had to contend, save to say the man made my life a misery and revelled in every moment of it. He must have lain awake at nights, working on schemes to make himself progressively more vexatious; probably discussing them with the long-suffering Madame Chahi. My life might have been made easier had I yielded to his shameless demands: to provide him with various items of stationery and other equipment, as well as providing a position in my department for one of his female relatives. It's against my personal honour to surrender to a blackmailer; especially a disreputable rat and he got bugger all from me. A transferee from a lowly engineering position, Chahi had only been in the security department for two years and I'd forgotten more about the business than he will ever know. He was the only Algerian to whom I confided exactly how much I earned, since it made me feel superior. Even with his under the counter bonuses, his salary wouldn't have amounted to a quarter of mine.

The third conspirator was a giant by the name of Meki, the manager of 2SP in Arzew. His name first came to my attention one Saturday morning, when I received a telephone call from the Prosur guard commander at Camp 3. Without any prior information to IHI or Prosur, twenty members of 2SP had suddenly appeared at the main gate of the residential camp. Led by the burly Meki, they had told the Prosur chief that his crew were being replaced with immediate effect. The Prosur guys were made of sterner stuff than I'd ever imagined and, at the prospect of their livelihoods being taken away at a stroke, they refused to allow Meki's men into the camp.

Five minutes later, a similar assault on Camp 10 produced the same result, only this time the Prosur boys pulled the iron gates closed, locked them and refused to allow access to anyone. This could easily have presented me with a serious problem, given that all the IHI personnel lived in Camp 10. At Monsieur Wally's request, however, they announced they would be willing to open the gates for me. Thank goodness I'd been so benevolent when it came to handing out biscuits and sweeties to the lads at night.

I went to see the Sonatrach boss responsible for our operation and demanded to know what the hell was going on. He was as much in the dark as me, or so he maintained. I needed to know immediately whether it was Sonatrach's intention to replace our troops with their own security men. Following several calls in Arabic, a Sonatrach command decision was made—Prosur were to pack their bags and clear off. I journeyed up to the camps, conveyed the ill tidings to the men and asked them to leave without causing a riot. It's true that Prosur were under contract and couldn't be removed arbitrarily and that the action by 2SP was both illegal and immoral. These matters would need to be settled at a later date, however. Not unnaturally and with my full accord in fact, they ignored my request, made their weapons ready and battened down for the duration. Several 2SP members were bloodied during the conflict, which was to last for 36-hours. By lunch time on Sunday, the TV cameras were in situ and the boys lost little time in airing their well-founded grievances. The sieges of Camps 3 and 10 were in full swing.

A high-powered management and security meeting was swiftly convened at GP1Z. Lazreg, Meki and Chahi had overstepped the mark badly and they knew it. When cornered, Algerians are prone to speak either in Arabic, or in a mixture of Arabic and French; both of which are equally unintelligible to me. Vocally supported by the other two musketeers, Lazreg dominated proceedings, although only the Arabs present knew what the hell was going on. In the end, Lazreg was forced to confront me in French, whereupon he brazenly accused me of overreacting to the incidents. I lost my temper at this juncture and told it as it was. Nobody makes a scapegoat out of me and, after this farce, it was irrelevant to me whether I stayed in

Arzew or not. I enquired whether he considered it managerially moral to unilaterally replace my guards, in violation of written contracts and without the agreement of Sonatrach or IHI. He couldn't answer. My next poser was to ascertain whether he was aware that armed guards were specified in the contract for the camps, whereas his men didn't have the right under Algerian law to bear arms. He couldn't answer my second question either. When I enquired whether he intended to override the contracts signed by IHI and Prosur for camp security, he reverted to Arabic. The wise Monsieur Dahmane, Sonatrach's project manager, came up with a solution which, whilst absolutely unacceptable to me, meant my boys at least retained their jobs. The Japanese site manager took the line of least resistance and, interested only in keeping the peace, accepted his proposals without quibble. Camp 10 was handed over to 2SP and Camp 3 to Prosur. This resulted in vastly overstaffed security teams at both locations, but my men were still in employment and the dirty players were able to pocket their bonuses.

My work in Arzew necessarily brought me into contact with several vagabonds to whom I would cheerfully have done a mischief and the Lazreg, Chahi and Meki team were at the top of my hit list. In Algeria though, it's all too easy to have a person's throat cut for the price of a packet of fags and I was frequently forced to bite my lip rather than attempt retribution.

Returning from leave following this distasteful event, it came as a pleasant surprise to discover both Lazreg and Meki under suspension. Even Sonatrach have some ethical personnel in their upper echelons it seems. Rumour had it they were not only involved in the scam to replace Prosur, but had also connived in the theft of a petrol tanker from a fuel storage depot. Some months later the venal swine were both reinstated, to conspire and cheat anew.

In my view, the IHI security department required a minimum of six personnel to function anything like efficiently. Including me, we numbered precisely three: Yasmin, an overconfident, egotistical, albeit generously breasted Berber lady and Mohamed, an Algerian with a serious attitude problem. Mohamed had been appointed to run the department pending the arrival of an expatriate security manager. He had worked for me on a previous operation in Arzew and, whilst a very aggressive type of chap, he knew his stuff. In the interceding years, he had worked for IHI in a security role on a couple of small projects, but this monster operation was beyond a 28-year old who spoke only rudimentary English. Eighteen months previously, whilst engaged on IHI business, Mohamed had been seriously injured in a traffic accident. He had lain in a coma for three weeks, after which the company paid for him to be medically evacuated to Lyon where he remained in hospital for six months. His legs had been badly broken and were now full of screws, pins and titanium plates; worst of all though, the crash had left him with a severely altered personality. In short, he was barking mad! It's worth mentioning that the driver of the vehicle involved in the crash walked away from the accident unscathed, but then, he had been wearing a seatbelt.

Mohamed found it hard to accept demotion to the position of my assistant and clearly resented my arrival. Not only a liar and a cheat; he wasn't remotely dependable, was prone to puerile pranks, drank whisky to excess and, hardest of all for his subordinates to bear, he was a megalomaniac of the highest order. Known to his Algerian contemporaries as *le Diable*, I found it necessary to rein him in several times each week, whereupon he would behave for five minutes before resuming his unacceptable behaviour. I later discovered that, at the various meetings it was necessary for the pair of us to attend, he was in the habit of announcing himself in Arabic as the IHI

Security Manager, with me his faithful expatriate sidekick. This fact only came to my knowledge at the very end of my service; otherwise I'd have paraded him around every office in the area by the ear and made him put the facts straight.

Not even an IHI departmental head had the authority to sign letters addressed to outside agencies. This was the preserve of the Japanese Site Manager, who must have been pretty pissed off with signing his name scores of times each day, but this was the Nippon way of doing things. Normally I would never go though anyone's desk, but when Mohamed had been sick for several days and some documents were missing, I considered it expedient to open his drawers. Therein I discovered a file of letters, written in French and addressed to the Gendarmes, Algerian Army, Port Police and the Industrial Zone Administration. The signature block on each letter was in Mohamed's name, indicating that he was the Security Manager. Of these letters I had no knowledge and, more importantly, neither did the Japanese. I brought this to the attention of the IHI Administration Manager and he passed the information onto Tokyo. A formal letter of warning was issued to Mohamed.

With one outrageous exception, IHI departments and sub-contractors followed the security regulations without quibble. Our rules were tried and tested for work on a large industrial site in Algeria; other regulations were instituted at the insistence of the Gendarmerie Nationale, the Algerian Army and the organisation responsible for security within the Arzew Industrial Area and were not negotiable.

Construction of the new gas storage tanks, a huge undertaking, was the remit of Italian subcontractors Bentini. One ought to have sensed trouble with this rabble I suppose, since one of their engineers was called Valter Mussolini! Their general manager, Alberto Zuccini, was almost unique for an

Italian, in that he actually led from the front. One example he demonstrated so ably to his men was that, when you're the only storage tank constructor in town and therefore irreplaceable, you can ignore security regulations with importunity, with no prospect of ever being brought to task. Over the months I was able to demonstrate, by means of a plethora of evidence, outrageous violations of every security regulation pertaining to expatriates working in this dangerous country. For example, Bentini kept an apartment near Oran airport where parties were held at weekends; Zuccini had an apartment in the nearby village of Portauxpoules where he entertained his secretary and the Sheraton Hotel was the company's regular watering hole. Their senior personnel were regularly seen in the surrounding towns and reports of them travelling further afield were not uncommon. All missions to these venues were required to be made with a gendarme escort; an obligatory requirement for every expatriate travelling outside the industrial zone.

Access and egress to and from the industrial zone was controlled by armed police officers at one of four gates, imaginatively numbered 1-4. Since every mission involved leaving the zone, Bentini's apparent carte blanche to travel outside without an escort demanded investigation. My spies told me money was being paid to the head of the industrial zone police force, Monsieur Chaa; so I invited Monsieur Chaa to my office to join me in a cup of char. He flatly denied any accusations of wrongdoing until, purely by chance, who should enter my office but Zuccini! I put my accusations to him in the presence of Chaa and an embarrassing silence ensued. Reams of paper regarding the misdemeanours of Bentini were penned to IHI and copied to the Gendarmes, Algerian Army, Sonatrach, the Italian Embassy and the owners of the industrial zone. Nothing whatsoever was done to rein in the Italians; the response of those in authority regarding Bentini making a mockery of security regulations, was to put their heads in the sand and keep on taking the graft!

There were an abundance of other severe annoyances designed to make this a bloody awful job; my main gripe being the fact IHI wouldn't pay me! Having submitted my bill and timesheet for the first month's work, I was contacted by the pay department in Tokyo. They were unable to pay salaries into private accounts apparently and it was obligatory for me to provide them with details of my company account, along with copies of the following documents:

    a.   The Memorandum of Association.
    b.   The Articles of Association.
    c.   Certificate of Incorporation.
    d.   An Example of my Company Business Card.

Why wasn't I told this before they dragged me out to Arzew? A trip to Lloyds Business Banking section in their Leicester branch would have sorted all this out for me at a nominal charge. Now abroad, I needed to deal with Lloyds International Branch in the Isle of Man, who put me onto a company in Dubai that could form a limited company for me; but at an outrageous cost. The trouble was I was now marooned in Algeria and needed original copies of bank statements and utility bills, which were at my home in the Philippines. It's debatable whether Algeria or the Philippines has the most inept postal service in the world, although I'd probably opt for the latter. From Manila, it took 35-days for an express letter containing these documents to be delivered to me in Arzew, whereupon they were sent to Dubai by DHL, for work to begin on forming my company. It took several months before the financial world was stunned by news of the formation of Walter Payne Associates Limited, which had been a complicated transaction for sure. I banked in Leicester, my company banked in the Isle of Man, my solicitor was in Dubai, I worked in Algeria, lived in the Philippines, my company was incorporated in the British Virgin Islands and my inside leg measurement is 31 inches.

After my first three months of work, I returned to the UK for my fortnight's leave and spent it all asleep on my mate Bob's settee. I'd received neither a penny piece, nor a yen note, by way of remuneration from IHI, which was academic really, since I was too tired to venture out to spend anything in any case.

Returning in mid-April, I was still worn out and swiftly came to the conclusion there had to be more to life than working, eating and sleeping. Despite the lure of the filthy lucre, I wanted more of an existence than simply working myself to death. Other selfish considerations, like the desire to watch sport, get my leg over occasionally and to eat something other than raw fish and boiled rice may have coloured my decision. Suddenly, the prospect of me struggling on until the end of June seemed a mountain just too high to climb and I decided to pack it in. To my great disappointment, I discovered there was no escape clause to my contract, although a chat with Hata san solved my problems in an instant. He was keen for me to be part of his team and allowed me to change the terms of my contract, to a very reasonable routine of 2-months on and 2-months off.

Just the same, by the beginning of August things in Arzew were getting badly on my nerves. Yasmin had been sacked, although our numbers had increased to the recommended six, including two large bosomed females; but the antics of Mohamed were becoming increasingly impossible. No less than three of the four office staff had consulted the site doctor with Mohamed induced stress related disorders; the other had laid a formal complaint against him. All of them were being bullied unmercifully, always behind my back or, if I was present, then he'd torment them in Arabic. What a talent. I approached the Algerian in charge of local employment several times regarding this evil character. We had both known him for a considerable period of time on previous contracts and were in full accord that Mohamed was a severely changed man. He also concurred that, in his view, he was no longer capable of carrying out his duties. In true Algerian fashion, however, nothing was done. I also approached the IHI administration manager on a host of occasions, finally convincing him my department and IHI would be better off by granting extended leave to Mohamed. I even offered to pay his salary for the period of his absence.

The truth regarding IHI's constraints when dealing with their wounded hero and my *bête noire* finally came out when the administration manager visited me at home one evening. Whilst agreeing with my assertions, he gave me four reasons why the man could never be sacked, no matter how shabbily he performed:

1. He had been hurt whilst working for the company and the Japanese felt they had a moral obligation to keep him in their employ.
2. IHI had invested immense sums of money in his hospitalisation and welfare; a by-product of which was enormous goodwill towards the company from many quarters. To jettison him now would probably have the reverse effect.
3. His father held a high-ranking position with Sonatrach, the Algerian conglomerate with whom IHI was contracted.
4. His mother was the manageress of the Arzew Labour Office and provided all the local labour for the site. Keeping on her good side was imperative to the war effort.

So, as we said in the Army, I was pissing against the wind. Despite complaints from every quarter, this chap was not going to be moved by the spineless Japs. It was obvious to me, if not apparent to my Japanese masters that the security department would have to function either without Mohamed, or me! As a younger man, I'd have taken radical action to ensure the victory was mine, but there was no fight left in me. I was both physically and mentally spent working in this environment. The problems were myriad and a vast proportion could be attributed directly to Chahi's intransigence and Mohamed's gross inefficiency. The caustic combination of workaholic, racist Japanese and inept, smelly-arsed Algerians had made life very trying for one of Her Majesty's subjects in exile.

Access to the camp was controlled directly by me and, arriving at work on Tuesday morning, I discovered the entrance blocked by a sixty-ton crane. About the existence, ownership and destination of this abnormal load, I had no prior knowledge and so instructed the guards to have the vehicle moved to an adjacent parking area until the matter had been investigated. Returning to the entrance ten minutes later, I was verbally assailed by a diminutive Japanese person—in French, as he couldn't speak a word of English. The giant vehicle was on his charge it appeared. What the bearded Nip lacked in height, he certainly made up for in mouth, for he simply wouldn't shut up and continued to berate me roundly in his badly fractured French. Electing to adopt my most threatening pose, I towered over the poison dwarf and was unsporting enough to step on his feet. All to no avail it seemed, as he continued to rattle on. Finally, rather than clout him around the ears, I elected to walk away and leave him and his crane outside the site. At this, he lost his self-control completely and ran after me, screaming loud enough in French to be heard back in Osaka:

"Come back here at once!"

"I beg your pardon?" I asked.

"Come back here immediately," he replied.

"Listen short-arse. The last time someone of your nationality saw fit to order an Englishman to do something against his will, we dropped atom bombs on your stinking country. Furthermore, the last time someone as small as you insulted me in this fashion, I ensured he spent a protracted period in hospital. Now, before I do you some severe damage, desist from talking and I'll explain the situation to you."

He desisted, I explained and the crane entered the site.

The stunted Japanese wasted no time in laying a complaint against me though and, shortly afterwards, I was required to explain the incident to the administration manager. Not for a moment would I confess to any wrongdoing but, in retrospect, consider that the incident might have been handled rather more diplomatically. I'm sure the matter would never have escalated the way it did had I not been so totally sick of the whole shambles this project had turned into.

On Wednesday, one of Mohamed's supreme howlers was uncovered. Since application forms for access badges to the port area needed to be completed in Arabic, it had been necessary to entrust him with the undertaking. After a month of farting around, progress had been minimal and the main sub-contractor had complained. The Japanese are serial complainers it seems and, in true IHI style, a forgathering was called. Those seated around the impressive conference table were three representatives of the main sub-contractor; with a liaison engineer, the administration manager, Mohamed and me representing IHI. Prior to the conference, the sad facts regarding our abject failure to obtain the port badges came to light and it was clear that Mohamed had subjected me to some 'mushroom' treatment. He'd kept me in the dark and fed me lots of shit. In view of this, I was willing to put my hand up, admit our failings and give an assurance things would be rectified as soon as practicable.

First, however, there needed to be the usual introductions around the table. On this occasion though, instead of using English, the *lingua franca* throughout the site, the liaison engineer opened the batting with a monologue in Japanese that lasted several minutes. I felt compelled to interrupt proceedings, contending that since the security department was under scrutiny here, matters needed to be conducted either in French or English.

"Oshigawa san only make introduction Payne san," explained the administrator.

"That may well be, but how are Mohamed and I to know? Be good enough to conduct the meeting in English or French."

At this juncture, one of the sub-contractors leaned across the table, cocked his head to one side and glared at me. Thirty seconds of his slant-eyed scowling proved sufficient for my quick temper.

"Is there something interesting about my face mister, or are you mentally retarded?"

"I speak Ingrish," he replied.

"Not very well, let me assure you. In any case, what has your peculiar behaviour to do with my honourable mother tongue?"

"No understand."

"Let me put it to you in the simplest English. Either you stop leering at me immediately, or I'll render you incapable of slurping noodles for a month."

"Prease Warry san," interjected the mild mannered administrator, "You always big gentleman before now."

"Not when faced by ignorance and arrogance of this nature. I'm now leaving this meeting and you can try and sort things out without me. If and when you decide to speak a language understood by all present, please inform me."

I marched back to my office, to be joined five minutes later by Mohamed. He had clearly been tasked to persuade me to return to the meeting, but there was no prospect of that in my current state of mind. I sat for a while in angry contemplation and decided to leave IHI and Arzew at the earliest opportunity. I'd had my fill.

Leaving Algeria wasn't as simple as one might imagine; I'd been on site longer than a month and would need to produce my work permit at the airport before they would allow me to depart. Since this document was held by the administration department, it was obvious a swift departure and release from my contract would call for a little guile. My old friend the site doctor was summoned and, upon his arrival in my office, I used the ever dependable 'stress' ploy—it never fails. He knew he was being subjected to a bluff, but signed me off for three days just the same. I left with the crowd for Camp 10 at the prescribed hour, having first cleared my desk, deleted private stuff from the computer and grabbed all my personal gear. I wasn't returning. The administration manager came to see me that evening, as I knew he would. He was very understanding and, provided I arranged a replacement security manager, he promised to let me leave as soon as possible. A call to a former SAS man of my acquaintance resolved the minor problem of finding a successor.

I sat in Villa 40 for four blissful days; it felt as if a huge weight had been lifted from my shoulders. The administration guys were finally able to offer me a flight ticket when, at the eleventh hour, an economy seat presented itself on the Oran to Lyon flight. Lyon wasn't ideal by any means but I snapped the opportunity up, since flights out of Algeria during Ramadan were at a premium. All Algerians with a bolt-hole abroad make their exits before they are subjected to the strictures of the fast, something which is strictly observed in the country. My emotions as I left Camp 10 for the last time were those of total, blessed and overwhelming relief.

During many years of working in Algeria, my flights to and from the blighted land had always been made in Air Algérie's first-class cabins. This time, instead of ascending the steep flight of stairs to the airport lounge and a complimentary cup of coffee, I made for the other ranks' waiting room and found a plastic chair on which to while away the hours. My departure coincided with that of a throng of aged desert Arabs, bound for a pilgrimage to Mecca before they snuffed it. To a pilgrim, they were attired in white gowns, with several yards of white bandage wrapped around their heads to complete their ensembles. The turbans may have been sensible headgear when mounted upon a camel in the desert but, to me, seemed highly impractical as travelling titfers. The desert men weren't mountain fresh and the waiting room stank of an objectionable melange of reeking oxters, Arab arses, Ramadan breath and mothballs. It came as a blessed relief when the announcer called them forward for their flight to Jeddah, whereupon the majority sped, gazelle-like, to the departure desk. A few tarried to expectorate in the waste-bins, have a last rectal scratch, ritual belch or voidance of wind. Alas, with their departure and with no more smelly bums or fetid feet to enjoy, the flies all descended upon the lone Englishman instead. I was left to wonder what the pilgrims' dormitory in Jeddah would have smelt like next morning.

Thirty minutes later, the announcer called for steerage passengers to board the flight bound for Lyon. I dawdled to the desk and, on the way, put my St John's Ambulance Brigade skills to good effect by treating Ramadan's first victim of the fast. A buxom wench had succumbed to the heat and lack of liquid, so I undid her top button and plied her with a diet coke. This won me the undying thanks of her panicky husband, whilst simultaneously consigning me to Islamic damnation in all probability. The exigencies of my medical duties relegated me to being the last passenger to get on the bus to traverse the airport apron, before it stopped near the aircraft. Here, it was necessary to 'recognise' your suitcase prior to boarding the plane, whereupon handlers would throw it onto a trolley and load it into the plane's hold. Even before descending from the bus, it was clear my expensive Samsonite suitcase wasn't among the few remaining pieces of luggage on the tarmac. A loader, dressed in a violently luminous yellow jacket, was made cognisant of the fact and he promptly hot-footed to the main airport building. He returned a few minutes later, only to give me his 'it's not in there' shrug and then report to his foreman. A summit meeting of loaders ensued, before one of them ran to the rear of the plane, where an expensive Samsonite suitcase stood in supreme isolation. It was mine! The explanation for my case's seclusion was that it was London bound; a rationale which seemed to satisfy the Oran (Es Senia) Airport Baggage Handlers' Union, if not me.

I boarded the old Boeing, only to discover seat 30C in the very last row, adjacent to two malodorous lavatories. My neighbour in 30B considered it fashionable to travel in an underarm hair exposing singlet, thereby making an enemy of me for life and the man in 29C was snoring loudly, even before the plane left the runway. After a great deal of pushing, shoving and raised voices, the plane finally took to the skies and within minutes we were over the Mediterranean. There was reasonable order among the masses for a few minutes; until the captain's injudicious decision to turn off the 'fasten seatbelt' sign signalled a mass outbreak of bladder ailments amongst the passengers. A queue to use the unsavoury toilets formed by my left arm and didn't decline numerically until the stewards came around with the nosebags thirty minutes later. Given this was the first day of Ramadan, it surprised me to see so many people tucking into their halal chicken with such obvious relish. One shabby individual making a visit to the toilet later in the journey caused consternation, by smoking in the toilet and causing a fire when he stubbed out his cigarette butt in the waste bin. The stewards, for once called upon to do more than play silly games in the rear galley, took the man seriously to task. I saw him at the baggage carousel in Lyon just the same, so no punitive action appeared to have been taken. This was undoubtedly one of history's most uncomfortable flights. In stark contrast, my business-class flight on British Airways from Lyon to London was blissful, despite the homosexual purser taking a shine to me. I played along with him, thus ensuring the speedy delivery of copious quantities of red wine and cognac to seat 1B.

Back in the Philippines, it took me several weeks to get over the lassitude brought about by my last tour in Arzew. Just the same, within two months my feet had begun to itch once again.

When I left the Retreat House in Cambridgeshire a few years previously, the minister in charge of the spiritual side of things wrote me a card, on which he hit the nail on the head concerning my attitude to life. He referred to me as, "Somewhat of a wanderer on the face of the earth." No matter what I do, I'm always looking to see what's on the other side of the hill—it used to be a mountain, but hills are enough for me these days. The other side of the hill on this occasion was the UK, where two further jobs in the church had presented themselves. One was the post of warden at an almshouse in the Malvern Hills and the other, the selfsame post at the Hind Sisters' Homes I'd rejected exactly a year previously. The incumbent of the post had lasted barely as long as I'd stuck Arzew out.

I went for an informal visit to the set up in Malvern and was delighted by the magnificent old buildings, church and gardens comprising the complex. During a chat with the Anglo-Catholic minister-in-charge however, it became apparent he was taken aback to discover I'd never been confirmed into the Church of England, despite me having made it perfectly clear of my Methodist leanings when submitting my application. We never broached the subject, but I was certain he would have refused me the Eucharist in his church and that wouldn't have been acceptable. The perceived possibility of being turned away from the altar rail bothered me considerably, since I would have resented having confirmation being forced upon me. Then, the size of the honorarium they offered was minute and the designated accommodation contained not a single stick of furniture. The only place to sit down in the warden's house, it appeared, was in the toilet. I expected better and promptly withdrew my application.

A few days after deciding against embarking on a career in the almshouse game, a peculiar incident occurred at Boots the Chemist in Leicester's Gallowtree Gate. I'd gone into the busy pharmacy to have a prescription filled and saw two signs suggesting which queue to join: 'Immediate Collection' or 'Collection Later'. Since there were three people in the 'immediate' line, I judged the empty 'collect later' row to be a better bet. After all, I had no pressing engagements and the first race at Newmarket wasn't until noon. As I approached the lady behind the counter, a voice boomed:

"Oi, the fucking queue is over 'ere!"

"Are you talking to me old chap?" I enquired.

"Yea! The fucking queue is 'ere, get in it."

Not convinced he was able to read, I invited him to join me in re-reading the signs. Boots in Leicester is always packed and so, playing to the crowd, I belittled his lack of comprehension, shabby attire and poor personal pride in that he was unshaven. He was also chided for his ignorance, in imagining he was at liberty to talk to an obvious superior without first having been granted permission.

"You're asking for a good 'iding," he declared.

"And you, my friend, are a pathetic little man who oughtn't to be foolish enough to take on a person who is clearly your better in every way."

Returning to the counter to confirm I could deposit my prescription and pick it up later, who should follow me but my newly made acquaintance. He was clearly intent on fisticuffs and the more I ignored him, the more aggressive he became. Finally, he took a seat and waited for me to finish my business. As I strode past the ignoramus and towards the exit, he arose to confront me.

"You and me, outside!" he declared.

"Willingly," I replied.

He was stopped in his tracks by a security guard; one of the biggest and broadest women I've ever seen. Fearing an imminent fight in the store, the counter staff had summoned her to the pharmacy. The CCTV recording had seemingly shown my opponent to be the absolute aggressor and Wally Payne, the mild-mannered victim. Who says the camera never lies? How fortunate for me there was no sound on the recording. She ordered him to stay in the store and asked if I wished to lay a complaint. Declaring myself a pacifist and non-complainer, I thanked her for her intervention and left the premises to the cries of, "You're a fucking coward!" from my opponent.

Emerging from WH Smith's a few minutes later, a *Daily Telegraph* tucked under my arm, who should I espy scouring Gallowtree Gate and still in a state of ferment? It was the bounder from Boots, by my troth. I sneaked up behind him.

"Looking for someone?" I enquired.

He turned quickly, but nowhere near quickly enough. A single, well-delivered straight left was sufficient to rearrange his teeth, sit him firmly on his backside and remove any desire he might have had to pursue the matter. I made my cowardly way down an alleyway and into the marketplace, to mingle with the pre-Christmas shoppers buying their Brussels sprouts. My conduct was undignified and inappropriate for someone of my age and station in life but, until I find a better way of dealing with louts, a punch in the teeth will have to suffice.

On Boxing Day I flew to the Philippines for the final time. My spouse had been making life uncomfortable for me in recent times and she continued in the same vein upon my arrival back in Cavite province. After several weeks of unhappiness I finally gave up the unequal struggle, both with her and her country and, on the Ides of March, headed for Hong Kong once again.

Chapter 16

Wally Payne – The Old Colony

I WAS BACK in Hong Kong; dragging a couple of pensions it's true but, long after I ought to have been put out to pasture, panglossian Payne continued working in an endeavour to replenish his personal privy purse. I am, alas, a living example of the old adage that a fool and his money are soon parted and words like reckless, cavalier and foolhardy are inadequate when it comes to describing the manner in which I've treated my fortune. In mitigation for my crass stupidity, I'd been ably assisted on my journey to pauperism by a profligate spouse; a woman with no concept of financial prudence whatsoever and who is, in all probability, a direct descendent of the prodigal son. A Malawian once told me to "Look after the tambala and the kwacha will look after themselves." On reflection, perhaps I ought to have paid more attention to my tambala, or even married one of Nwachukwu's kinswomen. It was my own choice to see the world in style however, before becoming too frail to climb up to the Parthenon under my own steam. What's sadder than watching the blue rinse and colostomy bag brigade trying to enjoy their fortunes when it's too late? The back of the aeroplane never good enough for me either; not once I'd experienced the pure pleasure of sitting in the posh end. Furthermore, eating in a hamburger joint will never do for me, not when there's a decent restaurant situated just around the corner.

Having finally and irrevocably convinced myself that, despite having seen a considerable number of summers, I needed to start my life afresh, I activated my oft considered

Philippines Escape Plan and fled to the former British Colony of Hong Kong. After two nights in the Silvermine Beach Hotel, I caught wind of the fact a New Zealander of my slight acquaintance was leaving his apartment in Wang Tong village empty for a 6-month period and, even at the last moment, was anxiously seeking a house sitter. In my desperation to have a roof over my head, it never occurred to me to contemplate why there had not been any other takers for the role and snapped up his offer. Within ten seconds of occupying the first-floor property, the reason became blindingly obvious. It was absolutely honking! Being a former military man, well used to battling adversity and finding an answer to the direst dilemma, the solution was obvious. No, of course I didn't clean the place myself; I hired two Filipina girls to sort it out while spending a pleasant day at Sha Tin Races. So, for 6-months, I had a base from which to formulate the next stage of my life.

During those six months, I tried my damndest to find some way of earning an honest dollar. Although finding a position within the security industry was, in reality, the last thing I wanted, it was in this area that I concentrated my efforts just the same. At least I could produce a reasonably impressive CV if required. To be brutally honest, the possibilities of landing a job of any description in Hong Kong at my age were slim indeed, but I had to make the effort. During this period I was set to be a warehouseman in a factory; the 'ghost writer' for a perfectly wretched book written by an Israeli; a stand-in bar manager at Rosanna's; the security manager of a petro-chemical site in Kazakhstan; a part-time salesman in a book shop; the operations manager of a security company; a risk assessment operative of a Singapore-based security outfit and, believe it or not, the risk assessment officer of another rotten security company. I'd prostituted myself around pretty well but, in the event, none of the possibilities bore fruit.

During what was to prove a financially lean period, I did at least manage to earn some money in the field forced upon many of the British 'hopeless cases'—by teaching English. As it transpired, I turned out to be rather good at the job and, after starting by teaching a professional pianist once a week, I developed a clientele of no less than eight students. Being a teacher wasn't a task I enjoyed in the least it must be confessed, but it gave me the choice of evading the supermarket shelf dedicated to products whose sell-by dates were about to expire and also to select butter once again, rather than enduring cheap margarine.

Ample free time between lessons gave me the opportunity of engaging in my passion of walking the rugged tracks on Lantau Island, although one particular jaunt was to give me an adrenalin rush altogether more extreme than I'd bargained for!

It's an odd fact, but you can walk a route times without number and yet still be oblivious to something perfectly obvious. The concrete path leading off the Mui Wo to Tung Chung track was certainly overgrown, but easily discernable if you were wanting to venture left and through to the valley that lay hidden from view. I had just never noticed it before. Within ten yards the path became so overgrown as to be almost impassable, although the concrete was still solid enough underneath the mass of foliage. After 200 yards, the track crossed a small stream and headed uphill for a further furlong, before coming to an abrupt stop at a grave site. Such paths are a common enough feature on Lantau Island, although this 'horse shoe' grave had clearly not been visited for its annual Ching Ming grave cleaning for a very long time.

Approaching the tomb to pay my respects, I became aware of something substantial moving in the bushes to my right. Expecting to see nothing more intimidating than a large lizard, to my absolute horror I espied the head of an exceedingly large Burmese python! I froze; the python stopped and our eyes met.

To my good fortune, the serpent appeared disinclined to take on a man sporting a Leicester City jersey and, with a disdainful look, he slithered casually down the slope and into a dense thicket. This was one hell of a big snake, many metres in length and with a girth almost as thick as my well-developed, beautifully proportioned thighs. My rapid about-turn would have delighted any drill sergeant and my descent back down the path was swift in the extreme. I was left to contemplate just how foolish my compulsion to go off the beaten track alone really is.

My monetary problems were all self-inflicted and, whilst seeking neither sympathy nor alms from anyone, two people took it upon themselves to help their comrade in distress. Luke, a restaurateur and licensed victualler of some renown in the old Colony, who was a friend and my erstwhile business partner in a spectacularly ineffective foray into the security equipment business many years previously, pressed a considerable sum into my palm. Then David, a friend of decades and the guy who sat next to me in church for years before defecting to the ranks of the choir, slipped a large cheque into my breast pocket. I will never forget the largesse of either of these two friends and I'm pleased to announce they were both reimbursed once the tide turned in my favour.

Being a firm adherent of the little known saying, "Faint heart never won a financial tap when you really need it," I wrote to numerous friends and relatives of means explaining my predicament, but stopping short of directly asking for funds. In almost every case, there was a modicum of sympathy for my predicament and occasional good wishes for a brighter future, but offers to bail me out proved mightily elusive. Their lack of charity was noted and, to quote Ko-Ko in 'The Mikado', "I've got a little list." In fact, it's a rather extensive list and, when I finally land the EuroMillions jackpot, I will be equally as generous to them as they were to me! All too soon, the New Zealander returned to repossess his modest dwelling place and I steeled myself to claiming a bed space on Mui Wo beach with the rest of the bums.

As if by magic, however, another example of the most outrageous good fortune that has seen me survive so often when all seemed lost, manifested itself once again. The aforementioned Luke, showing friendship and compassion transcending by far the call of duty, offered me a job. As well as the very decent salary specified in my contract, addendum clauses provided for free accommodation and a generous food and beverage allowance in any of his six licensed premises. Needless to say, he didn't need to make the offer twice. So, after a period when I could foresee precious little in the way of a bright future in the Orient, life was suddenly about to take on an altogether rosier glow. At the time, I wondered if it would ever be possible for me to repay him for this magnanimous gesture. Appointing me as his office administrator must have been something he needed to think long and hard about, since Luke was well aware of my renowned volatility. It was important for me to convince him that the years had mellowed me somewhat. Shortly after starting work and when even I was beginning to believe the propaganda regarding my new-found tranquillity, an incident occurred that might easily have cost me dearly had it ever become common knowledge.

Macau has never been one of my favourite places; it's just too small and, since becoming the gambling capital of southeast Asia, it's a tawdry spot in my view. What has always made the journey to and from the former Portuguese enclave even more unpalatable for me are the rugby scrums at immigration. Once a vessel disgorges its passengers, the race to make it to the front of the queue to face the arrival officials is undignified to say the least. For this reason, I've always travelled first class, a method whereby the posh passengers are guaranteed a thirty-second start over the steerage bums. Arriving back in Hong Kong after a trip to Macau's splendid Venetian Hotel, the eight elite passengers from the 1530 hrs Cotai Strip Ferries vessel had negotiated the first set of steps ahead of the field scurrying along behind and I was about to turn through 180 degrees and onto the first of four escalators leading to the arrivals area. At the corner stood an exceedingly large and exceedingly clearly marked rubbish bin and, a nanosecond before making my right turn, a diminutive Chinaman, possibly a retired jockey, came up on the inside rails. Well, this little Asian wasn't taking my ground and I made sure he collided with the rubbish bin rather than pip me at the post. The bin clanked off the wall and ricocheted across the corridor, to smite a fellow first class Filipino lady passenger a mighty wallop, just below the knee. A loud curse in Tagalog followed and I turned to remonstrate with the impatient bin-bouncing bounder, pushing him firmly backwards and onto his bottom.

It was conceivable, I suppose, that this impatient clown was in an almighty rush to get home for his teatime noodles, or had he perchance simply forgotten to take his prescription Valium that day? In any case, the 100lb weakling arose and launched himself at me, swinging his weighty duty-free bag in the direction of my head. Even a long-retired pugilist like me would have been ashamed to have allowed such a wild haymaker to find its mark and I simply swayed back. Quickly regaining my upright stance, I discovered him standing directly in front of me, hopelessly weighed down by his heavy bag, which was on the floor and still in his grasp. His unguarded face, snarling in anger, was a mere foot from my left fist. It was just too inviting an advantage to pass up and he was cracked firmly enough in the phizog to lay him on his back. This was no ordinary idiot though, but a thoroughbred, for he arose and came careering forward for a second helping; walking straight into a punch that conclusively ended the contest in favour of the British heavyweight.

Quite how he managed to make the Arrivals Hall before me is unclear, but there he was, bleeding nicely and laying his complaint to the police in a noisy fashion. Speedily gluing into place the false moustache I invariably have secreted upon my person for such eventualities, popping on my sunglasses and adjusting my flat cap to an innocent angle, I was able to pass close enough to the aggrieved, two policemen and a Canadian lady witness to hear what was going on. The Canadian lady had been directly behind me at the time of the fracas and I heard her announce, "It was entirely the fault of the Chinese man officer; the old European man was totally innocent." The reference to 'old man' smarted more than a little but, in the circumstances, may the good Lord bless the Dominion of Canada.

I took a circuitous route back to my quarters, just in case he had any meat cleaver bearing chums who might want to test the efficacy of their weapons on me. Alas, I'd proved once again that a teenage thug never reforms, but simply grows up to be an old thug.

During my years in Luke's employ, there was never an occasion when my performance was less than professional and he frequently saw fit to remark that employing me as his administrator was certainly one of his better decisions. He had good reason for these comments as, from the outset, I became his archivist; record-keeper; office-minder; advisor; confidant; tutor; chaperone; speech-writer; wet-nurse and foster parent. It was me who covered up his gaffes, lied on his behalf, kept his secrets, sold his properties for more than they were worth and rewrote all his letters in English, rather than what passed for English in Lancashire. On reflection, I may even have been underpaid. Luke was the owner of six successful bar/restaurants, a dozen valuable flats and a junk. It would have been two junks, but for an oversight that wouldn't have occurred had I been his administration manager at the time. He had failed to insure his second vessel and, the day after the policy lapsed, a typhoon struck Hong Kong and sent Junk No. 2 to the bottom of the South China Sea. He had become a rich man by taking the odd risk, sometimes pushing the borders of legality; possessing an uncanny sixth sense of knowing when to buy and sell, as well as, by his own admission, huge slices of good fortune. He was also something of an enigma. For the most part charismatic, witty, fine company and generous to a fault, there was, alas, an altogether darker side to his personality. The happiness and contentment his financial success ought to have afforded him was denied, by the firmly held conviction that everyone was trying to cheat him out of his money. Many of his staff members, although in all probability totally innocent of any misdeed, were to fall victim of his suspicions. Mercifully, I was spared the ignominy of being considered a villain, until immediately prior to my departure from his employ that is.

By virtue of his position, Luke was obliged to socialise with his punters, often late into the night. Not being a man to shirk his responsibilities, it was a task he undertook with relish and his appearance in the office before mid-afternoon would cause raised eyebrows. Had he restricted his nocturnal overindulgences to sampling the fruit of the brewer's, vintner's and distiller's arts, then all may have been well. It was when pills, powders and potions began to influence his demeanour that things started to go awry. There were an increasing number of occasions when his manner gave me reason for concern; as irrationality, mood swings, verbal aggression, tantrums, rudeness and eccentricity became ever more discernible.

He was thoroughly tired of the licensed victualler's game and, had the right offer come along, I'm convinced he'd have taken the money and run. Since he was getting richer by the day, however, there was no real need for him to take anything other than a top offer. This was a subject upon which he sought my counsel on a regular basis. Rather than sell a money-making empire, I urged him to work less, take time off to travel and enjoy the fruits of his labour. He concurred with my suggestions and decided to travel, once he'd been convinced that I would contact him on a daily basis to report any horrors. In addition, the accountant would send him the 'scores on the doors' before he'd risen from his slumber and the Chinese managers who couldn't, or wouldn't, grasp the concept of a chain of command, could call him directly to tell tales. Apart from flying lessons down in Durban, which kept him occupied for a couple of months and the odd visit to the UK, Spain or the Philippines, his primary port of call was always Thailand.

With the heartfelt blessings of his real pals, he lived his life and ran his empire as he saw fit. Similarly, his sexual exploits were his own business too. That said, some of his performances down on Thailand might best be termed 'odd'. More stories regarding the Kingdom of Thailand presently.

It might be considered a testament to my stupidity, but I've always been inclined to scorn the heat and humidity of Hong Kong summers, by taking to the hills regardless of what the weatherman might have to say. In July 2010 however, my body gave me a reminder that I was no longer destined for Olympic greatness. One of the tracks leading up from the Shek Pik Catchwater branched a few hundred feet up the hillside, the right-hand fork clearly marked: "Permanently Closed due to Serious Landslips." The Country Parks Commission had even seen fit to erect a wooden barrier across the path to reinforce the edict. Well, it had the appearance of a wooden log, but a closer inspection revealed it to be a plastic lookalike. Such a directive normally equates to an invitation on vellum for me to give it a bash but, despite having stopped a couple of times to ponder the option when I'd previously passed that way, the isolation of the area should things have gone wrong meant good sense had prevailed. I elected to wait until company was available before taking on this incline. That company materialised in the shape of Tony Taylor, a former Royal Signals sergeant, who agreed to have a bash at the overgrown track with me. On this particular Saturday morning, I found it hard going from the outset, although it didn't immediately register. Once Tony and I reached the out of bounds area, it was down to me to take the lead along the badly overgrown path, since I'd had a dabble at it previously. Once a track is declared closed in Hong Kong, nature takes over with a vengeance and there were sections of this climb where the route was barely discernible. The slope would normally have been child's play to Tony and me just the same, but the incline was having a serious effect on me this day. I developed serious wind, the sweats, palpitations, dizziness and a general weakness that finally brought me to my knees. Like a battered boxer, I arose groggily and kept struggling on before Tony, good former soldier that he is, called an end to the contest and ordered a strategic withdrawal. I actually considered the possibility of a heart attack and gave some serious thought to the fact my end might be nigh. My partner later confessed to fearing for my prospects of ever getting back down the hill. Just the same, plucky old dog that I am, we reached the seldom used road at the foot of the mountainside. My partner pushed on the mile or so to the main road and waited there in the hope of finding a taxi to come and pick up the walking wounded. A modest hill saw my legs give way again and I simply sat on the road, breaking all records for producing wind and making a serious attempt on the Guinness Book of Records top score for palpitations per minute. Not for the first time that morning and fuelled by my famed hypochondria, I doubted my ability to make it back home.

An Australian cyclist appeared, took one look at the sorry-looking apparition sitting slumped on the road and dismounted.

"Shit mate," he remarked, "you look really crook. Can I help?"

"That's very kind of you chum, but what can you do for me on a bike?"

"Good point cobber. At least take a decent rest and good luck."

By my reckoning, the Aussie's 15-gear bike constituted this road's quota of vehicular traffic for the day but, to my astonishment, the thoroughfare was graced a few minutes later by the appearance of a rather swish Mercedes. Clearly my countenance hadn't altered greatly since the Good Samaritan Australian had peddled away, for the driver stopped his car, wound down the window and enquired in a thick French accent:

"Is it that you are OK monsieur?"

"To be honest chum, no, I'm not."

"In this case, can I lift you to some part?"

"Are you French?" I enquired.

"Yes I am."

"Then fuck off you French bastard; there are some of us who haven't forgotten Crecy, La Rochelle and Rouen you know! And where were you buggers in 1940? Hiding behind the Maginot Line I suppose!"

At least that's what I should have said; but instead, I muttered a heartfelt, "Yes please." He all but lifted me into his car and must have regretted his moment of benevolence, as mud and sweat was quickly transferred onto the plush leather of his front seat. He turned his car around and took me to meet up with Tony at the main road. My mumbled *'merci mille fois'* was hopelessly inadequate for such a manifestation of camaraderie. Somehow, by bus, ferry and taxi, I made it back home to Wanchai. In later months I returned to this area several times, in the hope of seeing the Frenchman and adequately thanking him for his help that day, but he was never to be found.

Weeks of severe and debilitating wind, palpitations and dizziness followed my exertions above Shek Pik; none of which could be explained to the satisfaction of my friendly Scots doctor chum. Closely following someone's wordy account of a book he's just read, a long-winded report of a recently watched film or the details of a latest diet, surely the most tedious thing on earth must be a list of someone's medical woes. Just the same, I'll defy you not to be impressed by the range of tests I underwent during the weeks following my failure to recover from the morning jaunt. Several armfuls of blood revealed that my prostate, sugar levels, cholesterol, liver, kidneys, blood count and goodness knows what else were all within the necessary parameters. An ECG revealed the heart of a lion and I briefly toyed with the idea of contacting the Deed Poll people, since Walter Coeur de Lion has a certain ring to it. The thought of a body scan had me scouring the Internet for more details, as my mild claustrophobia wouldn't have allowed me to enter one of those full-body jobs without a fight. In the event, it was just like going in and out of a giant-sized Polo mint and the result revealed there was nothing awry with my innards in any case. There followed an endoscopy, which, apart from being uncomfortable, showed a reasonably healthy stomach for a man who has abused the organ unmercifully over the years. With their last throw of the dice, my medical advisers prescribed a colonoscopy!

When I'd had my endoscopy, they injected me with enough sedative to induce a mildly calming effect upon a 90 lb Chinese lady of advanced years. It did nothing at all for me. So, on the day they were about to put a hosepipe into my bottom, I demanded something rather stronger and, consequently, suitably desensitised physically and mentally, recall little about the event. Whilst undressing for the procedure, the nurse was at pains to tell me to place my trousers and underpants on a bed in the changing room. The reason for this wasn't apparent, until I was aware of the same lady pulling them onto my nether regions once the colonoscopy had been completed. I've had many a lady remove these garments over the years, but can't ever recall a woman putting them back on me before. The result of the procedure was negative.

It took me several months to get over whatever it was that floored me at Shek Pik and still the doctors could offer no diagnosis to explain the event. I put my walking boots to good use again, but as the summer humidity set in, I vowed to give best to the steeper of Hong Kong's hills.

And I was as good as my word, taking things reasonably sedately on the hiking front during the steamy season. Saturday remained my primary day for walking, often in the company of Buzz Langille, an amiable workmate in the Group's office—or 'orifice' as we preferred to call the place. The pair of us set off one October morn to climb the oft suggested, but as yet unconsummated Mount Stenhouse; not a particularly lofty, but still challenging peak on Lamma Island. This particular 'best laid scheme' was to turn into a nightmare.

Buzz's knowledge of the hill was restricted to having seen it at a distance during seven years of residence on the island; mine to having huffed and puffed my way to the top some two decades previously. Just the same, the supremely honed athletes reached the summit without a hitch, where a convenient trig point served as a dining table as we preened ourselves, ate our sandwiches and discussed the descent. A cursory glance at a map of the area, which lay undisturbed in my backpack, would have confirmed there was only one way down. From up there on high however, there appeared to be two alternatives. Buzz dithered, maintaining the more obvious route to be both difficult and dangerous, whereas my fuzzy memory indicated the path heading straight ahead to be the better bet. Since my suggestion to steam ahead, 90 degrees in the wrong bloody direction met with no objections, away we trotted.

Ominously, the track petered out after only half a mile, forcing us to blunder downwards through never ending stretches of head-high thickets and steep scree. It was an extremely tired couple of adventurers who finally made it to the foot of Mount Stenhouse and the adjacent shoreline. With Buzz confessing to feeling knackered and me feeling very much the worse for wear, we belatedly consulted the map. It served to confirm that we were miles off course and probably in something of a pickle. What had appeared from on high to be a track leading out of the area turned out to be nothing more than a deep stream; there was no chance of attempting a coastal route back to civilisation and the hills behind us were guarded by huge boulders and covered with impenetrable shrubs and grass. In retrospect, the sensible thing to do would have been to rest and then retrace our steps, but that would have been too much of an ordeal. Instead, we attempted to scale the boulders protecting the hills to the east. At this point my dizziness and palpitations started again, so we retreated to the seashore where I took shelter from the sun in the shade of a large rock.

Realising his comrade was in some kind of distress, Buzz made his way to the shore and tried to convince a couple of fishermen bobbing around in a fragile looking boat that it would be to their financial advantage to take us around the coastline. They were adamant that the shoreline was far too dangerous to attempt such a rescue and suggested he call 999. Jeopardising my reputation as a doughty and pugnacious hill-walker, I reluctantly agreed with Buzz that our best option would be to contact the emergency services. Wouldn't you know it, there was no telephone coverage! Why should there be? Nobody lived within miles of our current location. The brave Nova Scotian gritted his teeth and headed off alone, back over the boulders and up the hill until he was high enough to make contact; returning to assure me a rescue vessel would arrive presently and take us to safety.

I was still feeling dreadful. The palpitations and stomach pain were constant and an irregular heartbeat was causing me to feel distinctly apprehensive. For a considerable period we scoured the sea around the headland for anything resembling a rescue boat, until the futile exercise was interrupted by the sound of helicopter rotors. They had only sent the Emergency Services 'A' team to save me! I really didn't fancy the idea of being winched up into a helicopter hovering high above the sea and rocks. There was nothing for it though, but to steel myself in readiness for the experience. The pilot spent several minutes satisfying himself that his aircraft was in exactly the right position for a rescue; simultaneously soaking both of us to the skin with sea-spray, when down the rope dangling from the chopper slid a medic.

This was one highly experienced and proficient medical man. He listened to my tale of woe, diagnosed the problem, declared an evacuation to hospital the most prudent course of action and produced a winching harness from his backpack; all in quick time. There was, after all, a fuel guzzling helicopter up above us, consuming gallons of avgas a minute just to keep hovering. As he lifted my left leg to attach the canvas strapping around the top of my thigh, I let out an almighty scream.

"You having heart pain, Mr Warry?" he asked anxiously.

"No, just clamp in my reg," I reassured him, my perverse sense of humour clearly unaffected by the trauma.

With me attached to the medic by several square yards of webbing, I felt marginally more comfortable. If anything snapped, we would at least be dashed to our doom on the rocks as a team. Prior to instructing his winch man to hoist us heavenwards, the medic asked Buzz if he wanted to travel back in the chopper too. In words he was to bitterly regret within the hour, when the very same helicopter and crew returned to rescue him from a hilltop, he assured the medic he was feeling strong and would plod onwards. Bidding my walking companion a fond farewell, I then closed my eyes as the medic and his wounded charge ascended. There was a slight bump as we collided with the open slide door of the helicopter, whereupon the crew dragged me inside. They put me on a bed, stuffed oxygen outlets into my nostrils, took my blood pressure, listened to my heart and took all my personal details. Before there was time to enjoy the view over Victoria Harbour, we descended to the helipad in Central, where I was transferred to an awaiting ambulance. As if to indicate that my medical condition was far from serious, the ambulance dawdled towards Eastern Hospital at an exceedingly moderate pace and, to my disappointment, without the use of flashing blue lights. The whole rescue effort had been highly professional just the same and I later wrote to the officer in charge of the service, to commend him and his men for their efficiency.

Upon arrival at the casualty department, my irregular heartbeat was deemed to be sufficient cause to keep me in overnight for observations; whereupon someone pushed me up to Ward 5 in a wheelchair. My clothes were sodden so, before being ordered into bed, a nurse presented me with a shabby gown that was several sizes too small for my magnificently proportioned frame. To my considerable surprise, the garment bore the logo 'PYNE', as did all the other medical accoutrements on view. How thoughtful of them to provide me with personalised bed wear I thought, even if they had omitted the first vowel of my surname. I was later to discover the hospital, known throughout Hong Kong as the 'Eastern', is more formally known as the 'Pamela Youde Nethersole Eastern'—PYNE. There was a comforting view from the ward window, which looked out over the enormous Chai Wan graveyard. At least it wouldn't be too far to travel should things take a turn for the worse.

The entire hospital staff wore facemasks at all times, a hangover from the days of SARS and Bird Flu perhaps, and I never did see the face of the splendid doctor who attended to me during my stay. He instructed his staff to draw several vials of my O+ lifeblood for analysis, take my blood pressure at rather too frequent intervals and attach a heart monitor to my person. If you've never been wired up to a heart machine and never seen evidence of your irregular heartbeat on the monitor, then you've missed a treat.

I was required to drink copious quantities of water to counteract dehydration and, in the early hours of the morning, when all the staff appeared to have deserted their posts, the requirement for me to void urine became a priority. No amount of bell-pressing succeeded in summoning the services of a face-masked nurse, however. Where were they when we needed them? When the situation became critical, a command decision needed to be made, lest the bed linen become soiled. I pulled the plug from the heart monitor and came very close to putting the PYNE record for the 50m sprint from Ward 5 to the latrines, whilst trailing yards of wires, in severe jeopardy. En route, I'd espied the 'heart resuscitation team' scurrying in the opposite direction and, upon returning to my bed with my bladder registering optimum emptiness, I was roundly chastised by them before being presented, not with a gold medal, but a couple of cardboard bottles to see me through the night. Thirty-hours after admission, the faceless physician prescribed some tablets, advised me to take things easy for a while and arranged an appointment with the consultant ten-days hence.

The specialist merely confirmed my remarkably good state of health, but then ruined the whole experience by adding the obligatory 'for your age' suffix. He assured me that future hill-walking was to be recommended and I decided that Tiger Hill might be an appropriate target for Saturday's solo jaunt.

The summit of Tiger Hill was bagged inside a couple of hours, which left me wondering why I'd been overlooked when the Army's Mount Everest team was selected. Feeling in such fine fettle at the summit, I eschewed the easier way down into Discovery Bay in favour of an altogether steeper descent. Things were still going well, until I espied the faintest of tracks that had never been obvious on previous walks along this route. I elected to wander along it, until coming across a wide stream bed. A subsequent confirmatory visit to this area revealed that it was at this point I made my serious mistake. The track, although barely discernible, actually carried on over the stream and down into Discovery Bay. Ignoring Hong Kong Radio's sage advice for walkers, broadcast with tedious regularity:

1. Never walk alone.
2. Always carry a surfeit of water.
3. Never, but never, tackle streambeds unaccompanied,

I veered erroneously to the right and headed down the stream. At least there was plenty of water! This was a beast of a watercourse to tackle, with roughly 25 waterfalls of varying heights needing to be climbed down, or around, with the utmost caution. An abundance of water-filled pools, slippery rocks and areas where it was obligatory to climb into the bush at the side of the stream to negotiate the cataracts, made this a stern challenge indeed. I'd made a mental note of having blundered my way down a dozen waterfalls, when my boots suddenly slipped on an expanse of wet rock sloping downwards at a 45-degree angle towards an ominously deep-looking pool. There was nothing to grab in an effort to arrest my speedy downward slide towards a soaking, although my acceleration was reduced momentarily, when I went over a cunningly located rock that did something very nasty to my coccyx. My entry into the pool wasn't elegant by any stretch of the imagination. Mind you, for someone who hadn't swum a stroke for at least two decades, my breast-stroke appeared to have lost little of its power and grace.

Drenched and somewhat apprehensive about what mischief might have been done to the base of my spine, I battled on; only to slip again on another section of slick rock. This time, my right leg finished up rammed between two boulders that stopped my descent towards another drenching, but held me fast. There were some ominous-looking holes in my leg when I finally managed to extricate myself. A sore backside, an even sorer leg and two sprained wrists, the result of a third tumble, resulted in me taking the matter of a safe outcome to this adventure to a Higher Authority. My prayer was swiftly answered, as the manicured lawn to the rear of a posh accommodation block suddenly hove into view through the scrub. I was bruised, battered and bleeding, but would live to fight another day. Was it a lesson learnt? Not really!

The two incidents I'm about to relate were particularly manic, indicating to me that all wasn't well with the way Luke was choosing to fill his time in Thailand. I received a call in the early hours of the morning from Luke's father in Spain, explaining that he had received a disturbing telephone call from his son's good friend in Cardiff. The gist of Luke's call to Wales had been that he believed he had been poisoned down in Thailand and was about to die. All subsequent attempts to phone him back had gone unanswered it appeared. His father asked me whether he had left an address or contact number by which we might locate the prodigal son. I did have an address in Pattaya, which was a mansion hired by him and another Hong Kong entrepreneur. I'd insisted upon this information before he departed on his adventure. Furthermore, I had a good friend who was the British Consular Correspondent in an adjacent Thai province to the area where Luke was getting himself into trouble. Thanks to my Consular friend, his equivalent in the province that included Pattaya and my administrative nous, the profligate one was located and repatriated to a Hong Kong hospital with all haste. Tests revealed quantities of rohypnol in his body; somebody had slipped him a Micky Finn. A couple of days later he was released from hospital, leaving me to feel that my efforts on his behalf had been more than acceptable. A year and a half later, my self-congratulatory feeling was to be shattered, but more about the unsavoury matter later!

To most people, the rohypnol event would probably have served as a warning about what might befall the unwary reveller down in Thailand, but Luke was made of sterner stuff. Some months later, my phone rang once again in the middle of the night. It was Luke, calling from Bangkok with a perfectly shocking revelation.

"I'm in real bother Wal. My jaw is broken, so are some of my teeth and I have a lump on my elbow the size of a cricket ball. My passport and wallet are in the hotel, but I don't know where it is, or even the name of the place. What shall I do?"

A considered response from 1,500 miles distant and without all the facts to hand would be difficult, but I might have suggested getting into a taxi and hot footing over to the British Embassy. Before I could respond with any profound counsel however, he suddenly rang off. It was several hours before he called again, this time from Bangkok Airport, where he was waiting for a plane back to Hong Kong. Luke was eager to explain why he'd rung off so abruptly and to give me the run down on the previous 24-hours of strange happenings. This story beggared belief!

It transpired that he had been tracked down by his assailant as he was making his initial call to me and had been forced to ring off. This aggressor, whilst possessing all the physical attributes of a female, was actually a creature of debatable chromosomic antecedence. For the remainder of this tale, I shall refer to this person as a female of the species, but would be reluctant to put any money on the fact. Luke had apparently spent the previous night in a hotel with this lady and next morning, having declared himself highly satisfied with her performance, donated sufficient Thai baht to enable her to depart for a morning's exercise in retail therapy. As a serial libertine nonpareil, however, he used the time the lady was absent on her shopping spree to engage the services of another female. This substitute, he confessed, had been used without him taking the necessary precautions—a criminal omission for a man with his experience in this part of the globe.

When the previous evening's star reported back for her next shift, Luke was presumably under the influence of something to render him loquacious in the extreme because, after another coupling with the 'star', he elected to reveal the full story of his daytime tryst. This information wasn't received with the best of grace and it became a case of 'Let Battle Commence'. The lady smashed a heavy table onto the floor and broke off one of the legs, thereby producing an implement perfectly weighted and shaped for close-quarter combat. Wading into Luke like a black-belt Kendo exponent, she succeeded in fracturing the lad's jaw and breaking a couple of his teeth with the first blow. He took up a defensive position hiding behind the hotel room curtain, but was unable to fend off the table-leg wielding lady, sustaining a couple of meaty whacks to his ribs and another to the elbow that produced a truly magnificent swelling. He had then fled the hotel and phoned me.

A foreigner in Thailand has very little chance in a legal battle with a local; the bias of the police in favour of their fellow kinsmen ensures this well-documented fact. After finding our boy, the lady took full advantage of the situation and drove him, broken bones and all, to the local constabulary. His inability to speak any Thai rendered him ignorant of exactly what was going on and, thus, he was unable to put up even a basic form of defence. He was ordered to pay a sum of money to the police, allegedly to smooth matters over and prevent further legal action being taken, but a bribe in reality. A further sum needed to be paid as financial restitution for damage to the hotel room and then came the final ignominy— he was driven to a goldsmith's establishment, where he was required to stump up a considerable sum to buy the lady a weighty amount of gold. Thereafter Luke was at liberty to depart for the airport and a flight home. Did he learn a lesson from this incident? I doubt it very much.

I have a huge store of tales about the man's antics that would make your eyes water, but feel compelled to keep them confidential to spare the blushes of people still known to me. In fact, because of the kindness he showed to me upon my return to Hong Kong, I would never have spilt the beans regarding his indiscretions at all—were it not for libellous comments he subsequently made about me. *Revanche!*

As an employee of the Group, things appeared to be going along swimmingly and, despite getting on a wee bit, it seemed a safe assumption that my position was secure for as long as I wanted it to continue. In addition to my salary from Luke, I was also earning a monthly fee from a clandestine American organisation involved in the investigation of the illegal manufacture and importation of cigarettes. It was all very hush-

hush, but didn't even require me to leave my desk. US$1,000 a month for less than an hour of form filling; nice work if you can get it. As if preordained in my life, however, things have a habit of souring swiftly and my rapid departure from Hong Kong was nearer than I'd ever dreamt possible.

During a week when Luke's behaviour reached new heights of paranoia, he appeared to have set Thursday aside to extend his horizons and engage in a spot of Wally bashing. Unlike the remainder of the office staff, who had been bullied pitilessly for spurious reasons over the years, I'd been exempt from any attacks until this date. He called me into his office and, without offering me a seat, promptly accused me of misappropriating three cheques.

"When do you imagine you gave me three cheques?"

"Four months ago, before I went to Durban."

"Why would you give me cheques, when you have both an accountant and a book-keeper in your employ?"

"I told you to hang on to them and now they're missing."

"Have they been presented at the bank?"

"No."

"Then I suggest you look elsewhere for them; in your desk drawers perhaps, along with all the other detritus."

"I distinctly remember giving them to you," said the man with a memory span of ten minutes, always provided the wind was in the right direction.

"What day is it Luke?"

"Friday."

"It's Thursday! You don't know what day of the week it is and yet you have the crystal-clear recollection of giving me three specific cheques to safeguard four months ago! The sole reason you gave me the cheques, not three but several hundred pre-signed cheques, was that I was the only person left in the office. You had arrived late as usual and all the others had gone home. The cheques were placed in the safe, for which only you and I know the combination and next morning, by which time you were on your way to Durban, I passed them over to the accountant. This accusation is simply not acceptable and I'm leaving your employ with immediate effect. Your flat will be vacated by tomorrow morning and I'll leave the keys with Buzz."

With that, I packed up my stuff, closed the computer down and went home. For all my warts and blemishes, fiery temper and confrontational manner when faced with selfishness, stupidity or corruption in others, I remain painfully honest. It was the questioning of my integrity that proved to be the last straw as far as working for this company was concerned.

I had watched him bully his office staff for too long. He had driven the wholehearted, consummately honest and hard-working accountant firstly into a psychiatrist's chair and then resignation; the huge Canadian, who was big and powerful enough to eat him for breakfast had been browbeaten into submission in the certain knowledge that, with a wife and baby daughter to support, he badly needed to hold onto his job; the dim-witted book-keeper had been bullied into saying 'yes' to anything and the decent, honest Chinese dogsbody who handled huge sums of money and stock, had once been falsely accused of stealing a box of crisps. A box of crisps, for goodness sake! I'd accused Luke of being a bully many times and he invariably took severe umbrage at the accusation. The truth hurts!

That same evening, Luke called round to see me in my flat; not to apologize, but to tell me of his nonsensical plan for the future of the company. As if I cared any longer! My services, he declared, would no longer be required. He wanted me to stay in his employ though and take on an alternative venture, one not associated with the licensed trade. He suggested I returned to the UK for a period of leave and then he would call me back once the new company had been established. How gullible did he think I was? Having been assured, on numerous occasions, just how crucial my contribution to his company was, I found it impossible to comprehend why my position was now deemed irrelevant. He had seemingly earmarked a female employee to assume a newly formed General Manager's role at the two establishments in Wanchai and the outlet in Tsim Sha Tsui, Kowloon. In addition, she would manage one of the bars in Wanchai and also take over the administration of the group. A tall order indeed was my first thought, especially for a woman who ran the only place in the chain that made a loss, was highly unpopular with her staff and also with many of the dwindling number of customers. So, an unpopular female who couldn't write anything like presentable English, was to be the panacea to cure all the ills within the Group. Could the fact he'd had sexual relations with this woman only a few days before she married a gullible Mancunian have influenced his decision? It was a question I was wicked enough to ponder.

Having wet-nursed Luke for three years, I knew damned well that the administration role was way above her capability. Expecting her to cope with all the additional responsibilities was simply absurd. There were certainly problems with the set-up in Wanchai, but I refused absolutely to accept that any fault lay at my door. With the exception of Luke himself, it was perfectly clear to anyone with a modicum of sense what was wrong with the company. It wasn't necessary to look any further than his office!

I was hurt and disappointed with what I'd just heard and didn't want to listen to any more of the nonsense he was spouting. The generous glass of my finest Cognac with which he'd been plied was unceremoniously withdrawn and I ordered him to vacate my flat. He was at pains to point out that the apartment was, in fact, his property and that I wasn't in a position to order him out. It was a fair comment, but I countered by reminding him of my volatile nature, to which he was in imminent danger of being exposed. He departed. By breakfast time next morning the flat was cleaned, my humble chattels removed and I was in the house of a friend on Lantau Island. Two days later, I was back in England and a twenty-year friendship had bitten the dust.

Within two months I was back in Hong Kong, house sitting for a friend who was away on a long sabbatical. Luke had heard of my arrival and called to ask me to join him for Sunday lunch. We enjoyed some splendid fare, although the conversation was restricted to talk of life's more important subjects: football, beer prices and sex. Before returning to Discovery Bay, he asked if we could meet again two days hence, to discuss more serious matters. Whether he wanted me to consider returning to work for him I was never to ascertain, for he pulled one of his regular stunts, by failing to turn up for the meeting. My text, to ask him the reason behind his non-appearance, resulted in him arranging an alternative rendezvous. He failed to turn up on this occasion either and I have never seen him again.

One of Luke's former employees invited me to dinner at his home. During the repast, he appeared most anxious to get something off his chest and informed me of the lunch meeting and conversation he'd had with our former boss, only a few days after the rohypnol incident in Thailand. He expressed his extreme regret for not having me made privy to this information immediately after the event, but he felt I ought to know now, even at this late juncture. Luke had apparently talked openly about the incident and had expressed the view that my actions to resolve matters had been just too slick and efficient. The fact I had his father's telephone number; knew exactly where he was staying and the fact I had a personal friend connected to the British Embassy appeared all too convenient, he'd remarked. I knew his father's number because, not only did he give me his card, but it was him who had phoned me with the initial information. At my insistence, Luke had informed me of the location for his sojourn in Thailand before he departed on the ill-fated mission and it was merely by a happy coincidence I had a contact within the British Embassy. Luke's damning comment had been that he believed Wally Payne was the mastermind behind the whole affair! I was incandescent with rage.

An e-mail to Luke, asking him to confirm his slanderous allegations, met with a typically flippant response. A second e-mail, penned in less amicable terms, demanded an apology before I resorted to legal action for slander. My good name had been besmirched and the minimum requirement to appease me would be a humble apology. It has never been forthcoming and Luke would be well advised to remember that I can make a formidable adversary. I remarked previously that it would be a difficult task indeed to be able to repay Luke for his kindness to me in my hour of need. Following the revelation that he considered me to be the prime suspect for masterminding his poisoning in Thailand, I consider my debt to him has been discharged in full.

With absolutely no prospect, or indeed without any burning desire to find an alternative source of employment in Hong Kong, I elected to remain in the Far East just the same, until my daughter finished her schooling in the Philippines. I still harboured the hope she would choose to accompany me back to the UK to undergo her tertiary education and I wanted to be close at hand. Given that a couple of my former Military Police brethren were living over in Thailand and that Hong Kong isn't a place to stay for a prolonged period on a budget, I opted to spend some time down in their chosen retirement location of Hua Hin, a couple of hundred miles south of Bangkok. Hua Hin is something of a poor relative when it comes to benefitting from the lucrative 'sex and sunshine' trade that makes Thailand such a magnet for the proliferation of European lower classes; 40-million of whom flock to the kingdom annually. One of the palaces of HRH the King of Thailand is located in the town, something about which the locals are inordinately proud. Consequently, they tend to behave accordingly and dress modestly, albeit casually. It wouldn't be seemly to be seen in shorts and a vest by a member of the royal family after all! It must vex the locals considerably, therefore, to be confronted on a daily basis by a plethora of tattooed European lowlife. Tourists invariably sport vests, preferably of a style displaying as much underarm hair as possible; shorts with hideous floral designs and cheap flip-flops. If that doesn't instantly identify a male European holidaymaker, then the hideous sunburn, can of lager in one hand and a Thai female young enough to be his granddaughter clinging onto the other surely will. In addition to the 13-day and 12-night mob, there are numerous older expats living permanently in Hua Hin. Without waxing too highbrow, they remind me of the shipwrecked souls in Tennyson's 'Lotus Eaters'—the majority having no intention, or more likely the finance to ever return to their native shores. Attracted by a very reasonable cost of living, cheap rents and alcohol, obliging females on every corner and steaming hot weather, perhaps they've made sagacious decisions.

I spent another couple of months over in Hong Kong, when a former barrister friend asked me to housesit for him once again, before returning to Thailand to await my daughter's decision as to whether she wanted to stay with her mother in the Philippines, or accompany me back to the UK. I lost and returned to the UK, primarily to get under the umbrella of the much maligned, but free, National Health Service. Despite a contented year ensconced in the Land of the Prince Bishops, notwithstanding a fortnight spent as a guest of Sunderland Royal Infirmary, the inability to settle still afflicts this rolling stone. As this volume is brought to a close, I can already feel my feet itching, especially when the wind whips in off the North Sea. Thailand is unlikely to enjoy my company again, although Hong Kong could easily attract me back. Time will tell.

9716558R00224

Printed in Great Britain
by Amazon.co.uk, Ltd.,
Marston Gate.